Trusting God

Learning to Walk by Faith

Trusting God

Learning to Walk by Faith

Trust in the LORD forever,
for in God the LORD we have an everlasting Rock.
—Isaiah 26:4 —

Dr. David R. Reagan

McKinney, Texas
www.lamblion.com

Dedicated to
the faithful and generous
Prophecy Partners
of Lamb & Lion Ministries

First edition, 1987

Second revised edition, 1994

Third revised edition, 2015

Copyright © 2015 by Lamb & Lion Ministries
Library of Congress Catalogue Card Number 2015900145
ISBN Number 978-0-945593-23-2

Lamb & Lion Ministries
P.O. Box 919
McKinney, Texas 75070

Cover photo from Getty Images.
Photographer: Andrew Parfenov.
Cover design by Trey Collich.

All scripture quotations are from the New American Standard Version, © The Lockman Foundation.

The poem on page 176, "Epistle," by Carl Sandburg, is taken from *Complete Poems* by Carl Sandburg and is used by permission of the publisher, Harcourt Brace Jovanovich.

Table of Contents

Preface 7

Part I. The Mission

1) Avoiding God 11
2) Meeting God Halfway 14
3) Limiting God 17
4) Reaching out to God 21
5) A Transforming Miracle 24
6) Discovering God 28
7) Wrestling with God 34
8) Surrendering to God 37

Part II. The Ministry

9) Walking by Faith 49
10) Receiving Blessings 58
11) Relying on Prayer 63
12) Believing in Miracles 69
13) Leaning on the Spirit 78
14) Preaching with Power 93
15) Living out of a Suitcase 99
16) Maintaining a Sense of Humor 114
17) Teaching the Future 128
18) Filling the Airwaves 135
19) Adventuring Abroad 154
20) Walking in the Footsteps of Jesus 173
21) Growing in the Lord 194

Part III. The Message

22) Knowing the Season 207
23) Recognizing the Season 213
24) Understanding the Urgency of the Season 219
25) Living in the Season 226
26) Responding to the Season 232

Postscript: 1994

27) Looking Back Over Seven Years 239

Epilogue: 2015

28) Celebrating Milestones 255
29) Experiencing the Impact of Technology 259
30) Making the Transition to Television 262
31) Producing Video Programs 270
32) Focusing on Writing 278
33) Developing New Forms of Ministry 285
34) Continuing Involvement in Missions 290
35) Replicating Our Ministry 298
36) Receiving Financial Miracles 302
37) Dealing with Criticism 306
38) Continuing to Laugh 315
39) Evaluating Success 320
40) Looking to the Future 329

Preface

In 1987, when I took a Sabbatical rest from my extensive travels, the first project I devoted myself to was the writing of this book.

The Lord laid the concept of the book on my heart in the fall of 1986 while I was holding a meeting at a church in Covington, Georgia. I awoke one morning with the idea, and by noon I had prepared an extensive outline of the entire book! I was astonished at how smoothly and quickly the thoughts and words flowed. This experience convinced me that the project was from the Lord.

The writing went just as quickly and easily. I began in January and had the first draft completed by mid-February. It was the first of many writing projects that I completed during that Sabbatical year, and as the year progressed, I became convinced that the Lord was steering the focus of my ministry away from meetings and seminars toward publishing.

An Encouraging Response

The book was well received. It went through three printings. And I received hundreds of letters from people all over the world whose lives were touched deeply in a positive way by what I had written. The most common comment I received over and over was, "I found myself weeping one moment and laughing the next."

Those letters continued to come, and the testimonies they contained convinced me that I should spend a portion of my second Sabbatical year revising the book for republication, and so we issued a second edition in 1994.

Praising God for Special Blessings

And now, as I prepare this third edition for publication, I am overwhelmed as I look back over 35 years and see all the blessings God has given me and the ministry in response to the faltering step of faith I took back in 1980 when I gave up my academic career to preach the soon coming of Jesus.

I praise God for His faithfulness.
I praise Him for His patience with me.
I praise Him for surrounding me with dedicated staff
    and trustees.
I praise Him for loving family members.
I praise Him for our Prophecy Partners.
I praise Him for giving us such an expanded out-
    reach all over the world.
I praise Him most of all for the salvation He has
    provided through the gift of His Son who
    died for our sins.

As I said in the preface to the very first edition of this book, it is my earnest prayer that this book will encourage you to trust in God more than you ever have before. There is no walk like the faith walk because "without faith, it is impossible to please God" (Hebrews 11:6).

Dr. David R. Reagan
Allen, Texas
January 2015

Part I
The Mission

"Here I am, Lord — Send someone else!"

Avoiding God   1

I spent 20 years running as hard as I could from God. It all began in 1959 when I graduated from the University of Texas.

I had gone through college in three years, and I was exhausted. I decided to lay out for a year and work for my dad. I intended to use the time to rest and decide whether I would go to law school or graduate school.

Within a few days after I moved back home, through a bizarre series of circumstances, I found myself serving as the minister of a little country church in Groesbeck, Texas. I knew then that God was calling me to be a minister.

But I didn't want to be a minister. I wanted to be a politician. I dreamed of being a governor or serving in the Congress. So I rejected the Lord's call, and I rationalized it by saying, "I'll be a politician for Jesus." In reality, I wanted to be a big shot for Dave Reagan.

Pushing the Lord Aside

I served the little country church for a year and then went off to a Boston graduate school to study international politics. The school was called The Fletcher School of Law and Diplomacy. It was owned and operated jointly by Tufts and Harvard Universities.

Up to that point in my life I had been greatly blessed. I had been born into a Christian family, raised in the church, received an outstanding education, and fallen in love with a beautiful Christian girl whom I had married.

But when I departed for Fletcher, I began running from the Lord, and my fortunes began to change. I failed to earn my master's degree on time because I could not pass the foreign language exam. I had never experienced academic difficulties of any type before in my life, and this failure was a bitter pill. But I was stubborn, and I persisted.

I became one of the first in my class to earn a doctorate. But I found no satisfaction in this accomplishment. In fact, I hated every moment of it. Writing the dissertation was pure drudgery to me, so much so that I have looked at it only a couple of times since the day I completed it. It was simply a necessary step in earning a union card for university level teaching — a doctor's degree.

Searching for Meaning

I looked forward to teaching with great enthusiasm, believing that it would fill the vacuum I felt so strongly in my soul. But it didn't. I shifted to a career in academic administration. I thought life would take on new meaning if I could only escape the confinement of the classroom. It didn't.

Finally in 1972 I decided to put the academic life behind me and seek the fulfillment of my childhood dreams. I entered politics. I filed to run for Congress and, again, through a bizarre series of circumstances, I ended up as a candidate for the Republican nomination for governor of Texas! I was only 34 years old. It was a heady experience.

It was also a terribly disillusioning experience. I had always been politically motivated by altruistic considerations. I dreamed of honest government that would serve the needs of the people. I found that most people involved in politics are driven by selfish motives. I had my head in the clouds. I spoke of lofty goals like revising the outdated Texas constitution. I discovered that people were more concerned about dollar-and-cent issues.

Once again I tasted the bitterness of failure. I placed third in a field of seven. I railed against God in my heart. "How could He let me down when I wanted to do so much good in His name?"

Feeling Empty

During the next few years I focused on paying off my campaign debts. I returned to higher education and served as president of one college, dean of another and vice president of a third. I moved almost yearly, giving little consideration to the effect of such a nomadic life upon my wife and two daughters. All that mattered was my career.

I achieved a lot in worldly terms. I held prestigious positions. I made a lot of money. But there was no fulfillment. I continued to feel empty inside.

Moving in a New Direction

Then one day I got a brilliant idea. I decided to go into business. My dad was a very successful businessman, and he had urged me for years to get out of the ivory tower and live in the "real world" by starting a business.

It suddenly occurred to me that I could kill two birds with one stone. I could get my earthly father off my back by going into business. At the same time I could get my Heavenly Father off my back by establishing a church-related business. I announced I was going to open a Christian book store and supply center. I thought it was a pure stroke of genius!

Meeting God Halfway 2

My dad wasn't too excited about the type of business I had in mind. He would have preferred something more down-to-earth like a plumbing supply distributorship.

But he encouraged me to take the step. My younger brother was already a successful businessman. Dad felt that at long last there might be some hope for me!

Hoping to Please God

I was more concerned about the reaction of my Heavenly Father because what I wanted more than anything else in the world was inner peace. I knew that could only come from God.

I didn't know anything in those days about how to seek God's will. I just knew God had called me to be a minister, and I figured that He would jump with joy when I finally stopped running away from Him and took one step in His direction by starting a church-related business.

I was wrong. I was to find out the hard way that God is not interested in our meeting Him halfway. He has gone more than halfway in sending His Son to die for our sins. He expects us to yield fully, not partially, to His will. But I didn't understand that then.

I jumped into the project with great enthusiasm. I believed it had to succeed because it had the blessing of both my physical and spiritual fathers.

Taking the Plunge

I spent a year and a half getting the business set up. I had to find a location, purchase a building, secure the fixtures, review the trade magazines and order the stock. It was to be the largest Christian store in Dallas — much more than a mere book store. We were going to offer Christian music, Bible school curriculum, religious art, church supplies, choir robes, fiberglass baptistries — you name it.

During the year and a half it took to get the business started, I had no income. My wife and I sold every asset we had, including our house, to generate the money necessary for such a grandiose business. What we couldn't afford, we secured through loans granted on my dad's credit. It never occurred to me to start small and grow. No, my store had to be the biggest and best.

I called it Renewal House. The name proved prophetic, for God used it to renew me.

I operated the store for a year and a half. Our volume of business grew steadily each month, but never fast enough. There was too much overhead and too much interest on loans. Finally, the day arrived when I had no operating cash left. I called the bank for more. The answer was "No!"

Experiencing Failure

I'll never forget that day. Three years of my life — every waking moment — had gone into this project. Now I faced bankruptcy. Failure again.

It was more than I could bear. I became physically ill. I descended into a pit of depression.

A few days later I had to put the "CLOSED" sign on the front door. That was a tough moment. I looked out the window at the homosexual bar that was located right across the street from my store. The place had standing-room-only every night. The money was rolling in. I wanted to scream, "Why me, God? Why not that den of iniquity?"

Just then the owner of the bar drove up in his four-door Jaguar and parked out front. He was wearing an expensive-looking suit. He stood by his car for a moment, lighting a cigar. It was as if Satan was taunting me, saying, "Look how I reward those who serve me!"

The emotional distress intensified later that day when I called the bank to get the total on how much I owed. The answer stunned me: "Your loan balance is $100,000." One hundred thousand dollars! I could not even imagine that much money. Where would I get it? How could I avoid bankruptcy and total humiliation?

Limiting God   3

I desperately needed God. But I didn't know how to reach out to Him.

I had grown up in a legalistic and sectarian church. We believed we were the only ones who had the truth. We believed the rest of the so-called "Christian world" was terribly deceived. We consigned them to hell and believed they deserved it because, after all, they didn't agree with us!

We believed the Bible was the Word of God, but we did not believe in the God who was revealed in the Bible. Our God was a God of Nostalgia. He was the "Grand Old Man in the Sky." He was a God who once performed mighty deeds in Old Testament and New Testament times — but who ran out of gas at the end of the First Century. He had gone into retirement. The age of miracles had ceased.

Putting God in a Box

If I wanted to experience God, I had to go see a movie like *The Ten Commandments,* in Technicolor and Panavision, with a cast of thousands. I would sit there in awe as I witnessed Cecil B. DeMille re-create the miracles of God dividing the Red Sea, leading the Children of Israel with a cloud and feeding them with manna. I would drive home with goose bumps, yearning for such a God today — a God of power who was concerned about me and my problems.

But I didn't believe in such a God. My God was an impersonal God who had more important things to worry about than my problems. Furthermore, even if He were concerned, He couldn't do anything because He no longer intervened in human affairs — except, of course, to bug me to preach!

My church had rejected more than the power of God. We had set aside the whole realm of the supernatural. We did not believe in demons or angels. They too had retired at the end of the First Century!

We knew nothing about spiritual warfare. We thought our battle was with flesh and blood. We knew nothing about the power of the Word, the power of prayer or the power of the name of Jesus.

Our faith was all past tense — directed at the Cross. Our faith did not relate to the present or the future. Regarding the present, our attitude was that God had given us a rule book and minds. We were to follow the rules and use our minds to cope rationally with the problems of life.

Our faith did not relate to the future because we ignored God's Prophetic Word. Also, we were caught up in works salvation, and therefore we were all uncertain about our eternal destiny. The future was unknown. We tried not to think about it.

Living in a Spiritual Vacuum

Our faith was really in our church. We trusted in the church because we were told that our church was right about everything. We took pride in our church. We took glee in putting down other churches.

We were debaters. We liked to prove that other people were wrong. By age 15 I had pages in the back of my Bible that were designated for every major denominational group. On each page I had a list of proof texts that I used to attack that particular group. We had a zeal to prove we were right about everything.

This was before the days of Christian radio and television and Christian bookstores. Our ministers could keep us in isolation from the rest of the world. We talked only to ourselves.

Sorting Out the Holy Spirit

Another aspect of our rejection of the supernatural was our treatment of the Holy Spirit. We mainly ignored the Spirit. Our preachers felt that any emphasis on the Spirit would lead to "dangerous emotionalism." The Holy Spirit was the great taboo topic of our fellowship.

This caused me some real problems as a child. The only version of the Bible that we used was the King James. It used the term "Holy Ghost." That was confusing to me. I felt like the Holy Ghost was supposed to be something good, but all the ghosts I had ever heard about had been evil. I would go on Boy Scout campouts, and we would sit around the campfire at night and tell ghost stories. We were good at it because we would all end up sleeping in the same tent!

I kept asking myself how a ghost could be good. One Saturday morning when I was about 12 years old I found the answer. I got on a city bus in Waco, Texas where I grew up and went downtown to the Strand Theater where I paid nine cents to see a cowboy double feature. Between the features they stuck in a serial and a cartoon.

As I watched the cartoon that morning, my theology of the Holy Ghost suddenly crystallized. The cartoon was "Casper, the Friendly Ghost." It dawned on me that the Holy Ghost is like Casper — always there to help you out, to pick you up, dust you off, encourage you and help you win your battles.

I didn't have any more trouble with the Holy Ghost until I was 16. At that age all the boys in my church went through a rite of passage called "Young Men's Bible Training Class." We were taught how to pray, teach, serve communion and prove that a Methodist was going to Hell.

I caused quite a stir the night we studied the Holy Ghost. The teacher began by asking, "Who can identify the Holy Ghost?"

I jumped at the opportunity. "The Holy Ghost," I blurted out, "is like Casper, the Friendly Ghost!"

I almost received the left foot of fellowship that night.
The teacher turned me every way but loose. He told me in no
uncertain terms that Casper had nothing to do with the Holy
Ghost. "The Holy Ghost," he explained, "is the Bible."

That's right. We were taught that the Holy Spirit is an
inanimate object — a book. If we wanted to get the Spirit, we
would have to memorize the book. The more verses we
committed to memory, the more of the Spirit we would
receive.

Reaching Out to God 4

The point is that as I stood there that day in the mid-1970s facing the chilling reality of a failed business and a $100,000 debt, I had no inner spiritual power to help me cope with the crisis.

Let me take that back. I did have the power, for I had received Jesus as my Savior many years before, and on that day I had received the indwelling power of the Holy Spirit. But I didn't know that. I had never plugged into the power. I had never released the power of the Spirit in my life. Instead, I had stifled and quenched the Spirit.

I thought the Spirit was a book. I did not realize that the Spirit is a personality, that the Spirit is the supernatural presence of God in the world today, and that He dwells within believers.

I could recite the five steps in what our church called "The Plan of Salvation." I could also recite what we called "The Five Acts of Worship." I could give you chapter and verse to substantiate several dozen of our pet doctrines. But I had no power to cope with a business failure and a $100,000 debt.

Wallowing in Self-Pity

So I did the only thing I knew how to do — I threw a pity party. I wallowed in self-pity. And as I did so, I sank deeper into the pit of depression.

I finally became so despondent that I decided to kill my-self. I felt like I just couldn't face the disgrace and pain of such a failure. Also, I was mad at God. How could He let me down so miserably when I had, at long last, deigned to meet Him half way? In my emotionally perverted reasoning, I decided that by taking my life I would teach God a lesson! I know that sounds weird, but when you are deeply depressed, you don't think too clearly.

For several days I plotted my demise. Just as I had everything carefully planned, I suddenly got a strange thought: "Why not try God?" That was a strange thought for me because I didn't believe in either a personal or a powerful God. Looking back on it today I can only conclude that the thought must have come from the stirring of the Spirit within me. I had quenched the Spirit, but the Spirit was still there and, like Casper, He was trying to minister to me in my time of need.

I tried to suppress the thought, but it would not go away. Over and over it came to me: "Why not try God?"

Calling for Help

I finally decided to follow the prompting. I got on the phone and called several friends. I asked them to come to my house. When they arrived, I explained my predicament and asked them to pray for me. One by one they prayed. Their prayers were lifeless and unbelieving. They no more believed in a personal and powerful God than I did.

As the prayers droned on, I became agitated. "This won't do," I interrupted. "None of you are praying with any mean-ing. You don't understand, I need a miracle! Let's try again and this time, pray with some faith!" I could hardly believe those words came out of my mouth. But they did. My friends started praying again, this time with some fervor.

God performed the miracle the very next morning, and it transformed my life. You could start guessing right now and guess till the Lord returns, and you would never guess how God answered our prayers.

Being Shaped by God

You see, when God responds to a cry for help, He does so in a manner that is always designed to minister first to the inner man, to the spiritual nature. It's not that He's unconcerned about the physical man and the physical and emotional pain; it's just that His priorities are different from ours. We want to be ministered to from the outside in. He ministers from the inside out, because that is the only kind of ministry that has lasting effects.

If you were to guess how the Lord answered our prayers, you would most likely assume that some man walked in my store the next morning and offered to buy the business for $100,000. That would have been truly remarkable, but it would not have had a transforming effect on me. I would probably have written it off to "coincidence" rather than recognizing it as an answer to prayer. Most likely, I would have sighed with relief and gone on my way continuing to try to meet God halfway.

God answered my prayer miraculously, but He did it in a way designed to get my attention, to convince me that He truly is a personal and powerful God who is on the throne, hears prayers and still performs miracles. He also used a method that was designed to transform me more into the image of His Son.

A Transforming Miracle   5

Here's what happened. The next morning I went to the store and started calling around trying to find a buyer for my fixtures. I was standing at the front counter talking on the phone when I heard a knock at the front door. I turned and looked at the plate glass door and saw an Oriental man and woman standing there. The man was grinning from ear to ear. I pointed to the sign hanging on the door and turned my back on the couple. The sign said, "Closed: Going Out of Business."

The man resumed his knocking. I got mad. Couldn't this fellow read? Why did he have that big grin on his face? The last thing I wanted to see was someone happy. Misery really does love company.

I put the phone down, went to the door, opened it about an inch and shouted, "Can't you read? We're closed!"

"Oh yes sir," he replied, "I know you are closed. I'm interested in buying your fixtures."

"Oh!" I replied. "Come in. Come in."

I locked the door and went back to the phone while the Oriental man and lady looked around the store. When I finished talking, the man came up to me, still grinning, and said, "Thank you, dear sir, for letting me see your store." He was almost nauseating in his politeness. He continued to grin and started bowing in the Oriental style. Then he started apologizing! "I'm very sorry, dear sir, but you do not have any fixtures I'm interested in. I'm opening up a different type of store."

A Probing Question

I escorted him and the lady to the door. The lady walked out, but as the man got halfway through the door, he suddenly stopped, turned to me and said, "I discern that you are troubled in the spirit. Do you want to talk about it?"

Talk about getting angry. I was livid. Who did this guy think he was? I replied in my "best" Christian manner, "What's it to you?"

"Well," he replied, "I assume from the nature of this store that you must be a Christian. I am too. And I discern that you need ministry. Would you mind if I shared with you what Jesus Christ has done for me in my life?"

I didn't want to hear his story. I wanted him to leave. But what was I to say? It was like when someone asks if they can pray for you. You may not want them to, but you hate to say no.

"I'm awfully busy," I said, as I glanced at my watch in irritation.

"It won't take but a moment," he replied. He grinned again.

"Okay, okay," I said, "but make it quick."

He turned and said something to the lady in a foreign language, and she left. I locked the door again, and we went to my office. When we sat down on the couch, he put his arm around me and began to pat my shoulder sympathetically. Again, I was outraged. Who does this guy think he is? He hardly knows me, and he has his arm around me.

But I soon forgot my anger as he began to tell his story.

A Fascinating Story

"When I was a small boy, my father came home one day with terror in his eyes. 'The Communists are coming,' he said, 'and they are going to kill us because we are devout Christians.'

"He told each of us to get two pillow slips and to go to the living room. He started running all over the house gathering up items which he piled in the middle of the floor. 'Put these in the pillow slips,' he said, 'and tie the tops.'

"We were a very wealthy family, but all we took with us that day was what we could stuff into those pillow slips. We fled into the jungle, and we threw ourselves upon the Lord because we didn't know how to survive in the jungle. There were 12 of us in all. We wandered about aimlessly crying out to God to save us.

"Finally, after three weeks, we made it from Hanoi to Saigon, and we rejoiced over the Lord's deliverance.

A Repeat Performance

"We began our life anew. Many years later I came home one day to my family and my aged parents with that same look of terror in my eyes. 'Get the pillow slips,' I yelled. 'The Communists are coming again.'

"You see, I was a translator at the American Embassy. I had been informed that the Embassy could not arrange for all my family to be flown out. I would not leave without them. So, once again, we had to flee. I knew if we stayed we would be executed because I had worked for the Americans.

"We fled into the Mekong Delta and, again, we began to cry out to God for deliverance. After wandering for several days, we made it to the South China Sea where we discovered a boat full of refugees about to depart. God had saved us a second time!

"But when the boat got out to sea, it started sinking. There were just too many people on it. Some people panicked and began to push others overboard. Some even threw their children into the sea. We got on our knees and started calling out to God. Soon, a merchant ship appeared and took the survivors on board. God had saved us a third time!

"We were taken to the Philippines where we were put with thousands of other refugees in a concentration type camp. We began praying that God would give us a new home.

A year later the news came that we were being adopted by a Bible Church in Dallas, Texas. God saved us a fourth time.

"So, here we are in a new land starting our lives over. God is so good. He loves us, and He answers our prayers. Lean on Him. He will deliver you."

A Changed Attitude

I looked at the man with tears in my eyes. Before I knew it, I had my arms around him, hugging him in thankfulness for insisting on sharing a story I had not wanted to hear.

When he left, everything had changed. Yet, nothing visible had changed. I still had a failed business. I still owed a bank $100,000. What had changed was me. I no longer felt depressed. I was no longer wallowing in despair and self-pity. I had hope. I knew in my soul that God had heard my prayer and that He had sent that man to assure me that if I would trust in the Lord, everything would turn out all right. God had used an Oriental man from halfway around the world to get my eyes off myself and onto His Son.

I had no problems compared to the problems that man had faced. If God could solve his problems, He surely could handle mine.

Discovering God   6

God had gotten my attention, but He did not yet have me.

During my years of running from the Lord I had developed many sinful attitudes, thoughts and habits. I was in bondage to pride and lust. I wrestled daily with a hot temper. I still dreamed of worldly success.

I still had a long way to go before I could become a useful servant of the Lord's. I had to get to know God as a personal, caring and powerful God. I had to get to know myself — to really know myself — by honestly facing up to my faults. I had to learn how to surrender myself to God's will and then how to live on the power of His Spirit rather than the power of my flesh.

Viewing the Bible Differently

The Lord began the process by giving me an insatiable appetite for His Word. I had grown up in a Bible believing church. Theologically we proclaimed the Bible as the revealed Word of God, and we stood on the authority of the Scriptures. But in practice, we put our traditions above the Word. We played games with Scripture.

When the Word contradicted our doctrines, we either spiritualized the passage or we dispensationalized it. We spiritualized by saying that the passage didn't mean what it said. We dispensationalized by arguing that the passage had ceased to be valid at the end of the First Century.

We also tended to use the Bible as a debating handbook. Rather than reading it to seek truth or simply to allow the Holy Spirit to minister to our hearts, we approached it as though it were the Texas Code Annotated. We looked for proof texts to justify our doctrines and to prove others wrong.

As I started reading the Bible anew, The Spirit led me to read it in a different way. Rather than searching for proof texts, I found myself reading for the sheer joy of it. As I read, I began to make some amazing discoveries. For example, prophecy began to make sense, if I would just believe what it said.

In fact, the whole Bible began to make more sense to me as I began to accept what it said as meaning what it said and as being applicable to me today. As a trained academic, I had always approached the Bible as literature to be analyzed, categorized and theologized. I now became aware that it was written to be believed and acted upon.

It was difficult, but I began to put aside the rationalizing, the spiritualizing and the dispensationalizing. As I did so, I found that the Word began to transform me. For the first time my eyes were opened to my own faults rather than the faults of others. Time and time again I was brought to my knees in repentance. The Word became a spiritual mirror reflecting my inadequacies compared to the perfection of Jesus.

Seeing God in a New Way

I also began to discover some important things about God. First and foremost was the revelation that He is the same yesterday, today and forever (Malachi 3:6 and Hebrews 13:8).

What a discovery that was for me! God had not retired! He is alive and well. He is still the same God as the one revealed in the Bible — a God who is sovereign, personal, loving, caring, powerful and who still intervenes in history in response to the faith of those who seek Him. I could hardly contain my joy.

Tasting the Lord's Discipline

The Word was not my only teacher during those difficult days following my business failure. I was also shaped and molded by the Lord's discipline.

After I sold off all the assets of my business, I still owed the bank $60,000. I negotiated a deal to pay off that debt by agreeing to pay the bank a minimum of $1,000 a month. That obligation meant that my family and I were going to have to learn to live on a greatly reduced income. Our whole lifestyle was transformed almost overnight.

Prior to the business failure, my income had been increasing rapidly almost every year. But like most Americans captivated by materialism, no matter how much I made, it was not enough. I always needed a bigger house or a larger car. Suddenly, we had to learn how to live a frugal lifestyle. Most of what I earned each month went to pay off the debt. So we mainly lived on my wife's income as a first-grade teacher.

It was the discipline of the Lord. It wasn't easy, but it was another spiritually transforming experience. We were delivered from materialism. We learned how to live simply, how to count our blessings, how to be satisfied with what we had. We began to learn about how to trust in the Lord to provide our basic needs.

Playing at Christianity

But we were still pretty much what I would call "cultural Christians." By that I mean that my wife and I had been born into Christian families, raised in the Church, and considered Christian values to be an integral part of our lives. We attended church regularly and made sure that our children were involved in all the church's activities. In short, we were a typical American churchgoing family.

The problem with that is that we were not committed disciples of the Lord. Like most Christians, we had accepted Jesus as Savior but not as Lord. We had received His Spirit into our lives, but we had never released the power of the Spirit. For me the Spirit was a resident but not president. He resided but He did not preside. My ego was on the throne of my life.

I still needed a lot of the Lord's discipline. I began to taste it when I decided to take one more step in the direction of the Lord's will for my life. I had been preaching part-time on the weekends for a church in Irving, Texas. When the business collapsed, they asked me to become their full-time pastor. I agreed.

Moving a Step Closer

At long last, I had given in to the Lord's will for my life. I expected to be blessed mightily. I looked forward to receiving the inner peace that I so desperately desired. I was in for a surprise.

I was to learn that the Lord could not minister effectively through me because I still had not surrendered fully to Him. I had surrendered my career but not myself. I still had a lot of sin in my life that I refused to deal with. I still wanted to run the show my way.

I tried to run the church like I would run a university or a business. I set goals, organized committees and attempted to manipulate people to do what I wanted. I was involved in constant confrontations.

I was not filled with the Spirit. I did not know anything about spiritual gifts. I operated in the flesh. It was all I knew how to do.

God in His mercy blessed me in many ways during the three chaotic years that I served that church. As I said before, He got me immersed in the Word. He began to open my eyes to the things of the Spirit. He began to deal with the sin in my life. Through all the conflict, He taught me more about Himself, myself and other people.

Undergoing a Family Crisis

Near the end of that ministry I tasted the discipline of the

Lord again in a traumatic event involving our younger daughter. She became involved with drugs. Her whole personality changed. She became moody and tempestuous. Her school work declined. Family arguments grew more frequent.

All the signs of drug involvement were there, but we didn't recognize them. We could not begin to conceive that a child of ours could be having a drug problem. That was the kind of nightmare that afflicted other families, not ours.

But it did afflict us. One day it culminated with our daughter running away from home. She was only 16. She vanished completely. For three months we did not know if she was dead or alive.

During those awful days of waiting and wondering — days of weeping and searching — Satan attacked us with everything he could use. We were overwhelmed by self-condemnation. We felt judged and censured by some of our friends. Every news report seemed to contain a horror story about the mutilation death of a runaway. A special television documentary on runaways indicated that most girls ended up as prostitutes.

We felt totally helpless. In our helplessness, we turned to God as never before. My wife and I joined hands and got on our knees and cried out to God for mercy. We admitted our inability to cope with the situation and, like little children, we cried out to our Father for help.

A Spiritual Transformation

As we emptied ourselves and humbled ourselves before the Lord, we experienced the filling of His Spirit. We received a peace that was beyond human understanding. We felt assured that our daughter was in His hands and that everything would turn out okay if we would only lean on the power of His Spirit and trust in His mercy.

My wife and I were drawn closer to each other. Long lingering resentments evaporated. Pettiness dissipated. Love was renewed. God was working mightily through a tragedy to heal our marriage and to renew and deepen our relationship with Him.

Our daughter was found alive and well, living and working in a small town in Indiana. We had walked through the valley of the shadow of death and found that the Lord walks with you every step of the way if you will only let Him.

Feeling Confused

My experience with the filling of the Spirit motivated me to launch an intensive study of the Holy Spirit and spiritual gifts. It did not take me long to discover that I did not have the spiritual gifts to be a pastor. I did not have a pastor's heart. I did not have the love and patience to shepherd a flock of God's people.

By the time I made that discovery, I was already burned out from operating in the flesh and terribly confused. Why had God called me into the ministry without giving me the gifts to be an effective minister? I just couldn't figure it out.

I had run from the Lord as hard as I could run for almost 20 years. Then, when I stopped running and gave in to His will, He allowed me to fail again. Was He some sort of cosmic sadist?

I decided to chuck the whole thing. I resigned in disgust and returned to my career in higher education, accepting a position as vice president for development for a private, church-related university in Oklahoma.

I decided that I had misread God. I hadn't. God had simply been trying to teach me some things that I desperately needed to know if I was ever going to be an effective servant of His.

Now He was preparing to put me through a wilderness experience that was designed to move me into the center of His will.

Wrestling with God 7

Although the job I had been offered was an outstanding one, I had some strong reservations about it. The university was related to a denomination that had a very liberal reputation. I could not get excited about raising money to assist the propagation of theological liberalism.

I raised this point with the new president of the university who had offered me the job. He assured me that the school did not share the liberal viewpoint of the denomination that supported it. "We are located in a conservative area," he pointed out, "and we must maintain a conservative posture if we are to attract the support of our surrounding churches."

A Wilderness Experience

I was soon to discover that in religion, as in politics, the terms "conservative" and "liberal" are highly subjective. I quickly realized that what the university president considered "conservative" was to me nothing but rank liberalism.

Because I was suspicious from the start, I refused to move my family to Oklahoma. I decided to get an apartment and check out the situation. For the next six months I lived alone, commuting to Dallas on weekends.

I did not realize it at the time, but God had maneuvered me into exactly the place where He wanted me — alone and isolated. He was determined to get my undivided attention. He had set me up for a wilderness experience.

Confused Again

Disillusionment with the new job set in almost the moment I arrived on campus. The school had been thoroughly secularized. It was church-related in name only. Religion professors openly scoffed at the Bible. Fundamentalists were ridiculed. My worst suspicions proved true.

I was bewildered again. Why had God led me to this place? I was bordering on despair when I decided to go to my knees. I began to pray with a zeal I had never before experienced.

Every night I poured my heart out to God. "Oh Lord, why am I here? I'm so lonely, so empty, so confused. What is your will for me? What must I do to receive peace? Have mercy upon me, Oh Lord. Have mercy. Show me what you want me to do. I'm tired of running from You. I'm weary of being out of Your will. Close all the doors You don't want me to go through. Leave open only the door You want me to enter, and then give me the courage and faith to go through it. Please, dear God, show me Your will!"

Night after night I continued to pray and weep before the Lord. Finally, one night I became so exhausted that I shut up and simply knelt by my bed in silence. It was then that I heard the voice of God — not audibly. It was His Spirit witnessing to mine. The message was clear and precise: "Resign your job. Step out in faith and preach, 'Jesus is coming soon.' Preach, 'Flee from the wrath that is to come.'"

A Challenging Message

It was a "good news, bad news" message for me. The good news was the call to preach the soon coming of Jesus. The Holy Spirit had led me into an intensive study of Bible prophecy that had brought me to the conclusion that we are living in the season of the Lord's return. The message was heavy on my heart. In fact, like Jeremiah, it was burning in my breast (Jeremiah 20:9). It was a message I ardently wanted to proclaim.

The bad news was that the Lord wanted me to do it by faith. That scared me to death. I had taught a lot about faith and preached faith. But I never really had done anything by faith. I discovered there is a great leap from preaching to doing.

So, instead of saying, like Isaiah, "Here am I, Lord, send me," I began to make excuses like Moses did when he said, "Here am I, send Aaron." I waffled all over the place.

"But Lord," I said, "how will I support myself? I'm still paying on my business debt. And I've got a daughter about to start to college. How will I pay her tuition?"

Excuse followed excuse. I pelted the Lord with questions. The only answer I received was the same command: "Resign your job. Step out in faith and preach 'Jesus is coming soon.' Preach 'Flee from the wrath that is to come.'"

The Lord wasn't interested in my questions. His only concern was my obedience.

Continuing to Resist

But I wasn't ready to obey. I wanted to wrestle. I tried my old ploy of compromise. "Okay, Lord," I said, "I'll meet you halfway. I'll find a church where I can preach. That way I'll have an assured income. Then I will go out during the week to other churches and proclaim the soon return of Your Son."

The Lord wasn't impressed. His only response was a question: "Is that faith?" I knew it wasn't. But I didn't have the faith to do what He wanted me to do. I continued to wrestle with Him.

As I look back on the wrestling match and consider my incredible stubbornness and lack of faith, I can only praise God that He is so patient and full of loving-kindness. Instead of washing His hands of me in disgust, He began to give me supernatural confirmation of His will for my life. That confirmation was to radically change my life, propelling me into the center of His will.

Surrendering to God 8

One day in the midst of all this spiritual struggle, I went to the mailbox and discovered a package from an old friend in Houston. Inside was a cassette tape by Pat Robertson. The topic was "How to Seek the Guidance of God."

I later learned that it was one of a series of 12 tapes Robertson had done on spiritual guidance. Through my friend, God had selected this one tape for me to hear. The note that came with the tape simply said: "While I was listening to this tape, God impressed upon my heart to send it to you."

The topic and timing of the tape intrigued me. I listened to it immediately. In the middle of the tape Robertson suggested that if you are ever struggling with a career decision and you think you've heard God's voice as to what you are to do, you might put the guidance you have received to a spiritual test by using the Old Testament principle of seeking the confirmation of two or more witnesses. That advice witnessed to my spirit, and I decided to follow it that moment.

Launching an Experiment

I picked up the phone and called one of the godliest men I knew in Dallas. "Bob," I said, "you may think I'm crazy but I believe God has called me to resign my job and step out in faith and preach the soon coming of Jesus."

"That's great!" he replied. "What can I do to help?"

"I want you to pray about it for three days," I said. "Then call me back and tell me what the Lord has spoken to your heart."

He agreed. The three days seemed to drag by as I waited anxiously for his call.

Promptly on the evening of the third day Bob called back. "Dave," he said, "you'd better sit down."

"What do you mean?"

"I mean God has given a strong and clear answer to my prayers. You're not going to believe what has happened."

My heart began to pound, and I sat down.

"First of all," he said, "God has really impressed upon me in my prayers that you are to take this step of faith. Second, I have mentioned the matter to only two people and yet, in three days' time, I have spontaneously received commitments from people all over Dallas who have pledged to give $800 a month for the first year!"

I was stunned. This was far beyond anything I had imagined. I didn't know what to say. Talk about God hitting you over the head with a baseball bat! It was like He was screaming from the heavens, "Do it, David!"

Then Bob asked, "Are you going to do it?"

I should have been rejoicing, but I was frightened. I started scrambling for excuses.

"Well, Bob, I just don't know yet. You see, I'm running an experiment. I'm seeking confirmation from two witnesses. You're the first. I have to find another."

I thanked him for calling and hung up. I was scared — really scared. I had put God to the test and He had come through with flying colors. The ball was in my court.

Continuing the Experiment

I decided I needed to give the whole matter some careful thought. I put off seeking the second witness for several days. During that time I kept searching through my mind, trying to come up with the name of the second person I would call. I made list after list of names. I kept ruling out people for various reasons. "This one won't be honest with me. That one will tell me what he thinks I want to hear. I can't call her because she won't really pray about it." On and on the excuses went.

As I look back on that selection process today, it is clear that the real reason I ruled out so many people is because I was afraid they would confirm God's call. I was searching for some one who would say, "You're crazy — forget it."

Trying to Stack the Experiment

The ideal person who finally came to mind was a lady named Bernice. She was a widow in her late 70s who lived in Dallas. I had known her for about three years, though not well. Most of my contact with her had been through letters and telephone conversations.

But I knew her well enough to know that she was a gold-plated character. Somehow, she always managed to get a tape recording of every sermon I delivered in the Dallas area. She would listen to the sermon and then send me a five-page, single-spaced, typed letter in which she would take the sermon apart paragraph by paragraph. "Your introduction was weak. You should have used a different scripture to back up your point. You misused the scripture you quoted. You mispronounced the prophet's name." She was a real burr under my saddle. I felt like she was my self-appointed spiritual watchdog.

She was even more peculiar over the phone. She would answer gruffly with a phrase I could never understand. The words all ran together in what sounded like a command of a top sergeant. Finally, one day I got up enough nerve to ask her what she always shouted when she answered the phone. "I've never been able to understand what you say when you answer the phone," I explained, "Could you say it slower?"

"Of course," she replied in an irritated manner. "I say 'Rejoice in the Lord always.' And you are supposed to reply, 'And again, I say rejoice!'"

At long last I realized why our phone conversations

always got off to a bad start. I didn't complete the scripture verse that she was shouting at me!

Bernice never had time for pleasantries on the phone. If I asked, "How are you doing?" she would likely reply, "Not so hot. What do you want?" She was always anxious to get to the bottom line. One never knew when she might terminate the conversation. When she got tired of talking, she would just hang up, often without even bothering to say goodby.

Needless to say, I always got nervous when Bernice called me. I knew I was in trouble. So when I thought of her as the second possible witness, I did not relish the idea of calling her. But I knew she would shoot straight with me, and I felt it was likely that she would say, "You're nuts!"

Making the Crucial Call

"Hello Bernice, this is David."

"David who?"

"David Reagan."

"What do you want?"

We were off to a great start. I could tell she was annoyed by my call. I had caught her in a particularly bad mood. I was delighted. I felt sure this would be the end of my grand experiment.

I related the message I felt God had laid on my heart.

"Why are you telling me this?" she snapped.

"Because I want you to pray about it," I explained. "Pray about it for three days and then let me know what you think the Lord wants me to do."

"Okay, I'll do it." She hung up. No goodby.

I smiled and thought, "That's the end of that." But I was in for a big surprise from the Lord.

Receiving a Shock

Three days later Bernice called back. She spoke like a person transformed. No gruffness. No staccato commands. I could hardly believe it was her.

She was excited. "David, you're not going to believe

what has happened!"

"What?" I asked, now frightened by her positive tone and obvious enthusiasm.

"Well, first of all, God has really confirmed your call in my prayers. There's no doubt about it! And guess what? I've received an inheritance of $3,000 since you called. And if you will resign and start the new ministry, I will give you $1,000 of my inheritance."

Never in my life had I been so shocked. Could this really be Bernice? Was she really speaking words of encouragement? Had I heard her correctly? Did she just offer me one-third of her inheritance?

I don't know how long I stood there in amazed silence, but I was brought back when I heard her shout, "David, are you still there? Speak to me!"

"Yes, Bernice, I'm still here. It's just that I'm sort of flabbergasted by all this."

A Double Whammy

"Well, I've got more good news," she said. "Aren't you driving a university car?"

"Yes."

"Won't you need a car in the ministry?"

"Yes."

"Well, I've got one for you!"

That's when I nearly lost it. I dropped into a chair and just sat there limp. Then I heard something really strange. Laughter. Yes, Bernice was laughing! I didn't even know she knew how!

"What are you laughing about?" I asked.

"Well," she paused and giggled like a little child, "don't get too excited about the car. You see, it's a holy car."

"A holy car? What's a holy car?"

"It's one that's been prayed over on the side of the road many times!"

In short, it was an old junker. But that was irrelevant. The only thing that mattered at the moment was the fact that God had motivated this grand old lady to give me a car and part of her inheritance.

"Are you going to do it?" she asked.

Again, incredibly, I waffled. Again, God had hit me over the head with a two-by-four to get my attention. What more confirmation could a person ask for? But I was scared and just didn't have the faith to take the step.

"I'm running an experiment," I lamely explained. "I'll call you back in a few days."

Continuing to Doubt

I remember sharing this story with an Episcopal priest friend of mine. When I got to this point in the story, he stopped me and said, "I'll bet I know what you did next."

"How do you know?" I asked.

"Because I've been there."

"Okay," I said, "tell me what I did next."

"Well, being the great man of faith that you are, I figure you got on your knees and asked God for a third witness."

"You've definitely been there," I replied.

I'm ashamed to admit it but that's exactly what I did. "Lord," I cried out, "you've overwhelmed me with these two confirmations. But Lord, I may have stacked the deck. I may have called people I knew would say yes. Lord, I want to make certain of Your will. So, Lord, if You really want me to do this, then You send a third witness — an unsolicited witness. If You'll do that, Lord, I'll take the step of faith."

Playing Games

I was still playing games with God. I knew I hadn't "stacked the deck." The Lord's will for me had been con-firmed. I was just scared and kept pointing to my precarious financial situation — the need to pay-off the debt and the need to send my daughter to college.

But there was a deeper fear that I didn't want to admit because it was rooted in pride. My greatest fear was what people would think of me.

After all, I was a distinguished academician with a doctorate from a Harvard graduate school. I knew what sort of things people would say about a fellow — any fellow — who suddenly started preaching the soon return of Jesus. Both family and friends would write me off as a candidate for the guys with the butterfly nets.

So I squirmed and made excuses. I sought a third witness. Any other god would have zapped me with a lightning bolt. But the God I was dealing with was the God who is full of patience and longsuffering. He continued to prod me like a little child.

A Third Witness

The very next morning after talking to Bernice and praying for another confirmation, God sent the third witness. He came in a most unusual form, and I learned that when you are seeking God's guidance, you should be sensitive to receiving it from strange sources.

The witness was one of the greatest preachers of this century, Dr. Martin Lloyd-Jones. No, he didn't appear at my door. At least, not in person. God sent him to me through a magazine article.

The magazine was *Christianity Today*. On the cover was a drawing of Dr. Jones. I didn't know much about him, but what I knew really intrigued me. I knew he had written several volumes on the book of Romans which had received worldwide acclaim. He had the reputation of being the foremost expository preacher in all of Christendom.

I decided to read the article before going on to the office. The occasion of the article was Dr. Jones' 80th birthday. It took the form of an interview:

Question: "What seminary did you attend?"

Answer: "I didn't go to seminary."

Question: "Where did you go to school?"

Answer: "I went to medical school and became a doctor."

Question: "How did you get into the ministry?"

Answer: "God called me. I put a note on my office door

that said 'I have gone to save men's souls.'"

Question: "Did you enter seminary then?"

Answer: "No, I never went to seminary. I simply started preaching. I would read a verse and comment on it. Then read the next verse and comment on it. That's all I've ever done."

A Crucial Question and Answer

The interview with this remarkable man went on for pages, surveying his whole career in the ministry. The next to the last question was: "Have you learned anything new in your study of the Bible in the last five years?"

"Oh yes," he responded. "Five years ago I began an intensive study of Bible prophecy, and it has led me to the conclusion that we are living in the season of the Lord's return."

My chest tightened with anticipation as I looked to the last question. God was about to speak to me.

Question: "If you were a young minister just beginning to preach, what would your message be?"

Answer: "Flee from the wrath that is to come!"

I could hardly believe my eyes. Those were the exact words God had laid on my heart.

A Joyous Release

"Thank you, Lord!" I yelled. "Thank you. Thank you. Thank you!"

I was on my knees praising God in prayer. The call had been confirmed in my heart. I was no longer full of doubt. The fear was gone. Resolve had replaced it. I knew what I had to do, and I was ready to do it, regardless — regardless of finances or reputation.

As I drove to the office I found myself slapping the steering wheel in glee one moment, shouting, "Thank you, Lord!" Then in the next moment I would shake my head in astonishment and ask, "But why me Lord? I'm nothing but a miserable sinner."

I've asked the Lord that question many times since, and

He has responded graciously in two ways. First, by reminding me that "there is no condemnation for those who are in Christ Jesus" (Romans 8:1). And second, by reminding me of my namesake, King David of Israel. The Lord has made it clear to me that the only people He has to work through are sinners. If we have put our faith in His Son, He has forgiven and forgotten our sins (Hebrews 8:12). He calls us to do the same.

Becoming a Fool

When I arrived at the university, I went directly to the president's office and told him I had decided to resign. He asked what I was upset about. I told him that was not the problem and explained that I was resigning because God had called me to preach. Having been a preacher once himself, the president knew there was no hope in trying to argue with someone who had received God's call.

So, he simply asked, "What church?"

"No church," I replied.

"Well then," he asked, "how are you going to preach?"

"I'm just going to step out in faith and preach wherever God opens a door."

"What are you going to preach?"

"Jesus is coming soon."

He looked at me in disbelief. "You're going to preach what?" he asked.

"That Jesus is coming soon."

He just shook his head in amazement, smiled and said, "When are you going to do this?"

It was the middle of March. I had decided to give him two weeks' notice.

"April the first," I answered.

He sat there for a moment and stared at me incredulously. Then he shrugged his shoulders and replied, "All I can say is that I think you have selected a most appropriate date!"

So, on April Fool's Day, 1980, I stepped out in faith. Twenty years of running from the Lord was finally over. At long last, with great timidity and only after prolonged discipline, I had said, "Here am I, Lord, send me."

Now I had to learn how to trust the Lord for everything in my life.

Part II
The Ministry

"There's never a dull moment serving the Lord."

Walking by Faith   9

The fear that had filled my life for 20 years regarding the Lord's call had dissipated completely when I finally surrendered to the Lord. But during the two weeks between that surrender and the termination of my employment at the university, Satan attacked me hard. I was once again filled with self-doubt. Had I made a rash decision? Was I needlessly jeopardizing my family? Would those who had made pledges be faithful to them? Would any church invite me to speak?

Once I made the decision to resign, the two fears that bothered me most related to my wife and money. How would my wife react? And how would I ever pay that business debt? God in His grace and mercy quickly dealt with both fears.

Gaining My Wife's Support

The Lord had blessed me with a beautiful, red-headed wife named Ann who had a disposition exactly opposite to the red-headed stereotype. Instead of being moody and volatile, she was stable and quiet — the perfect balance to me! We had grown up together in the same church in Waco, Texas and had been childhood sweethearts.

Ann had always been my number-one fan. I thrived on her support and encouragement. But she had withdrawn that support when I accepted the pulpit in Irving. "I didn't marry a preacher," she announced coldly and, with that proclamation, she withdrew into her own world of public school teaching. She was determined that no one would ever force her into playing the role of a preacher's wife.

Trying to minister without the support of your wife is impossible. The lack of that support had been just one more of the many reasons that my ministry at the church in Irving had failed so miserably.

I could tell that Ann was relieved when I left the ministry and returned to higher education. I therefore greatly feared her reaction when the Lord called me to step out in faith and start preaching again.

My fears proved to be misplaced. When I broke the news to Ann, I discovered that God had already miraculously prepared her heart for my decision. To my astonishment she reacted with enthusiasm, and I took her reaction as one more confirmation of the Lord's call.

A Precious Gift

One year to the day after the ministry was launched, I returned to Dallas from a pilgrimage to the Holy Land. When Ann met me at the airport, she handed me a present wrapped in paper that said, "Happy Anniversary." I was puzzled.

"It's not our anniversary," I said.

"I know," she replied, "but today is a very special anniversary for both of us."

With those words it suddenly dawned on me that it was the first anniversary of the ministry — April 1, 1981. I opened the package and found a framed certificate that my wife had personally designed. A friend had done the calligraphy. It had the logo of the ministry at the top. Then, in beautiful lettering, it said, "Presented to my husband, David Reagan, on the occasion of the first anniversary of our ministry."

At the bottom was a quotation from 1 Corinthians 4:10 — "We are fools for Christ's sake."

That plaque is my most prized possession. Every time I look at it I am reminded of God's grace and mercy and His miracle-working ability to transform a human heart.

Removing a Debt

My second most pressing fear was the business debt. I still had two years of payments to go. Where would the money come from? Again, God in His mercy moved swiftly to remove this mountain from my life.

The really neat thing is that He took care of the debt in a way that helped me to better understand the meaning of His grace. I needed that lesson because I was still carrying a lot of legalistic baggage from my religious heritage and my family upbringing.

Dealing with My Dad

Part of my view of God had been determined by my relationship with my dad. I suppose this is true to some degree in every person's life. The Bible reveals God as our Heavenly Father. Because of this imagery, it is only natural for a child's view of the Heavenly Father to be shaped by his relationship with his earthly father.

My dad was a strict disciplinarian. He gave little tolerance for misbehavior. He was fast with a belt. I admired him greatly and wanted to please him more than anything, but I always seemed to fall short. And I feared that belt.

I communicated that fear very effectively to my first-grade teacher. At the end of the very first week of school she told me I would have to stay after class for talking too much. She lined up the rest of the kids and started marching them down the hall to send them home.

When she got all the way down at the other end of the hall, she suddenly heard me start screaming, "He's going to kill me! He's going to kill me!" She thought someone was in the room trying to hurt me. She ran back and found me alone. I was hysterical. I kept shouting the same thing over and over.

When she finally calmed me down, I explained that my dad was going to "beat me half to death" for having to stay after school. She told me to run home as fast as I could.

Learning the Value of a Dollar

Years later when I was 11 years old, I started working for my dad in the summers. He had just opened a sheet metal shop, the first of many successful businesses that he would eventually own. I showed up for work that first day full of enthusiasm. He told me to sweep out the shop. I knew he was a stern taskmaster, so I gave this menial task everything I had. I swept every nook and cranny.

I was just finishing up an outstanding job and was about to sweep the last pile of dust out the back door when my dad walked up.

"What are you doing?" he asked in a gruff sort of way that startled me.

"I'm sweeping out the last pile of dirt," I said, wondering what I could possibly be doing wrong.

He pointed to the floor. "Do you see that rivet?" he asked.

I looked down and saw the glint of a shining rivet through the dust. "Yes sir, I see it."

"Well, pick it up! That rivet cost me a quarter of a cent." He then proceeded with a lecture on the value of a dollar. I needed to know the value of a dollar. But I also needed a word of encouragement about the job I had done.

Experiencing Grace

I stood in awe of my dad, fearful of crossing him in any way, and I projected that relationship onto my Heavenly Father. I felt I could never please God no matter how hard I tried. I had no concept of the meaning of grace.

As the years passed I came to a theological understanding of grace, but it was intellectual rather experiential, and it therefore did not penetrate my soul. God knew I needed to better understand what grace was all about, and He knew that my fear of my dad stood in the way.

So God touched me with His grace through my dad. Here's how He did it. My dad had used his outstanding credit rating to secure all the loans for the business I had started. But the banks had required my dad to personally guarantee the loans.

That meant that when the business failed my dad's credit was on the line. I was really anxious about what my dad might say or do. I kept waiting for him to read me the riot act. But never once did he speak a harsh word. Never once was he judgmental or condemning. Never once did he remind me that he had advised against going into such a business. He stood .by me and encouraged me.

But what would he do now that I was stepping out in faith to serve God? Would he panic over the remaining balance of nearly $25,000? Would he demand that I get a safe job that would ensure the continuance of my monthly payments to the bank?

Again, he said nothing. He remained silent about the matter until about six months after the ministry was established. Then he and mom called one night. "Son," he said, "your mom and I have been giving a lot of thought to our finances. We want to get out of debt, so we've decided to consolidate our assets and pay off all our debts. We want you to know that we just paid off the remaining $20,000 that you owe on the business debt."

The mountain was gone — just like that! No more worry about debt. One more fear defeated. Most important of all, my relationship with my dad had been transformed. He had reached out to me in love and given me an incredible blessing I did not deserve and could not repay. Grace experienced. How sweet it is.

Spiritual Discoveries

Over the next few years I was to learn a lot more about walking by faith, and I am still learning today. One of the first things I learned is that God does not call you to serve Him without spiritually gifting you to fulfill the task He sets before you. You don't have to worry about whether you are qualified to do God's will. If it is God's will that you are doing, He will qualify you.

I discovered, for example, that all my graduate training in international politics had been a perfect preparation for me to teach Bible prophecy. After all, most end-time prophecy is concerned with world politics. That brought a smile to my heart, for I realized that all the time I was running from the Lord, He was preparing me to serve Him when I got tired of running! What is it the psalm says? — "Even the wrath and rebellion of man goes to the glory of God" (Psalm 76:10). Jonah found that out the hard way, and so did I.

Another discovery I was to make is that God does not put a call on someone without preparing the way for them. When I took the step of faith, I literally had no idea where I would preach. I had broken with the denomination I had grown up in, and there was no way to mend the fences. The church of my heritage was militantly amillennial, even to the point of making the doctrine a test of fellowship. My studies had brought me to a premillennial position.

I had not become identified with any other denomination, so there was no particular group of churches biting at the bit to invite me to speak. Furthermore, the Lord had impressed upon my heart that the new ministry was to be transdenominational in nature. We were not to identify with any denominational group. We were to go wherever God opened a door, regardless of the sign over that door.

Accordingly, the board of the ministry was composed of people drawn from a great variety of denominations. They agreed on only three things: 1) that Jesus is Lord; 2) that the Bible is the revealed Word of God; and 3) that Jesus is coming soon. Through the power of the Holy Spirit, they put all their differences aside and worked together in love to spread the message of the soon return of Jesus.

Cutting My Teeth

My first opportunities for ministry came among a group of churches that constituted a small splinter segment of the church I had been raised in. These churches were anxious to have me speak because their distinctive feature was their premillennial outlook.

They considered me a convert to their cause, and I was invited to make their circuit of churches. But most of them soon lost interest in me when it became obvious that I had no intention of affiliating the ministry with them.

My ministry among these churches lasted for about two years. During that time I learned another lesson about the faith walk. God does not zap anyone with instant spiritual maturity. Growth in the Lord comes through hours of Bible study and prayer, fellowship with the saints, and obedient service in the Kingdom.

For two years I preached my heart out to small churches all over this country, most of them with only 40 to 90 members. I had a burning message in my heart that I yearned to share with millions, but I spoke only to dozens, and I began to wonder if the Lord would ever open a door for ministry to greater numbers.

As I look back on those years now, I see that God used them to fine-tune my message and to develop me. I had to show my faithfulness in small things before I could be trusted with greater responsibilities.

The world calls it "paying your dues." I considered it a time of refinement in the image of Christ. God was shaping me and my message.

The Breakthrough

My patience was rewarded the third year of the ministry when the Lord prompted the minister of a large church in Lexington, Kentucky to attend a prophecy conference I was conducting at a high school auditorium there. His presence led to an invitation to conduct a prophecy meeting at his church. God greatly blessed that meeting, and the reports of its success led to an avalanche of invitations from a great variety of churches all over the nation.

I'll never forget that meeting. The host pastor had a great sense of humor. When I arrived, we had a conference about the meeting. I didn't know him well, and I did not know his congregation at all.

"What kind of prophecy meeting do you want me to conduct?" I asked.

"What do you mean?" he replied.

"Well," I explained, "I need to know if you want me to jump into the depths of Revelation, or do you want me to deal with prophetic fundamentals?"

He thought for a moment, and then he said, "Dave when I got married, my wife told me to go to the store and buy her a cookbook. I asked her what kind, and she said, 'Find one that says, Number One: Stand facing the stove.' That's what we need here in the realm of prophecy. Assume we know nothing."

I proceeded on that assumption, and God poured out His Spirit.

Denominational Variety

In the years since, the Lord has continued to open a great variety of doors to an ever expanding audience. I have spoken to all kinds of churches — Charismatic and non-Charismatic, traditional and renewal, orthodox and unorthodox, dead and alive. You name it. I've been there.

A classic example of the variety is what happened to me one weekend in Abilene, Texas. I was invited to teach a Saturday afternoon prophetic seminar to a Full Gospel Businessmen's convention. After the session, as I was driving out of the parking lot, a man flagged me down. He asked if I had a place to speak the next morning. I said no. He asked if I could stay overnight. I said yes. He then invited me to speak to his Baptist Church at 9 a.m. the next day.

I went back into the motel where the Full Gospel convention was being held. As I was registering for a room to stay overnight, another man walked up and asked if I had a place to speak the next morning. I said yes. He asked what time. I told him. He then invited me to speak at his church at 11 a.m. His church was one of the largest Churches of Christ in the city. I could hardly believe it — speaking at both a Baptist Church and a Church of Christ on the same Sunday morning!

Another thing you learn in a faith walk is that God has a great sense of humor.

So, I spoke on Sunday morning at a Baptist Church and a Church of Christ. I drove back to Dallas that day and spoke that evening at an independent Christian Church. On the following Friday evening I preached at one of the largest Episcopal Churches in Dallas.

When the ministry started, I had no idea where I would preach. I still have no idea what door God will open next. But there has never been a lack of doors.

I now receive invitations to hold meetings four and five years into the future. I appreciate such invitations but I turn them all down. I figure that a fellow who is preaching the soon return of Jesus has no business making appointments two to five years in the future. So, I take it one year at a time.

Receiving Blessings 10

Supplying spiritual gifts and opening doors of opportunity are two important ways in which God responds to a step of faith. Another is providing needs. I learned that God provides all our needs as we lean on Him in faith — not all our desires or wishes or delights, but all our true needs.

The first need I had was a name for the ministry. I searched the Scriptures and called out to God in prayer. One day as I was driving along the highway praying about the matter I felt led to use the name Maranatha Ministries. The ministry had been called to proclaim the soon return of Jesus, and Maranatha is an Aramaic expression that means "Our Lord come!" (1 Corinthians 16:22). It seemed to be the perfect name.

Disappointment Leads to a Blessing

I was disappointed to find out several weeks later that someone else in Texas had already secured that name. It turned out to be a group in McKinney, a town just north of Dallas.

But God had a purpose in my pursuing that name. My pursuit led me to make contact with that group, and that contact resulted in the development of a friendship with the group's leader, a retired optometrist. He ultimately became a member of our board. Shortly after that, his Maranatha Ministry contributed five acres of land to our ministry for us to use as a headquarters site. God truly works in strange ways!

Another Biblical Name

When the Maranatha name was turned down, I earnestly began to seek the Lord for another name. Time was short. We needed to get incorporated and apply for tax-exempt status. We needed to print letterheads and brochures. We could do none of those things without a name.

The Lord quickly responded with a new name — Lamb & Lion Ministries. I got excited when He impressed that name upon my spirit. It was ideal. Our message was a prophetic one, and the two great prophetic images of Jesus in the Bible are the suffering lamb and the conquering lion. He has already come as the lamb. He will return as the lion. There was great rejoicing when the Secretary of State of Texas confirmed that we could use the name.

Securing a Logo

My next need was for a graphic emblem that would boldly express the ministry's nature and purpose. I had been attracted to the artwork of an illustrator for one of the largest Christian book publishers in America. I found out who he was and discovered that he lived in Austin, Texas.

I wrote him a letter describing what I needed and explained that the ministry was new and had no money. I indicated that the most I could pay for a logo was $100. In other words, I was boldly asking one of the finest religious artists in the country to draw me a logo practically free of charge!

I laid my hand on that letter and prayed that God would prepare the man's heart to receive my request. That was the first time I had ever prayed over a letter. It was to be the first of many times.

I waited anxiously for a reply. A month passed. No word. I needed to print letterheads. I was about to give up and go ahead with the printing without a logo when I received a packet in the mail. Inside was a drawing of the perfect logo, better than anything I could ever have hoped for.

God had heard my prayer. He had prepared the way for my letter. The artist's heart had been touched by my plea through the preparation of God's Spirit.

The ministry now had an outstanding visual identity — all practically free of charge. When God does something, He does it first class.

Pennies from Heaven

My greatest need was money. We had no cash reserves. No equipment. Not even an office. All we had were pledges totaling $800 per month and Bernice's car, which was almost beyond the pale of prayer!

The board put me on a salary of $1,000 per month with a housing allowance of $500. With my wife's income as a first-grade teacher, we could get by financially, assuming, of course, that my $1,500 would materialize somehow each month.

I had no idea where my salary would come from. Neither did anyone else except, of course, the Lord. He graciously supplied our needs each month, often in strange and miraculous ways. We would get right to the end of a month, need $700 to pay our bills, and then receive a check for exactly that amount from someone we had never heard of. It was an exciting way to live.

The Lord never supplied more than we needed. We ended each month with all of our bills paid. We began the next month broke. It kept us on our knees reaching out to God.

Operating on Faith

One of my most memorable experiences regarding money occurred at a church in central Indiana. Our financial rule for meetings was to go on faith, believing that the Lord would supply our needs through free-will love offerings. We had no fees.

On the second night of this particular meeting the pastor asked to speak with me privately. He explained that he and the elders had gotten into an argument about how to compensate me for the meeting. They all agreed that the church should cover my expenses. They disagreed over how to provide a financial gift to the ministry.

"I proposed that they pay you $100 per day or a total of $500 above expenses," the minister explained. "But they said they had never heard of paying a preacher that much. They proposed a gift of $300."

I assured the minister that whatever they decided would be fine with me. I reminded him that I had come in faith, believing God would supply our needs.

"I know," he said, "but I want to be fair. What we've decided to do is guarantee the ministry $400. We're going to take up a love offering on the last night of the meeting. However much it falls short of $400, we will make up the difference."

I assured him that would be fine. The next morning I called my office. It was the next to the last day of the month.

"How are we doing financially?" I asked.

"Not so hot," my office manager replied. "We need a total of $1,700 to end the month with all our bills paid. Will your meeting produce that much?"

I told him we could expect only $400 from the meeting. I asked him to get the staff together and have a special prayer session in behalf of the $1,700 we needed. I also got on my knees and started praying the same prayer.

Opening Heaven's Windows

That night a love offering was taken at the end of the service. After the service was dismissed, I went to the door to shake hands with people. I noticed that while I was saying my goodbyes to the congregation, the chairman of the board of elders began scurrying around the sanctuary gathering the elders for a special impromptu meeting down front. "Oh no," I thought, "the contribution has fallen far short of $400, and they are reconsidering their commitment to make up the difference."

When the meeting ended, the chairman walked up to me. He stuck out a trembling hand and said, "Dave, we've never had anything happen like this before in the history of this church." In his hand was a check. I opened it and nearly fainted. It totaled $1,725!

I praised God all the way back to my motel. Then I called my office manager at his home, got him out of bed and delivered the good news.

"You'd better total up those bills again," I told him. "You said we owed $1,700. We received $1,725. You know God never gives us one dime more than we need. You missed a $25 invoice someplace." And sure enough, he had.

Relying on Prayer 11

I learned quickly that the key to the faith walk is prayer. Earnest prayer. Daily prayer. Specific prayer.

The ministry was only six months old when one of the trustees came to me and said, "Dave, you are killing yourself. You're working night and day, doing everything yourself. You need an office manager."

In full agreement, I explained that there was nothing I could do about it. We just didn't have the money to pay the salary of an office manager.

"The need is there. God knows it and God will supply," the trustee observed. "All you have to do is step out in faith."

Playing Safe

But I couldn't take the step. My terrible experience with the business debt had made me overly cautious regarding money. I was paralyzed by the fear of debt and wanted the money in the bank before hiring the much-needed employee.

The trustee was persistent. Every week for a month he either called or came by the office to impress upon me the need for an office manager. He began to wear me down. Then one day shortly before Christmas, he stopped by and dropped a bomb on me.

"Dave, I've been praying daily about your need for an office manager, and God has impressed upon me that I should resign my job and go to work for the ministry. I'm going to do that immediately. I'll report to work on the first Monday in January," he announced.

"But Billy Jack," I protested, "I can't take that risk! How will I ever pay you?"

"You're not the one taking the risk," he wryly observed. "God will supply. Join with me and pray that God will meet the need."

We prayed together. God supplied. At the end of the first month, the money was there. Our monthly income had mysteriously increased just enough to cover his salary.

The Bible says we do not have because we do not ask (James 4:2). I've learned to ask and to ask in faith, believing God will hear and respond.

The Key to Revival

It took me only two or three meetings to realize that prayer is the key to a successful revival. If the meeting is bathed in prayer beforehand, mighty things will happen, regardless of the quality of my preaching. Souls will be saved. Lives will be transformed. If the people do not pray, as is often the case, nothing will happen. I can preach my heart out, and still nothing will happen.

One of my most dramatic experiences with prayer occurred at a dead meeting I conducted in South Texas.

The church was packed out on Sunday morning, with almost 400 present. There was little response to the invitation that morning. Although that was unusual, it didn't concern me too much because it was a traditional church, and it often took two or three sessions of a meeting in such a church before people would finally loosen up enough to come forward for prayer.

But when the service began on Sunday evening, I knew we were in trouble. There were hardly 100 people present. In four years of ministry I had never seen such a dramatic drop-off in attendance between Sunday morning and evening. The apathy was so thick you could feel it. I gave the sermon everything I had that night and nothing happened. People just stood there during the invitation and stared blankly. It was a real downer.

On Monday I began to pray earnestly for a spiritual breakthrough. But again, the crowd was small, the singing was listless and the interest was minimal. However, this time during the invitation, the Spirit began to move. I could see people coming under conviction. Some wept. Others hung their heads. Some grabbed the pew in front of them and visibly shook. But they wouldn't move forward. Their feet were in concrete.

We were involved in intense spiritual warfare. The key to victory was prayer. The next day I went to my knees again and cried out to God for a breakthrough. It didn't come. On Tuesday night the Spirit moved with power again. But once more there was a greater level of resistance. People were bleeding to death inside, but they would not come for ministry.

Wednesday was the last day of the meeting. I was wrung out from the intensity of the spiritual battle. Having prayed with zeal for the meeting, now I was the one who needed prayer.

Discovering a Prayer Warrior

I tried to pray, but the words wouldn't come. I decided to take a drive in the country. As I was driving out of the town, I saw a gaudy temporary sign on the side of the road with a big red arrow on it that pointed to a small building. The sign said, "Do You Need Prayer? If So, Come In!"

I drove on past, but I couldn't get the sign out of my mind. I needed prayer, Why hadn't I stopped? "Probably some shyster after money," I thought. I continued to rationalize my refusal to stop. The rationalizations didn't work. I felt compelled to go back and check out the place.

I knocked tentatively on the door, wondering if I would be greeted by a gypsy with a crystal ball. The Lord had a surprise in store for me. The door was opened by a classic "little old lady in tennis shoes." A sweet-smiling, delicately built, elderly lady greeted me. She had the radiance of the Lord all over her.

"Come in," she said, "I've been waiting on you."

Waiting on me? What did she mean by that? I looked around the room. All that was in it were two rocking chairs and a small table. Cookies and coffee were on the table.

She pointed to one of the rocking chairs and asked me to have a seat. She then pulled her chair right up to me, leaned forward and said, "What can we pray about?"

Still suspicious, I asked, "Do you charge?"

"Oh Heavens no!" she replied, with a hearty laugh. "I serve the living God, and He doesn't charge for His grace and mercy. Now, what do you want to pray about?"

"Well, first of all," I said, "tell me what you're doing here."

She patiently explained that God had spoken to her heart six months before and told her to come to this town and open a roadside prayer chapel.

"This town needs revival," she said.

I could sure agree with that! Again, she pressed me for my prayer request. But I had one more question for her.

"What did you mean when you said, 'I've been expecting you?'"

A Word of Knowledge

She smiled. "You probably won't believe this," she said hesitantly, "but God spoke to my heart yesterday afternoon while I was praying. He told me a preacher would come by this morning for special prayer. You are a preacher, aren't you?"

I was speechless. How did she know I was a preacher? I was driving an old beat-up pickup that I had borrowed. And I was dressed in a flannel shirt with jeans. I certainly didn't look like a preacher.

"Yes," I replied, "I'm a preacher."

"I thought so," she said. "The Lord told me you were coming. I got here early this morning, swept out the place and made this coffee and cookies for you. Where have you been? I've been waiting for two hours!"

I began to praise God for his grace and mercy. I proceeded to describe my plight to her in detail. She kept nodding her head knowingly.

"I understand what you're up against," she said. "That's why God sent me here. This town desperately needs revival."

Praying in the Spirit

She then began to pray for a Holy Ghost blowout at the church that evening. I thought she was going to pray Heaven down. Never had I experienced such boldness and power in prayer.

That night she came and sat on the back row and continued to pray silently all through the service. I could feel the power when I preached. I could sense the spiritual tension in the congregation building to a climax.

The dam broke when the invitation was offered. People came flooding to the front with tears streaming down their faces. Some dropped to their knees in repentance. Others hugged each other and offered words of encouragement. It was a beautiful spiritual scene. God had given the victory through prayer.

Walking at God's Pace

Another discovery I've made about prayer is that it is the key to pacing the faith walk. This is one of the most difficult lessons for any Christian to learn, particularly for those who are called into the full-time ministry.

If we are going to walk in faith, we must walk at God's pace, not ours. That's tough. Most of us tend to lag behind. The Lord has to drag us screaming and kicking every step of the way.

For ministers, the problem is usually just the opposite. We tend to run ahead of the Lord. Like Abraham when he sired Ishmael, we try to help the Lord out. We get enthusiastic about what we are doing, we get impatient with the

Lord's pace, and we start running ahead of the Lord. That always means big trouble.

I'm convinced that many of the ministries that are suffering severe debt today are in that condition primarily because they are not moving at God's intended pace for them. Our God owns the cattle on a thousand hills. He can supply every need. When we run ahead, He leaves the needs for us to meet. The result, too often, is desperate fund appeals that do not bring any honor to the name of Jesus.

God wants us to walk at the pace He desires. To do that, it is essential that we spend a lot of time on our knees seeking His will on every decision.

Believing in Miracles   12

A serious prayer life leads inevitably to a belief in miracles. I have discovered that most Christians do not pray very frequently. It is not surprising, therefore, that most Christians have rejected the miraculous.

Many have been victimized, like I was, by the ultradispensational teaching that the age of miracles ceased at the end of the First Century. Another problem is that many Christians have almost defined miracles out of existence by stating that a miracle must violate a law of nature.

The Bible says God is the same yesterday, today and forever (Hebrews 13:8). He does not change (Malachi 3:6). He is still a personal, caring and miracle-working God (1 Peter 5:6-7). He created the physical laws of the universe, and He can suspend them anytime He pleases. Unlike the moral laws, the physical laws are not inviolate.

Types of Miracles

But what most people overlook is the fact that there are very few miracles in the Bible that violate any law of nature. Most biblical miracles are of a different sort. They are miracles of timing.

Take Hannah for example. She prayed for her womb to be blessed, and it was. The Bible presents this as a miracle. But there was no immaculate conception. She had a husband. Her pregnancy was a miracle of timing.

Likewise, Paul and Silas were released from jail by an earthquake. No laws of nature were violated. Earthquakes are very common in Israel. But isn't it interesting that this particular earthquake occurred at the moment Paul and Silas were praying for deliverance — and it occurred in just the right place! It reminds me of another earthquake that served Joshua and the Children of Israel at Jericho.

Or consider Elijah who prayed that it would not rain in Israel. It did not rain for three and a half years, not until he prayed again for the rain to come. Did that miracle violate any law of nature? There is no law of nature that says it must rain in Israel every year. Israel often experiences severe droughts. The miracle was one of timing. The rain stopped and started in sequence with the prayers. The world calls it "coincidence." I call it "God-incidence."

A God-incidence

I personally experienced one of these God-incidences when I went to Lexington, Kentucky to hold a meeting at a large church with several thousand members. The church had taken seriously a call to prayer I had sent them in a letter. They had conducted special prayer services. Some had committed themselves to both prayer and fasting. Over 100 had volunteered to conduct an all-night prayer vigil, with a different person coming to the church to pray every ten minutes for a 24-hour period.

When I was informed about all this prayer activity, I got excited. I knew God would greatly bless their prayers with a mighty move of His Spirit.

I arrived for the meeting two days early because I had some other business to tend to in Lexington. I had hardly checked into my motel room on Friday afternoon when I was suddenly struck by an extremely sharp pain in the groin area. The pain was absolutely excruciating. I lay down on the bed hoping it would go away.

It didn't. It intensified.

I called a taxi and went to the emergency room of the

nearest hospital. Several hours later, after many tests and X-rays, the doctor informed me that I had a kidney stone that had lodged in my ureter. He told me that I should be admitted to the hospital immediately for treatment, including the possible insertion of a stint.

Despite the pain, all I could think about was the wonderful meeting I knew God had prepared for me through the prayers of the congregation. I knew we were in store for a spiritual feast, and I didn't want to miss it. So, I refused admission to the hospital.

The doctor told me I was crazy. He explained that if the stone started moving, I would experience even worse pain. I still refused admission. He then gave me some powerful pain-killing pills and warned me that they might knock me out completely. He therefore urged caution in taking them.

A Spiritual Battle

I went back to the motel still racked with pain. I threw the pills away, convinced that this was a spiritual battle. I believed with all my heart that Satan had come against me with the express purpose of keeping me from preaching. He knew the congregation was on the verge of a great revival, and he was determined to stop it. I was equally determined to stand against him.

I stopped praying for healing. I started praying instead for spiritual strength to stand against Satan. I rebuked him and called upon the name of Jesus for victory.

The pain persisted. I tossed and tumbled all night long, hoping I would awake to find the pain gone. It wasn't.

About noon on Saturday I got an idea. I picked up the phone and called a dear friend, one of the godliest persons I knew in Lexington. He had been born on the mission field in China and had later become a missionary to the Philippines. He was a man of prayer, and that's what I needed.

He agreed to come right away. He brought a friend with him. The three of us sat in my room and talked for about 30 minutes. Then, he laid his hands on me and prayed a simple, quiet prayer: "Lord, dissolve the kidney stone so that David can fulfill your purpose in the meeting that starts tomorrow. In Jesus' name, Amen." That's all he said. No fanfare. No theatrics.

We talked for another 20 to 30 minutes and then they stood up to leave. When I arose, the pain instantly left. I knew the Lord had dissolved the stone. Satan had been defeated. We rejoiced in thanksgiving to the Lord.

The next morning I shared the miracle of my healing with the church. They responded with enthusiastic applause that startled even me. It was a remarkable beginning to what proved to be one of the most Spirit-anointed meetings I have ever held.

A week later when I returned to Dallas I shared the story with a friend who was a radiologist. He was skeptical. "Maybe God did heal you," he said, "but we need to check it out." He put me through another battery of tests and X-rays, but he could not find a trace of the stone. Of course not; God had dissolved it!

The Power of Praise

Another miracle I witnessed occurred at a home worship service in north Dallas. About 25 people had gathered for an evening of devotional praise. Right before the service was to start, I was standing near the front door when I heard the doorbell ring. I opened the door, and there stood an old friend I had not seen for a long time. I reached out to shake hands with her, but she quickly drew her hand back.

"What's wrong?" I asked.

"Take a look at my hand," she replied.

She thrust her right hand toward me. On the top of her hand was an ugly, red blister, about the size of a silver dollar.

"I just burned my hand severely with some grease." she explained. "I heard about this worship service over the grapevine and decided to come. Then, right before I left the house, I spilled grease on my hand. I almost didn't come."

I offered my sympathy for her badly burned hand. By

then the worship service was starting, so we hurried to the living room.

All we did that evening was lift up the Lord in praise. But I have discovered that there is great power in praise. When we lose ourselves in love and adoration for the Lord, we open ourselves to His ministry. Psalm 22:3 says that "God inhabits the praises of His people."

The Lord's Surprising Ministry

The Lord's Spirit came that evening and was enthroned upon our praises. It was a service of quiet and reverent praise and worship. When the service ended, my friend came up to me with tears running down her cheeks. She was on the verge of breaking into sobs.

"What's the matter" I asked. "Is your hand hurting a lot?"

"Oh no," she said, "that's why I'm so upset. Look what the Lord has done."

Once again she held our her hand. The blister was gone. There was no redness. The hand was perfectly normal. I could hardly believe my eyes.

"When did that happen?" I asked.

"I don't know," she replied. "I have no idea except that it happened sometime during the praise service."

No one had prayed specifically for her. No one laid hands on her or anointed her with oil. She had simply lifted her hands in praise to God, and the Lord had responded by touching her with His healing hand.

A Gift of Healing

The Bible speaks of gifts of healing — in the plural (1 Corinthians 12:9). God gave me one of those gifts shortly after I began the ministry.

I was holding a meeting for a tiny church of only 30 souls. The church met in a shopping center in southeast Dallas. On the last night of the meeting I preached on "The Power of God." The purpose of the sermon was to convince people that God is personal and loving, that He hears prayers and answers them, and that He still performs miracles.

I used many Biblical examples to illustrate my points. One of the examples was the story of Hannah and how God blessed her barren womb. That story had always had a special place in my heart.

When I offered the time of personal ministry, the worship leader suddenly signaled for another man to come up and take his place. Then he motioned to his wife to come join him at the front.

The two of them came up to me and asked me to pray that God would enable them to have a child. They explained that they had one girl about seven years old who suffered brain damage at birth and could not walk or talk. They said they had been trying to have another child ever since the first one had been born, but the doctors had told them they would not be able to have any more children.

I looked them right in the eye and asked, "Do you believe that with God all things are possible?"

"Oh yes!" they replied in unison.

I laid hands on them and prayed that God would bless her womb.

A Double Blessing

Three months later the husband called me at the office. "You're not going to believe this," he shouted, "but my wife is pregnant!" He then began shouting, "Praise the Lord! Praise the Lord!" I joined him, and we had a Holy Spirit pep rally right there over the phone.

Three months later he called again. This time he was more subdued. His voice sounded almost awe-struck. "Dave, that was some prayer you prayed over us. Guess what? We're going to have twins!"

They did — two boys named Jonathan and James. I get an updated photo of them every year, and I keep it hanging on my office wall as a constant reminder of God's love and mercy and power.

Three years after the boys were born, their sister died in

her sleep. She was only ten years old. When I heard the news, I immediately understood why God had blessed that family with twins. He knew all along that He was about to call that little girl home. So He gave them two.

Praying for Babies

In the years since, I have prayed for hundreds of barren wombs, and I have a drawer full of photographs of babies born to women who had been declared "incurably barren."

One incident I will never forget occurred in a town in Oklahoma. I was holding a meeting at an independent church. One of the members of that church was the leading obstetrician in town. He called me one day at the motel where I was staying and told me that he wanted me to pray with a patient of his. "I've done everything I can for her," he explained. "It's up to God." He said she would get in touch with me.

About an hour later I received a phone call from a man who identified himself as the pastor of one of the largest Baptist churches in the town. He asked if we could meet for a get-acquainted chat. I agreed and offered to meet him at his office because the church was located right next to the motel.

"Oh no!" he said, "I don't think it would be wise for you to come here. I'll come to your room."

In a few minutes he was at my door. We sat and talked for over an hour. Our conversation ranged over a great variety of topics — church growth, evangelism, spiritual gifts and, finally, healing. All the time I was wondering why he had come to see me. The topic of healing finally brought him to the point of his visit.

"Let me tell you the main reason I came over here," he said. "My wife desperately wants to have a second child, but the doctors don't think it's possible. Her current physician suggested to her this morning that she let you pray for her. I wanted to check you out first to make sure you weren't some sort of loony faith healer. I've decided I'd like for you to pray for her."

I appreciated his concern for his wife and his desire to prevent her from being hurt further by some emotional and manipulative "faith healer." I rejoiced that I had passed the "loony" test!

He called her. She came over to the room. We sat in a circle, held hands and prayed. The next Christmas I received a beautiful photograph of that couple holding their new baby.

Breaking Hardened Hearts

The greatest miracles God performs today are often taken for granted. They are the internal miracles of the heart. I'm speaking of miracles like the sinner who repents and is delivered from bondage to sin. Or the backslidden Christian whose heart is suddenly transformed from apathy to zeal.

I'll never forget a dramatic moment at a meeting in Indiana where the Spirit of God fell mightily at the invitation time. Many responded to the Lord that morning, but the person who led the way was a woman who grabbed my hand, squeezed it hard, looked directly in my eyes and said, "I have a heart as hard as granite, and I want God to break it right now."

He did. She subsequently decided to devote her life to the Lord's service and became a member of my ministry's staff.

A Dramatic Response

The most memorable breaking of a heart by the Holy Spirit that I have ever witnessed took place during a meeting in California. It was the last night. When I offered the time of ministry, the Spirit began moving with great power. Many responded. I announced we would sing only one more verse of the invitation song.

As we started that verse, a fellow built like a Mack Truck stepped out into the aisle near the back of the sanctuary and started forward. As he advanced toward the front, he gained momentum. He was almost running as he got within a few yards of me. I thought I was going to be run over! Just as he reached me, he slammed on the brakes and embraced me with a big bear hug. Then he dropped to the floor in a convulsion of tears. I went to the floor with him.

He was crying and sobbing so hard he could barely speak. As I struggled to get to my feet, I whispered in his ear that I was going to get the elders to pray with him. He grabbed my arm and pulled me back down. "No! No!" he gasped between sobs. "Don't call the elders. I've got to talk to someone who doesn't know me." I helped him over to the podium steps and told him I would be back to pray with him after the service.

Saving Two Lives

He had composed himself by the time I returned.

"What can I pray with you about?" I asked.

He lowered his head and spoke softly. "These folks at this church think I'm a good Christian man," he said, "but I'm full of rottenness. You see, I've been plotting to kill a man for three months. I was going to do it this next week. But God's Word just got hold of my heart tonight, and I know now that I can't go through with it. I want to turn it over to the Lord."

I was stunned. What power there is in God's Word! Two lives were about to be saved as I knelt beside that man, joined hands with him and lifted up his hate-filled heart for God to heal. The deliverance was instantaneous, and he went home rejoicing.

Leaning on the Spirit   13

One of the central lessons I've had to learn in my faith walk is how to live on God's power rather than my own. It is a constant, never-ending struggle. I desire to lean on the power of God's Spirit, but I find myself continually falling back on self-reliance.

I often feel like Paul in Romans 7 where he said he had a battle going on within him between good and evil. "I desire to do what is right," he wrote, "but I end up doing the very thing I hate" (Romans 7:15-19). For a long time this internal war really baffled me. I couldn't understand why it was still going on even after I had been born again.

God's Potter

I sought the answer in God's Word, and I found it. I discovered that I am composed of body, soul and spirit (1 Thessalonians 5:23) and that the only part of me that was born again when I accepted Christ was my spirit.

My body will not be redeemed until the resurrection (Romans 8:23). The redemption of my soul — my mind and will and emotions — is a process that began at my spiritual rebirth and will continue until I either die or am raptured. In the Scriptures, that process is called sanctification. It is a process whereby God's Spirit, working as a potter, seeks to shape our souls into the image of Jesus (Romans 8:29 and 2 Corinthians 3:18).

In other words, our salvation is an on-going process. It begins with our justification (the salvation of our spirit), proceeds with sanctification (the salvation of our soul), and is culminated in glorification (the salvation of our body). For the believer, salvation is past, present and future.

This helped me to understand the struggle going on within me. Every time I tried to make a decision, my spirit, which is redeemed and in tune with God's Spirit, would urge me in God's direction. At the same time, my unredeemed soul, still in contact with the world, would pull me in Satan's direction.

The Lord has allowed struggles to come into the ministry from time to time. He has used these to teach me how to rely on Him rather than myself. Sometimes I have succeeded. Sometimes I have failed. But I have learned from all the confrontations that if I will trust in Him and rely on the power of His Spirit, He will deliver me.

Growing through Persecution

My most painful confrontation occurred shortly after the ministry was established. I got a call from a preacher in McKinney, Texas, a town just north of Dallas. He was ministering at a church that represented the heritage I had grown up in. He asked me if I would come over to his church and speak to a group of ministers about prophecy.

I was immediately suspicious. I knew that religious heritage well. I had spent 30 years in it. I knew the preachers were all militantly amillennial in their prophetic viewpoint. I also knew that there was nothing they loved more than to argue. They were in bondage to a spirit of debate.

When I was growing up in that church, debating had been one of our favorite pastimes. We would pick some cocky little bantam rooster and turn him loose on some "denominational preacher," and then we would yell for blood. It was anything but spiritually enriching.

I was not about to be drawn into such an ungodly event, so I declined the minister's invitation.

"But why?" he persisted.

"Because I know from experience," I said bluntly, "that you fellows are not interested in learning anything. You just want to argue. You're trying to set me up for a scalping."

"Oh no!" he protested. "You don't understand. This is a regular monthly meeting of all our ministers in the county. We invite someone to read a paper for an hour, then we question them for an hour, and then we all go have lunch together."

I was tempted to accept. The man sounded sincere. But I had too many memories of past experiences. I refused his invitation.

A week later he called again. Again, I refused. Then he came by my office. He kept assuring me that the invitation was on the up-and-up, that it was not a setup, and that he would take personal responsibility for keeping the meeting orderly. I was impressed by his persistence and his sincerity. With much reservation, I finally agreed to speak.

Dealing with Head Hunters

The moment I arrived at his church I knew I was in trouble. I spotted preachers who had driven in from as far away as 200 miles. Some of them I recognized as notorious "head hunters" — a term we used for self-appointed defenders of the faith who were always looking for a heretic to nail to the wall.

No one spoke to me except the host minister. The tension was thick. I was being glared at from every angle. I decided immediately that I would not mention the word "millennium." That word to this group would be like waving a red flag in front of a bull. They did not believe Jesus would ever put His foot on this earth again — and they were ready to fight to the death to defend that belief. I decided to speak on why I believe Jesus is coming soon for the Church. I focused on the signs of the times. I never breathed the unspeakable word, "millennium."

As I spoke, some stared blankly at the ceiling, others passed notes to each other, and some even pulled out books and read them! It was obvious they had not come to listen. They had come to sharpen their knives during the question-and-answer period.

When I finished, we took a ten-minute break. Again, no one spoke to me, but that was fine with me because I spent that ten minutes praying non-stop that God would enable me to hold my Irish temper and to deal with them in love. By the time the question-and-answer period began, the Lord was in control of me, and I was at peace.

On the Griddle

The host minister, who proved to be an honest and sincere man, had sensed the intense spirit of hostility. So, before he opened the meeting to questions, he gave a little speech.

"Gentleman," he said bravely, "I want to remind you that this man is our guest. We invited him to speak. He did not invite himself. I will expect you to treat him like a guest. Is that understood?"

No one said a word.

"Furthermore, I want to remind you that the next part of our program is a question-and-answer period. All I want are questions. No sermons. And the questions must be on one topic only — Bible prophecy. Is that understood?"

Again, only silence. The host minister then turned to an elderly gentleman and said, "Brother, you are our senior minister, so you get to ask the first question."

The old gentleman, who looked to be over 80, turned to me, glared, and then literally shouted, "I have only one question for you, and it doesn't have anything to do with prophecy!"

Somehow, instinctively I knew it was not going to be a friendly question.

"Young man," he sneered with contempt, "I don't care what you have to say about prophecy unless you can answer this question correctly: Do you believe in baptism?"

I had spoken for one hour on the Second Coming of Jesus, and all this fellow wanted to know was my position on baptism! And he had been told point-blank to limit his questions to prophecy.

"Of course I believe in baptism," I responded. "Now, what is your question about prophecy?"

"Wait a minute," he shouted. "You're not going to get off that easy. Let me put the question another way." He thought for a moment, and then he continued. "When you bring a person to Jesus, do you baptize him by immersion for the remission of his sins?"

"Of course I do," I responded again. "Now, what's your question about prophecy?"

The Acid Test

By this time the man was almost livid. The trap he had laid for me was not working. He waved his hands in protest.

"Wait a minute," he repeated. "Let me put the question another way." He paused dramatically. Then, he spit out the words that formed the acid test: "Do you believe that Baptists are saved?"

"Of course," I replied. "Now what's . . ." I never got the words out of my mouth.

He jumped to his feet and started screaming, "I thought so! I thought so! You don't believe in baptism! Anyone who believes a Baptist can be saved doesn't believe in baptism!"

While I was trying valiantly to figure out the logic of that statement, the host jumped to his feet, motioned for the elderly preacher to sit down, and proceeded to give his speech again.

Once more, he urged the men to be hospitable. He emphasized I was their guest. He asked them not to preach, and he requested that they limit their questions to prophecy. "Understood?" he asked. Again, only silence.

Another Assault

The first person to stick his hand in the air was sitting at the other end of the room. When he was called on, he jumped from his chair, ran to the front and stuck his finger in my face. He too was more than a little livid.

"I want you to know that I also disagree with you," he shouted. "I disagree with everything you said, particularly what you said about the millennium."

I could hardly believe my ears. "But I didn't say anything about the millennium!" I protested.

"You didn't?" He seemed amazed.

"No, I didn't even mention the word. All I said is that Jesus is coming soon. Do you disagree with that?"

"No," he said, "but I disagree with the way you said it!"

The man had obviously not heard a word I had said. Again, the host was on his feet trying to bring order to a hopeless situation. Again, he explained the ground rules.

The next question was, at last, a relevant one. "Why are you so obsessed with the Jews?"

I thanked the Lord for the question and then launched into a lengthy survey of why the Jew is so central to the understanding of Bible prophecy. By the time I finished that question I had new hope that the meeting could be salvaged. My hope went down the drain fast.

A Pious Judgment

The next person to be recognized stood up, buttoned his coat, straightened his tie, and then very slowly, deliberately and piously made a statement without ever looking at me. "Gentlemen," he said, "my Bible tells me what to do with a man like this. My Bible tells me to mark him and not to eat with him." He turned to me. "I hereby announce that I refuse to eat lunch with you!"

It was the last straw for the host. "I've had enough of this," he snapped. "I will not allow this man to be subjected to this abuse any longer. The meeting is adjourned."

"Wait a minute," I interrupted. "I didn't come here to cause trouble. I came to witness my faith. I don't want to mess up your lunch plans. I'll go home, and all of you can eat together."

"No!" said the host. "You're not going home. I invited you to eat, and I'm going to buy your lunch."

"No you're not!" someone shouted. Everyone turned to see who had spoken. It was a short fat man who had not said a word up to that time. "You're not going to buy Dave's lunch," he explained, "because I'm going to buy it!"

A Friend Indeed

I had found one friend, a man with a lot of courage. After the meeting was adjourned, I went up to this new-found friend, put my arm around his shoulders and said, "Brother, you've got a lot of class."

"Oh no," he protested. "I don't have any class at all."

"Yes you do," I insisted.

But he continued to protest vehemently, saying, "I've got no class," When I asked him why he was so insistent on that point, he replied, "Because I'm the minister of a non-class church!" We both broke into gales of laughter.

You're probably wondering what we were laughing about. Let me explain. The church of my heritage was so legalistic that it split into more than 25 different groups. They all used the same denominational name, but they wouldn't have anything to do with each other.

Since they all used the same name, they had to devise labels to differentiate themselves from each other. Some were called "Pre-Mills." Others were classified as "Antis." There were the "One Cuppers." And there were the "Non-Class" brethren.

These latter folks felt it was wrong to have Sunday School classes. The brother who stood by me that day was the minister of one of these "Non-Class" churches — and that's the reason he was so insistent upon denying that he had any class!

Eating with Lepers

Well, believe it or not, we all went to the same restaurant for lunch. Thirty men pulled tables together, sat in a corner and whispered. I sat on the opposite side of the restaurant with the host, the "Non-Class" minister, and a third man who joined us.

He turned out to be the minister of an independent Christian Church in the area. When I asked him what he was doing at the meeting, he smiled, put his arm around the "Non-Class" minister and said, "They're trying to convert the two of us!" So, I had lunch with the host and the two outcasts.

The whole experience gave me an idea of how Jesus must have felt when he was confronted by the Scribes and Pharisees.

A Surprising Invitation

I soon had another challenging experience with my former religious heritage. Thankfully, it turned out much better.

One of my trustees moved from Dallas to Houston and started attending one of the churches of my heritage. It was a somewhat less traditional church, with more openness and freedom, but it still had a lot of its denomination's hangups.

When people in Houston began to urge that I come down there and conduct a prophecy seminar, I asked our trustees in that area to scout out a site for the meeting. The trustee who had recently moved there called and suggested that I conduct the seminar on a Saturday afternoon at his new-found church. I reminded him that they did not share my prophetic viewpoint. He said he was going to ask them anyway.

I was astonished when he called back and said they had agreed for me to use the building. Not only that, they had also asked me to speak to their church on Sunday morning!

There were, however, two stipulations. The advertising for the prophecy seminar had to state that it was not endorsed by the church. And with regard to the Sunday morning sermon, I was free to speak on any topic except prophecy. I agreed to both stipulations.

Almost no one from the church was present that Saturday afternoon for the seminar. That didn't surprise me. The next morning I went to the church not knowing what to expect. I tried to prepare myself for the worst — some ugly public confrontation. The Lord had a surprise in store for me.

An Unexpected Topic

I arrived in time for Sunday School. One of the elders met me at the door and asked, "Is it true that you have just returned from Israel?" I told him that was right. "Well then," he said, "would you take over our adult class in the auditorium and tell us about Israel?"

I felt a flush of excitement. What an invitation! What an opportunity to talk about my favorite topic. "Let me ask you something," I said cautiously. "Will I be free to say anything I please about Israel?"

"Oh yes!" said the elder. I don't think he had any idea what he was asking for.

I jumped into the presentation with great enthusiasm. I decided to pour it on — to give them a panoramic overview of the Jew in Bible prophecy, from the Abrahamic Covenant to its fulfillment with the primacy of the nation of Israel during the millennial reign of Christ.

I expected to be thrown out at the end. Instead, another elder jumped up and began praising the presentation. "This has been fantastic!" he said. "I didn't know any of these prophecies were even in the Bible. How could we have overlooked them for so long?" I had often asked myself the same question.

At the morning worship service, I was true to my promise. I avoided prophecy. I spoke on faith. At the end of the service another elder came to the front and expressed his appreciation for both the teaching and preaching. He then asked if I would be willing to return that evening to speak some more on prophecy! I just couldn't believe what was happening. I said I would be happy to return — and started praising the Lord in my spirit.

Then the elder did something beyond belief. He said he knew the whole congregation had been greatly blessed, so he wanted to give them an opportunity to express their appreciation. "We were going to give this man $100," he said, "but we've been blessed far beyond that, so let's take up a special love offering right now!"

An Astounding Response

That evening I spoke for an hour on Bible prophecy and then opened it up to questions. The people responded enthusiastically. The questions were sincere and probing. They showed that the people were open and eager to learn.

As I left that evening, one of the deacons called me aside. He put a hand on my shoulder and shook his head in amazement. "Dave," he said, "you're not going to believe what a miracle God has performed here today."

He then told me something that shocked me. He said that one of their elders had been very opposed to my coming and had even spoken out publicly against me, branding me as a "false prophet." He explained that was the reason so few of their members had attended the seminar the day before.

"What I'm telling you," he said, "is that you walked into a very hostile environment. And yet, God turned it around in one day's time! Not only were you invited back this evening, but I have an unbelievable check to give you from this morning's love offering." He handed me the check, hugged me and said, "God bless you, brother."

The check was for $1,500. It was the largest single offering the ministry had ever received up to that time.

I was to be invited back to that church many times to teach and preach on prophecy. The hostile elder eventually left, and the church moved on to a deeper walk with the Lord, ultimately even changing its name to one that was truly nondenominational.

An Angry Confrontation

One of the strangest confrontations I've had in the ministry occurred in Ft. Worth, Texas at the office of a denominational administrator. His title was Regional Minister, but he was, in effect, the bishop of 400 churches in Texas and New Mexico. He had sent me a letter asking me to call his secretary and arrange an appointment for a "get-acquainted session."

I suspected that he had more in mind than that, but I didn't know what. I found out fast, as soon as I arrived.

"Have a seat," he said. "I'll be back in a moment. I'm going to get a witness."

"A witness?" I responded in surprise. "What do you need a witness for?"

"Because I'm going to read you the riot act!" he said.

That is exactly what he proceeded to do, once he got his witness in place.

"I want you to get out of my churches and stay out of my churches," he snarled.

"Why do you feel that way?" I asked.

"Because I don't want my people hearing your message about the Second Coming of Jesus."

"Why not?"

"Because it's a bunch of bunk. Jesus is never coming back! All you're doing is just frightening and confusing people. So stay out of my churches!"

My emotions at that point were very mixed. I was angry. Who did this guy think he was, speaking constantly about "his" churches? I was appalled. How could a man responsible for 400 churches be so unbelieving and apostate? I also felt sad. I kept thinking about all those people sitting in the pews of "his" churches, hungering for the Word of God.

As I listened to his continuing rebuke, I found myself at one moment wanting to jump up and denounce the man as an agent of Satan, while at the next moment, I wanted to get on my knees and pray for him. I really didn't know what to do.

I just sat there and prayed for the Lord's peace as the man continued to rail against me.

A Sad Revelation

"There's another thing about you I don't like," he said. "You're a Salvationist."

That really caught me off guard. I had been called a lot of names in my life, but never a "Salvationist." He had used it as a slur, but it really didn't sound so bad. I was confused.

"What do you mean by that?" I asked.

"You're one of those guys who thinks that a fellow can kneel down in a field while chopping cotton and ask the Lord to come into his life — and thus be saved."

"Okay," I responded, "I confess. I'm a 'Salvationist.' What are you?"

I'll never forget his answer. In one sentence he summarized the apostasy of so much of Christendom: "I believe that every person on the face of the earth who is growing more mature is in the process of being saved."

"Does that include Buddhists? Hindus? Atheists?"

"Everyone!" he snapped. "As long as they are growing more mature."

No, he was not a "Salvationist." He was a Universalist masquerading as a Christian. He claimed to follow Jesus, but he was standing there denying the essentiality of the atoning blood of Jesus. Salvation was equated with maturity. The Cross was irrelevant.

As I stood to leave, I noticed a statement framed on his wall. I thought it was a peculiar one for his office. It said, "We speak where the Bible speaks. We are silent where the Bible is silent."

A Desperate Call

A confrontation of a totally different type took place in New Mexico a few years later. It was a tough one — the type that can easily generate bitterness. The experience impressed upon me again the importance of turning such things over to the Lord.

It all began with a desperate phone call from a distraught young minister whom I had met only once before. He begged me to come to his church immediately and conduct a revival. He said they were in a terrible condition and needed some encouragement.

He explained that their senior pastor had suddenly resigned several months before and had left them with an enormous debt on a new building. Since that time the attendance had dwindled, the contributions had dropped off sharply, all the staff members except him had been released, and the remaining members were about to lose their building to the bank.

It sounded beyond hope to me, but the young man was so earnest and persistent that I decided to go, if at all possible. It was early December when he called. I explained that I was booked solid for meetings during the next year except for the month of January — a month when most churches try to avoid special meetings because of unpredictable weather.

"Any time would be fine," he said. "Just come fast!"

I flew to New Mexico in late January. The young man met me at the airport, and en route to the motel it became painfully obvious that he was on the verge of a full-fledged nervous breakdown. He began to weep as he told me about his plight.

He had been the youth minister. When things started falling apart, all responsibility had been dumped on him. He was currently serving as youth minister, education director, pulpit preacher and janitor! And they had not given him any increase in salary.

A Deceitful Act

The meeting was well-attended despite the fact that the congregation had dwindled down to less than 100. I had held five meetings at different churches in that area, and all those churches supported the meeting by bringing vans and buses full of people each evening.

As I do with all my meetings, I had gone there on a faith basis, meaning that I would rely on love offerings to meet my expenses and compensate the ministry. Each evening one of the church's leaders made a plea for an offering, indicating that everything given would be passed on to Lamb & Lion Ministries. This is normal procedure.

The morning I was to fly out, the young preacher, still weeping, drove me to the airport. As I got ready to board the plane, he handed me an envelope.

"Don't open this until you get on the plane," he said. "When you open it, you will understand what I'm up against."

The envelope contained a check for $125. I was horrified. The church, or rather its leaders, had stolen the offering! They had kept it to make their building payment. I was handed a token that didn't even cover my expenses.

The Lord's Justice

As I said before, it is easy to get bitter about experiences like this one. As I sat there on that plane, I felt myself getting madder and madder. "Why those guys are nothing but a bunch of crooks," I thought. And then I turned my rage on the Lord. "Lord!" I thought, "why did you let this happen?"

His answer to my heart was short and simple. "I thought you came in faith. If you did, then believe I have it under control. Forgive and move on."

It was hard to do but, by leaning on the power of God's Spirit, I was able to overcome the bitterness and forgive.

And, as usual, God poured out His blessings. The plane I boarded that day was not going back home. It was headed for California where I had a meeting scheduled at a large church in the Los Angeles area. The offerings of the people at that church totaled $6,000 — the largest offering the ministry had ever received.

Another God-incidence

And, speaking of "God-incidences," I discovered that the

distraught young man in New Mexico was a "Timothy" of the church in Los Angeles. He had gown up in that church and had been encouraged by them to become a minister.

When they heard about his condition, the leaders of the church arranged for the young man to fly to California immediately. They put him up in an apartment and just let him rest in the Lord for six months before they found him a new ministry position. He was one of their spiritual invest-ments, and they were not about to lose him.

As Jeremiah put it, "The steadfast love of the Lord never ceases. His mercies never come to an end. They are new every morning" (Lamentations 3:22-23 — RSV).

Preaching with Power   14

Learning to lean on the Lord is always the most difficult in those areas where you are naturally talented. After all, why do you need the Lord's help when you have the natural talent to handle it yourself? Isn't your talent "God-given"? So, when you rely on your talent, aren't you really relying on God? It is so easy to rationalize away our unwillingness to yield to God and operate within His will and by His power.

My greatest natural talent has always been my public speaking ability. I won more contests than I could keep count of in junior high, high school and college. I was versatile. I excelled in dramatics, declamation, poetry interpretation, debate — just about anything that required me to open my mouth! When I was a junior in high school, I won first in the State of Texas in oratory. It was only natural that I should gravitate into a profession like teaching, where a gift for gab would be a great plus.

Preaching in the Flesh

When I finally yielded to the Lord's call on my life and began to preach at the church in Irving, I expected to excel at preaching without any difficulty whatsoever. A rude shock awaited me.

I quickly discovered that natural talent is not the key to effective service in the Lord's kingdom. No matter how much I polished my sermons or rehearsed them in front of a mirror, they just did not seem to have any power. They were often insightful, even eloquent and inspiring, but they were devoid of spiritual power. It was maddening.

The Lord impressed the problem upon me from time to time in a very interesting way. Once in a while someone would say to me, "Oh thank you. You said something in your sermon today that I really needed to hear. I was blessed." When I would ask what it was that I said, I realized that almost invariably it was something that was not contained in my sermon notes!

The blessings from my mouth always seemed to come forth at those infrequent moments when I would let my guard down and venture to say something I had not intended to say. That was puzzling — until I turned to the Word and began an intensive study of spiritual gifts.

Understanding Spiritual Gifts

I soon discovered that there is a great difference between a gift and a talent. Talents are natural. Gifts are supernatural. The Word teaches that every one of us who is born again receives at least one spiritual gift at the time of our rebirth (1 Corinthians 12:4-11). We may receive more than one. If we are good stewards of the gifts we receive, we may even be given additional gifts as our walk with the Lord progresses.

We are often gifted in an area of natural talent, but not always. A person who is a naturally talented singer might be gifted by the Spirit to use that talent for the Lord's glory, but then, again, the person might not be. When they aren't, we usually tend to write off their inability to sing Christian music effectively by saying "they have no feel for it." The truth is that they either have not been gifted by the Spirit or else they have quenched their gift and are relying upon their natural talent.

An example would be two singers who are going to sing "The Lord's Prayer." The first, operating in the flesh, might sing the song perfectly and receive a standing ovation. The second, leaning on the Spirit, might sing the song most imperfectly and receive no ovation because the listeners are too busy weeping and repenting of their sins. The second singer has allowed himself to be an empty vessel through whom the power of God can be manifested.

Applying the Truths

It is so difficult for us to empty ourselves of self. It is particularly difficult in the areas where we are talented. We would rather trust ourselves than God.

So it was with my preaching. I wanted to wow people with my oratorical prowess. I often did. But they went away empty because I had not shown them Jesus. I had shown them me.

I struggled with this problem for several years before I experienced a breakthrough. Once again, the agent was Martin Lloyd-Jones, the man whose magazine interview had served as my third and conclusive "witness" when I was trying to decide whether I should resign my job and preach the soon return of Jesus.

Someone gave me a copy of his marvelous book on preaching. Right in the middle I found the key. He wrote, "When preparing a sermon, work on it as if everything depended upon you. Then preach it like everything depended on the Spirit."

Abandoning Manipulation

My sermons soon began to evidence a new power, real power, as I learned to yield to the guidance of God's Spirit in the pulpit. I lost interest in impressing people with my skills. I became obsessed with lifting up Jesus. I had learned that even when we are serving God, we need Him more than He needs us.

I quickly applied these new-found truths to the part of the sermon that I dreaded the most — the invitation. Evangelists are judged by results, as evidenced by the number of people who march down the aisle at the end of the sermon. There is, therefore, always a temptation for an evangelist to use emotional, often manipulative, techniques to get people to respond. I hated such techniques and yet, when I would finish offering an invitation, I would often feel that I had been manipulative.

I decided to turn the whole invitation process over to the Lord. I prayed for His guidance, and the answer He impressed upon my heart was to stop preaching invitations altogether. "Rely on the power of My Word and My Spirit," He told me.

I responded by changing the way I ended my sermons. Instead of shifting into an invitation plea that constituted a mini-sermon, I simply ended the sermon with a prayer. Then, following the prayer, I would announce that we were going to have a "ministry time." I would ask all those present who needed prayer for any purpose to come forward. I would assure them that no public announcement would be made regarding their need. They would be prayed for personally and privately.

Experiencing the Spirit's Power

The first time I tried this new approach was at a meeting in Nashville, Indiana, a picturesque village about 45 miles south of Indianapolis. It was on a Sunday morning at a very traditional church. I was extremely nervous about the new procedure. I knew it would be most unorthodox for this particular church. But I felt convicted of God to try it, and so I did.

I'll never forget the result. The Holy Spirit fell with great power, and people began to come forward by the dozens for prayer. I had never seen anything like it in one of my meetings. Frankly, I almost went into shock. So did some of the more staid members of the congregation!

The telephones must have rung off the wall that afternoon because that evening we had a larger crowd than on Sunday morning! It was obvious that many had come out of sheer curiosity. Again, the Spirit moved with great power and, again, many came forward for ministry.

The word spread that we were having a "Holy Ghost

Blowout," and the attendance continued to grow. By the last night, Wednesday, we had almost 400 people present. The town had only 740 residents!

An Old Time Revival

God has continued to bless this approach to ministry. The greatest movement of the Spirit I have witnessed to date in one of my meetings occurred at a large church in Lexington, Kentucky. It was my third meeting there, but my first since the Lord had convicted me to use the new ministry approach.

The church's leaders had insisted that I conduct an "old timey, week-long revival." I had resisted that plea. My meetings were always conducted from Sunday through Wednesday. The modern-day attention span can't take more than about four days. Also, as you approach the weekend, there are just too many competing allurements for people's time.

But the church insisted, and I finally gave in. I did emphasize, however, that there would probably be very few people present on Friday and Saturday evenings.

Overwhelmed by the Spirit

I proved to be a poor prophet. The Spirit moved mightily each evening, anointing every aspect of the service, and the attendance grew steadily. Many responded for ministry, but not in the large numbers, proportionally, that I had experienced at the Nashville church.

Then, it happened on the last night — Saturday night! To my astonishment, almost 800 people were present that evening. When the ministry was offered, around 200 responded! People were on their knees all over the front of the building. There was literally no place left to walk. I stopped the musicians several times and called for visiting preachers and elders to come up and help us pray with people.

Unity in the Spirit

When the ministry time was finally closed, the host

minister made his way through the crowd at the front and stepped to the microphone. He was weeping.

"Folks," he said, "I have never seen anything like this before. I wish you could stand where I'm standing and see what I'm seeing. I see Christian Church preachers, Baptist pastors, Methodist ministers and even a Mennonite brother down here at the front praying with our people."

He stopped to regain his composure. "And I see someone particularly important. I see the minister of one of the largest Nazarene churches in our state down here on his knees praying with some of our folks."

He stopped again, called the man by name and asked him to stand.

"I want all you folks who are members of this church to take a good look at this man. He is the one who recently carried a large wooden cross down our main street, calling our city to repentance. His picture was in the paper. And everyone of you I heard talking about him did nothing but laugh and jeer. I want you to come down here tonight as soon as we dismiss and ask this man to forgive you."

It was a moving demonstration of the power of God's Spirit as people moved forward to hug a man they had ridiculed.

Living Out of a Suitcase 15

Seven years on the road will either drive you nuts or teach you how to rely on God. I spent the first three years ministering at small churches that were very concerned about expenses. That meant I always stayed at someone's house.

Usually it was some dear widow lady who was anxious to smother the visiting evangelist with hospitality — and I mean smother! I always take a lot of work with me when I'm on the road, and I quickly discovered that it was almost impossible to get anything done at a hospitable home. The hostess was always popping her head in my room to see if I needed something.

"Do you want a Coke? How about a cup of coffee? Want some cake? How about some brownies? You've just got to try my persimmon pie!"

Bless their hearts, as they put it, "I just want to make you feel at home." They meant well, but the harder they pushed, the more uncomfortable I felt. I just wanted to be left alone.

But I would rather be smothered in hospitality than have to wallow in filth. I've stayed in some homes so filthy that I made excuses not to eat for fear that I might die of ptomaine poisoning. Honestly, at one home I stayed in, dirty dishes were stacked all over the cabinets and kitchen table. Some had been there so long they had a green fungus-looking mess growing on them. That particular house was also knee-deep in cat and dog hair, and the bathroom smelled like an open sewer. My gracious hosts seemed totally oblivious to the fact that they were living in a garbage can.

Memorable Hosts

I once stayed with an elderly gentleman who I later discovered was manic-depressive. I didn't know what was wrong with him when I was there. All I knew was that he wanted to play board games all night every night. When I would finally insist on going to bed at 12:30 or 1:00 in the morning, he would then spend the rest of the night banging around in his wood shop, practicing the piano, or vacuuming. Needless to say, he was in his manic stage.

I experienced a contrast to his noise when I stayed with an elderly couple who absolutely refused to speak to each other. The man spent most of each day in his room with the door closed. He came out only for meals, which were eaten in deathly silence. Anything said was said through me.

"David, tell my husband to eat some more vegetables."

"David, tell my wife to mind her own business."

They had been married over 50 years, but it was a marriage in name only.

The strangest form of communication I ever encountered was at a home where the hostess talked to me through notes which she stuck on my pillow — or stuck on the wall or any other place she could find.

I arrived at her house at mid-day. She showed me the bedroom where I was to stay. I unpacked my things, took a shower, changed clothes and went downtown. When I arrived back at her house, the walls of my bedroom and bath were literally plastered with those yellow stick-on notes.

One on the shower door read, "Always close the shower door when you finish." The one stuck above the towel rack said, "Please fold your towels neatly before hanging them." There was one on my pillow that said, "You should use the other bed. This one has a hard mattress." There was even a note on the back of one of my shoes, "Please place your shoes completely under the bed." In my closet I found notes stuck to my suits telling me if they needed cleaning or pressing.

You can understand why I began to demand a motel room when I started ministering at churches large enough to afford one. Still, I found most churches wanted to avoid the expense. I would get a call from the minister — "I know you prefer to stay in a motel but . . ." He would then explain that he had the ideal place in some home where he could "guarantee" that I would not be bothered.

Milking Cows

One of those places was a "mother-in-law room" that had been built onto the main house. As the minister described it over the phone, it sounded ideal. A private entrance. A separate kitchen. A private bath. A completely self-contained unit with no door connecting it to the main house. I agreed to stay there, and sure enough, it turned out to be all that he had described. It appeared to be the perfect place for a traveling evangelist.

I settled in for the night completely content with my accommodations. About 4:30 a.m. I suddenly woke with the feeling that someone was in the room. Someone was! It was the ten-year-old daughter of my hosts. She was just standing by the side of the bed staring at me. Since I don't sleep with much on, I was relieved to find the covers pulled up. I jerked them up even more and asked what she was doing there.

"Just looking," she said.

"But why at this time of the morning?" I asked.

"Oh, I'm supposed to be helping my brothers milk the cow."

That didn't compute. But I was soon to find out what she was talking about. The father of this family was a stickler for discipline and responsibility. He had bought his children, two boys and a girl, a cow, and it was their responsibility to get up every morning at 4:30 to milk that cow. They used the kitchen in my quarters to strain the milk.

So, every morning at 4:30 the three of them would come into my kitchen with milking pails clanging. The last morning

I gave up. I set my alarm for 4:00 a.m., got up, put on my clothes, and went out to milk the cow with them.

The Bottom Line

I don't want to leave the wrong impression. Most of my hosts were delightful people who blessed me with their loving-kindness. But what most people do not understand is that even in the most ideal circumstances, you can never truly relax while staying in someone's home. When you are on the road constantly, you need to stay where you can relax.

One of my preacher friends from California who has spent many a year on the road summed it up best, "You never want to have to stay in any place where you must put on your pants to go to the bathroom!" Amen.

Mountain Hospitality

The funniest story I've ever heard along this line happened to a preacher friend of mine who now pastors one of the largest churches in Louisville, Kentucky. In his early years of ministry he was holding a meeting at a country church in the hills of West Virginia.

The people there had an incredible concept of hospitality. They felt that the only way to be really hospitable was to have the visiting evangelist stay at a different home each night! That meant he had to pack and unpack every day of the meeting.

Every home he stayed at that week had an outdoor toilet, which was an adventure in itself. At the last home he stayed in he decided to make the trip down the path before turning in for the night. His mountain man host went to a kitchen cabinet and pulled out a flashlight and a roll of toilet paper. He handed them to my friend and pointed him toward the back door. My friend stepped outside and starting walking.

He said he walked a long way and still could not see the outhouse. Finally, he stopped and started shining his flash light all around him, looking for the little house. At that point, the mountain man, who was standing on the back porch, shouted, "Just out there anywhere will be okay!"

Motel Accommodations

Staying in homes can be a very trying experience, but motels are not exactly the Garden of Eden. In the years since I've insisted on staying in motels, I have had some memorable experiences.

Take for example the time I got locked in my bathroom at the Holiday Inn in Olney, Illinois. The door handle just spun around and around. Like most motel bathrooms, this one was about the size of a closet. I tend to be claustrophobic. The walls started closing in on me real fast. I tried yelling and beating on the walls. No success. I decided to wait on the maid, but then it dawned on me that is was 5 p.m. and the maid wasn't due in until the next morning.

I emptied my pockets and spent the next 20 minutes using my car keys and paper clips to get the screws out of the door handle. I then jimmied the exposed mechanism to get the door open. I haven't closed a bathroom door in a motel since that time.

My wife rarely travels with me since she is a first-grade teacher, but occasionally, when the meeting site is not too far away, she will go with me on Friday or Saturday and fly back home on Sunday. She went with me one weekend in late November to a meeting in the Houston area.

The man who met us at the airport told us that there was no motel in the small town where the meeting was being held. He dropped us off at a motel in a town about ten miles away.

"This is the closest motel to our church" he explained. "It used to be a Holiday Inn, but it recently changed hands. We hope it's in good hands."

It wasn't. A classic "Texas Norther" had blown into Houston that day and it was unusually cold for that time of year. I kept fiddling with the thermostat in our room, trying to get the heat to come on, but nothing I did seemed to work.

By bedtime it was so cold in the room we simply could not tolerate it any longer. I called the front desk.

"I can't get the heat to come on in my room," I said.

"Yes, I know," said the lady. "It's off in all the rooms."

"When do you expect to get it back on?" I asked.

I will never forget her answer. There was a long pause, and then she said, "Well, let me put it this way. We are praying for warmer weather."

Translated, that meant there was no heat and there wasn't going to be any. So my wife and I put on all the casual clothes we had brought with us and got back into bed. It proved to be a long, cold night.

The next morning we discovered that they also did not have any hot water. We had our bags packed and waiting when they came by to take us to the Sunday morning service.

Looking for a Phone

One motel I stayed at looked like the motel in the movie, "Psycho." It was a classic 1930s "tourist court." It was clean and neat, but it was old. I could have tolerated it except for one thing — there were no phones in the rooms. A phone is essential to me. I have to call my office frequently, and my wife wants me where she can reach me by phone.

I walked up the street about a block and found a telephone booth. I looked in the phone book and noted that the town had several modern motels. I decided I would tell the preacher that I just had to have a phone and that I would personally pay the difference in the cost of the motels. I rehearsed my speech to make it as tactful as possible. I decided I would deliver it that very evening when he picked me up for supper.

Well, before I could get a word out of my mouth, he said, "We need to stop at the manager's office on the way out. The owner wasn't there when you checked in but he's there now. I want you to meet him. You see, he's one of our elders, and he always lets the visiting evangelist stay here free."

I spent a lot of hours that week in a telephone booth down the street from my room.

Seeking a Phone Number

My greatest motel adventure took place at another classic "tourist court" in a small town nestled in the hills of eastern Kentucky. It was the only motel in the town.

As we drove to the town from the airport in Lexington, the two men who picked me up gave me a warning, "Our pastor says the motel where you're going to stay has only six good rooms. They are the ones numbered one through six. So, be sure to insist to the desk clerk that you be put in one of those rooms."

When we arrived, I followed their instructions, and I was given room six without any difficulty. The room was outfitted in what could only be described as vintage World War II army furniture. Everything was made of gray painted steel. The carpet and drapes smelled of years of cigarette smoke. The room had only one redeeming social value. It had a telephone.

I unpacked all my clothes and called my office to tell them where I was and how to get in touch with me. That's when I discovered there was no phone number on the telephone. I looked around for a phone book but couldn't find one. I told my office manager to hold for a moment while I ran over to the office to get the phone number.

My ensuing conversation with the middle-aged lady at the desk was something out of Alice in Wonderland.

"What's the phone number here?" I asked.

"Why?" she responded as if I had asked some sort of dumb question.

"I need to give my office my number. What is it?"

"I don't know."

"What do you mean, you don't know?"

"I mean I never call it."

"Look, lady, I'm serious. I need the number."

"And I'm serious. I don't know it."

I could see I wasn't going to get anywhere with her, so I shrugged my shoulders and turned to go back to my room.

"Oh! Wait a minute!" she shouted. "Here it is on these matches."

She handed me a book of matches. Printed on the cover was the motel name and number.

Missing a Dial Tone

After my phone call, I decided to take a nap. I had hardly laid down on the bed, when there was a knock at the door. It was the desk clerk lady.

"I'm sorry, sir," she said, "but you're going to have to move."

"What do you mean?"

"Well, I made a mistake," she explained. "We've got a big family reunion coming in, and they specifically reserved rooms one through six. They know these are our best rooms. So, you've got to move."

I couldn't believe that she actually admitted I was staying in one of their "best" rooms. I tried arguing with her, but her mind was set. I had to move. She handed me a key.

"It's upstairs at the other end."

Of course it was upstairs at the other end! But it didn't turn out to be as bad as I had imagined. Actually, it was just like the other room. The same interior decorator had done both. And most important, it too had a shiny new telephone.

I spent the next 15 minutes making trip after trip up and down the stairs to transfer all my stuff to the second room. Once I got everything situated, I picked up the phone to call my office again to give them my new room number. There was no dial tone. I checked the cord to see if it was plugged in. It was.

Downstairs to the office again.

"Ma'am, I'm very sorry to keep bothering you, but my phone won't work."

"What do you mean, it won't work?"

I could tell it was going to be another memorable conversation, "I mean it won't work. It's dead."

"That's impossible. We've got a brand new phone system. It was installed just last week. You just don't know how to work it."

I nearly bit my tongue off to keep from jumping on that remark. How ignorant did she think I was that I didn't know how to operate a simple telephone?

Up to the room we marched. She picked up the phone and listened. She checked the cord. She listened again. She slapped the phone on the side two or three times. She listened again.

"This phone doesn't work," she said confidently. "You're just going to have to do without."

"Oh no, I'm not!" I said. "I've got to have a phone, so get me another room."

Shuffling Doors

We trudged back down to the office. I was given the key to a third room. It was upstairs next to the one I had just moved into. I stuck the key in the lock and started to open the door. At that precise moment I heard someone yell, "What are you doing?"

I looked up. It was the maid. "I've just been assigned this room," I said. "I want to check it out."

"I wouldn't go in there, if I were you," said the maid.

"Why's that?"

"Cause there's a woman in bed in there."

I quietly pulled the key out of the lock and headed back downstairs.

"You mean that lady is still in bed? Why I thought she left an hour ago. Well, try this one," the room clerk said.

I was handed my fourth key. Upstairs again. This time I knocked first. Several times. No response. I stuck the key in and turned the handle. It wouldn't budge. I started wrestling with the knob. Along came the maid again.

"What are you doing now?" she asked.

"I'm trying to get this door open."

"Why?"

"Why? What do you mean, Why? I've been assigned this

room, that's why!"

"What? I swear, I don't know what's wrong with that crazy room clerk."

"What do you mean?"

"Why nobody's been able to get into that room for almost three months. The lock won't work."

Downstairs again. Apologies. A fifth key. Upstairs again. I was beginning to feel like an actor in a surrealistic play.

The door opened, and there was no one in the bed or shower. So far, so good. I picked up the phone. There was a dial tone. Everything appeared in order. I started moving my stuff to the new room. By the time I finished, I had worked up quite a sweat. I decided to turn on the window air conditioning unit before I lay down for a nap.

Click. You guessed it. Nothing happened. I looked to see if it was plugged in. It wasn't. I picked up the plug, and I could hardly believe my eyes. Two of the three prongs were broken off.

I still marvel that I didn't blow my stack. It was maddening, but it was all too funny. By the time I checked into the sixth room, I was enjoying a good laugh along with the desk clerk and the maid. The sixth room proved to be a winner. But it was still World War II, and it was upstairs.

Fighting Gluttony

Lodging predicaments are not the only ones you face while traveling. There is also food. I once read where one of the most famous evangelists who ever lived weighed almost 400 pounds when he died. I was astonished. "How could such a godly man become such a glutton?" I thought. I soon learned when I went on the road.

There are dear sweet ladies all over this country who pride themselves in stuffing the visiting evangelist. You sit down at tables that are groaning from the weight of the food on them, and then you are strongly encouraged to have two or three helpings of everything, whether you like it or not. Just when you think you're about to pop, out come the desserts.

What's really pathetic is trying to speak after such a feast. Your spirit feels heavy and your stomach churns. Your attention focuses on trying to muffle the burps as they constantly rise to the surface. You literally don't know for sure what's going to come out of your mouth every time you open it.

Trying Diplomacy

I put on 20 pounds quickly and decided something had to be done. I started sending out an advance letter to the host minister explaining that I eat only two meals a day — breakfast and lunch — and that I never eat before speaking in the evening.

It didn't work. As soon as I would arrive, the minister would say, "I know you don't like to eat supper, but several of our ladies always cook for the visiting evangelist, and they insisted on preparing meals. However, they told me to tell you that you don't have to eat."

Sure. Tell me, how do you go to a sweet lady's house for supper and just sit there sipping tea when you know she's been cooking her heart out all day long? No way.

Others handled the problem in another way, "Dave, I know you don't like to eat before you preach, so we've scheduled all your evening meals for after the services."

That's even worse. When I preach, I preach with all my physical, spiritual and emotional strength. When I'm finished, I'm really finished. All I want to do is go to bed. Instead, I often end up at someone's house eating a huge meal at 10 p.m. The result is that I end up going to bed at midnight or later — and with a full stomach that prevents me from sleeping soundly.

There seems to be no way around becoming a 400-pound evangelist. There are just too many sweet ladies who are determined to give you "just one good home-cooked meal."

Calling on Angels

In addition to lodging and food, the third aspect of living

out of a suitcase is, of course, travel. One of my granddaugh-
ters has gone with me to the airport so frequently that she
thinks I work in an airplane! When she sees a plane flying
over, she always points and says, "Look, Mommy, there goes
Paw-paw."

I'm thankful that when I first began to travel, my Bible
study led me to an understanding of the reality of the ministry
of angels. I had heard of "guardian angels" all my life, but we
had never studied angels in our church. I still remember how
excited I got when I discovered Hebrews 1:14 which says that
angels are ministering spirits who have been sent forth to
serve those who are in the process of being saved. Wow!
Angels available to serve me — what a thought.

When I saw how many airplanes were falling out of the
skies, I decided to use the ministry of angels to protect my
flights. I've been using that ministry ever since. Every time
I get on an airplane, I pray, "Lord, please surround this plane
with your holy angels and allow them to fly with us every
mile of the way. May they protect us and give us a soft
landing." I always conclude that prayer by asking the Lord to
post an angel at my house to protect my wife.

A Sobering Flight

Some of those angels have had to work overtime. I was
flying one time from Dallas to Denver. When we arrived over
Denver, we started circling. After circling for almost an hour,
the pilot made an announcement over the intercom.

"Ladies and gentlemen, I'm sorry, but Denver is in the
midst of a blizzard. We can't land at the moment, so we're
going to fly to Albuquerque and sit down there for a while.
Maybe the storm will blow over."

That announcement created a storm inside the plane. I
soon became aware of the fact that the plane was packed with
groups of skiers who were anxious to get to the ski slopes.
The word "blizzard" was music to their ears. "To heck with
the danger," they said, "let's land!"

But, no, we were headed for New Mexico. The mood

turned dark and surly. The flight attendants must have reported the situation to the captain, because he soon came on the intercom with another announcement.

"Ladies and gentlemen, I know you are very disappointed, so we have decided to provide drinks on the house! Have as many drinks as you please on us, and enjoy the delay."

The liquor began to flow. The mood changed. We sat on the ground in Albuquerque for two hours, but I'm not sure anyone noticed except me. By the time we made the landing in Denver, I was the only sober guy on board. People were feeling no pain. Since I was sitting mid-way back, about half the people got off the plane before me. They were singing and laughing and carousing. By the time I got to the gate, my host minister was in a state of shock. He was wondering what I was doing on a plane loaded with drunks.

A Dumb Flight

My wildest airplane adventure occurred on a flight from Dallas to Cleveland. I had held a meeting in Cleveland once before. Shortly after that meeting, I received an invitation to hold a prophecy conference in Lancaster, Ohio. As soon as I accepted that invitation, I started receiving letters from people at the church in Cleveland telling me they planned to attend. Based on those letters, I assumed that Lancaster was a suburb of Cleveland. I never bothered to check a map.

I made my plane reservations and informed the Lancaster church of my flight number and arrival time. Now Lancaster is located just outside of Columbus, Ohio, about 150 miles south of Cleveland. I had a flight booked for Cleveland. The people in Lancaster naturally thought I was flying into Columbus. You can imagine how surprised the elder was who came to meet me when he discovered there was no such flight number coming into Columbus.

Since he assumed that I was smart enough to reserve a flight to the correct city, he therefore drew the conclusion that the airline had put me on the wrong flight. When he explained this situation to them, they, too, drew the same conclusion.

No one suspected that I would be so dumb as to fly to the wrong city.

The airline officials began scrambling around trying to come up with a solution to "their" mistake. At one point they asked the elder if I was in any way related to President Reagan! He told them I was not, as far as he knew. They told him that if I were related to the president, they were going to radio the plane to make a special landing in Columbus! Who says connections don't count?

Rescued by Angels

Meanwhile, I was flying to Cleveland, completely oblivious to my dumb mistake. When I arrived, there was no one to meet me at the gate, but that didn't bother me because most of the time I'm met at the baggage claim area. I proceeded to the baggage area and, just as I was picking up my suitcases, I heard my name being paged over the public address system.

I picked up a courtesy phone and identified myself. The lady told me to stay right there. In just a few minutes, two porters came running up, grabbed my luggage and told me to follow them. They took off at a fast clip. I had no idea what was going on.

The next thing I knew, I had been hustled into another airplane. The plane was already loaded with people when I arrived. Everyone stared at me with the obvious question written all over their faces, "Who is this guy who's been holding up our flight?" I was directed to one of only two vacant seats. My luggage was stuffed in a closet up front. I kept asking what was going on. All I was told was, "You're in the wrong city."

As we took off, I turned to the person next to me and asked where we were heading.

"Orlando," he responded grumpily.

"Orlando! You mean Orlando, Florida?"

"Yes," he replied. "This is a travel club. We chartered this plane to fly us non-stop to Disney World. Who are you and why are you on here?"

I didn't know what to say. I couldn't get past the thought of Orlando. Why had I been put on this flight? As I was struggling for an answer to his question, a stewardess came up and began to apologize.

"We are sorry that we put you on the wrong flight."

"What do you mean?"

"You were supposed to be on the flight to Columbus. We put you on the flight to Cleveland by mistake. This is a charter flight to Orlando, but we're going to make a special stop in Columbus to let you off. Please forgive us for any inconvenience we may have caused you."

"Do you know where Lancaster, Ohio is located?" I asked.

"Oh yes," she said, "right outside of Columbus."

Suddenly it all clicked. I had booked the wrong city! They thought it was their mistake. It never occurred to anyone that I could be so dumb as to fly to the wrong city. I was so embarrassed that I kept my mouth shut and let them continue to believe it was their mistake. The result was a free ride to Columbus on a special chartered jet.

"He will give His angels charge concerning you, to guard you in all your ways" (Psalm 91:11). Thank you, Lord.

Maintaining a Sense of Humor 16

I was holding a meeting at a small church in Pekin, Indiana. One evening before the service a lady walked up to me and asked, "Do you have a sense of humor?"

"Lady," I said, "to survive in this business, you've got to have a sense of humor."

"Oh good," she said, "because I want to share something funny with you. Last night as my six-year-old son and I were driving home from church, I noticed that he was very quiet. 'What are you thinking about?' I asked him. 'The preacher,' he said. 'What about him?' I asked. 'Well . . . he sure can preach for a bald-headed man!'"

The evangelist's life may be filled with trials and tribulation, but it is also liberally sprinkled with a lot of good laughs, if you only have the sense of humor to enjoy them.

I'm convinced that God has a great sense of humor. He would have to have, otherwise He would never put up with us. I'm also convinced that those who serve Him must have a sense of humor to survive. The reason is that most of the laughs they will encounter will come at their own expense. It's one of the ways God keeps us humble.

Tongue-tied

I experienced an embarrassing slip of the tongue in a

sermon on cults. I was coming down hard on the evils of the cults and began to name them specifically — the Jehovah's Witnesses, the Moonies, the Christian Scientists. I then dramatically said, "But the worst cult of all, the largest and best organized and the one that is leading the most people to Hell, is the Masons." There were audible gasps all over the audience. I was startled. I had never received such a response before from a Christian audience to the identification of the Mormons as a cult.

I paused to reflect. That's when it dawned on me that I had said "Masons" instead of "Mormons." I didn't bother to correct it. I figured it was a Holy Ghost slip of the tongue because no Christian has any business being a Mason. I found out later that there were a lot of Masons in that particular congregation. I hoped they had a sense of humor. I also hoped they would be motivated to reconsider their Masonic commitment.

Grandiloquence

My verbal problems usually come when I get carried away with enthusiasm and start waxing eloquent. One evening I was preaching on the millennium. I was developing the point that when the Lord returns to reign, He will redeem the plant and animal kingdoms.

"They will be put back the way God intended them," I pointed out. "There will be no poisonous plants, no weeds and no carnivorous or poisonous animals. The wolf will lie down with the lamb, and the lion will eat straw with the ox."

That's where I should have stopped. But no, I had to go on and belabor the point.

"I'm hoping and praying that when God redeems nature, He will do away with the chiggers!"

It got a big laugh.

I didn't say it to get a laugh. I was serious. I hate chiggers.

For those of you who don't know what I'm talking about, let me explain. Chiggers are microscopic little critters that infest the grass during the summer months in the Southern United States. They jump on your legs, crawl up to a tender spot and then bite with such ferocity that a large, red welt rises up that itches like mad for three or four days. They are definitely a part of the Curse.

My wife happened to be present the evening I expressed the wish that God would do away with the chiggers. As we were driving home, she was very quiet. I could feel it coming. Finally, I asked.

"What's the matter?"

"I couldn't believe your remark this evening about the chiggers," she said with a sound of exasperation.

"Yes, I know," I responded. "I guess I got a little carried away."

"Oh, that's not the point."

"Then what is the point?"

"The point is that what you said shows that you don't understand Bible prophecy."

Those were fighting words. I started to launch into a testy defense, when she cut me short.

"You see, honey," she said calmly, "God is not going to do away with the chiggers. He's going to make you lie down with them!"

We both had a good laugh, but all the time I was thinking, "If He does, I hope He defangs those little boogers first!"

Interruptions

The Apostle Paul once had a fellow fall out of the balcony while he was preaching (Acts 20). I've never had that happen, but I've learned to hang loose and expect almost anything to happen. I've had to contend with electrical blackouts, leaky roofs, crackling public-address systems, screaming babies, snoring elders and even heart attacks.

Non-insulated public-address systems are one of the worst hazards. You can be right in the middle of making a crucial spiritual point when the system will suddenly pick up a CB transmission from some trucker, and the whole sanctuary will be filled with expletives of the worst sort. It's always difficult to recover from such a blow.

The funniest interruption I ever experienced occurred at a church in Jennings, Louisiana. It was on a Sunday evening. About 300 people were present. I was in the middle of my sermon when I began to notice a strange noise. It sounded at first like a low-level police siren. It was a steady, high-pitched, oscillating tone. I stopped and tapped the microphone. The sound continued.

I then noticed that people near the front were beginning to get tickled. Some lowered their eyes and giggled. Others covered their faces and muffled their laughs. One man got so tickled that he started shaking all over and finally laid down in the pew.

That was it. I couldn't take it any longer. I stopped and asked, "What's the matter?"

A fellow on the back row stood up and shouted, "It's Grandpa's new watch. The alarm has gone off, and he can't hear it!"

The whole congregation exploded with laughter as the man ran to the front, tapped the patriarch of the church on the shoulder and pointed at his new wrist watch.

It took a good five minutes to get everyone settled down again and back into the lesson. Then, believe it or not, the alarm went off again. And again, the elderly gentleman did not hear it.

The next evening when he arrived, he showed me a naked wrist and said, "Mother made me leave it at home." His wife smiled triumphantly.

Clock Watchers

Every church has one or more clock watchers. These are often stern and authoritarian sorts who are determined that no service will ever run more than 59 minutes, especially during the pro football season. They constantly check their watches in an exaggerated manner to impress a sense of time consciousness upon the preacher. They always give me the feeling that if I go one minute overtime, the floor will open up and swallow me.

The most unusual time watcher I ever ran across was a fellow at a church in Dallas. I was conducting a week-long prophecy conference, and every evening this man, who was one of the elders, would come up to me after the service and complain because I had not preached long enough! I thanked him for the compliment, but I told him that I didn't want to wear out my welcome. I like to leave people wanting more. But my explanations were to no avail. He continued to complain every evening about my "cutting it too short."

On the last evening of the meeting he met me at the door as I arrived and asked if he could borrow my wrist watch for a moment. I thought it was an odd request but, before I could ask why, I was besieged by well-wishers who wanted to ask questions about prophecy. While talking to them, I slipped off my watch and handed it to the man. He promptly disappeared.

I forgot about the watch until it was time for me to preach. When I started to the pulpit, I felt for it and then remembered I had loaned it to the elder. That didn't bother me because that particular church had three clocks on the walls — one on each side and one at the back. In fact, I had never seen a church with so many clocks. It gave you the impression that the whole congregation was made up of clock watchers. I found out that appearances can be deceiving.

For you see, when I looked to see what time I was starting my sermon, to my surprise I discovered that all three clocks had been draped! There was no way for me to tell what time it was. I've been looking for a clock watcher like that one ever since. It was probably the nicest compliment my preaching has ever received.

Worship Antics

The worship time has the potential to be even more unpredictable than the preaching time, simply because more people and equipment are involved. Music accompaniment tapes are always starting at the wrong time or else not starting at all, leaving the nervous singer facing an audience in awkward silence. There are the out-of-tune pianos, the squeaky electric organs, and the drummers who believe that loud is beautiful. There are the Sandi Patti copycats who try to mimic her beautiful singing and end up screeching on all the high notes.

There are the draggy song leaders who lead every hymn at a funeral pace. There are the peppy ones who come across as frustrated cheerleaders. There are choir members who sit slack-jawed, napping on and off throughout the service, and there are others so full of the Spirit that they do everything except jump the pews and hang from the chandeliers.

Personally, I'll take enthusiasm over deadness any time. It's always easier to tone down a fanatic than to resurrect a corpse.

Dry Bones

One corpse I vividly remember was the song leader at a fairly large church in Louisville, Kentucky. On the Sunday morning the meeting began, this character looked out at the congregation with sleepy eyes and a sour face. He suddenly growled out a Marine-like command: "Everyone turn to song number 234!" Then he literally barked the command: "That's song TWO, THREE, FOUR!"

I started turning fast in fear that if I didn't, I might receive a public reprimand.

"The name of this song," he snarled, "is 'Stand Up, Stand Up for Jesus.' But I don't want to inconvenience any of you, so we're going to sing it sitting down."

We proceeded to sing a stand-up song sitting down! It was really an "inspirational" moment. By the time I got up to preach, the people were in a semi-comatose stage. I felt like Ezekiel standing in the valley of the dry bones speaking to the Frozen Chosen.

I went back to the motel and got on my knees before God. "Lord," I cried out, "do something about that song leader. Some way or other get him out of the picture so that we can experience some real worship."

When I arrived back at the church that evening, one of the deacons called me aside. "We've got a problem," he said worriedly. "Our song leader got a call from his boss this afternoon and was told to go to Tennessee immediately. We don't have a song leader for this evening."

It was hard for me to keep a straight face. I wanted to shout "Hallelujah!" I had prayed that guy right out of the state! I assured the deacon that I knew a really good worship leader there in the city who would be glad to substitute. That evening we started worshiping the Lord.

Country and Western

The hardest act I've ever had to follow in a worship service was one that I ran into at a meeting in New Mexico. The church had invited a husband and wife team with a Western format to lead in worship. They were a very sincere pair, but they had come to entertain and not to lead in worship.

They dressed in cowboy clothes, performed funny skits, and sang old-time, down-home Western songs for which they had written Christian lyrics. The congregation, particularly the children, loved every minute of it.

My most difficult moment came on the night when the man suddenly jumped out of sight behind the piano. When he emerged, he was wearing a "50-gallon" cowboy hat made of styrofoam. It was literally about three feet tall and five feet in diameter.

He then pulled out a homemade bass fiddle composed of a broom handle attached to an upside-down washtub. He strummed on the fiddle and sang while wearing the monstrous hat. When he finished, he bowed to the wild applause, pointed at me and said, "And now . . . here's Brother Reagan!" As I said, it was a tough act to follow.

Stern and Drab

The most memorable worship group I ever encountered was a family of Mennonites in central Indiana. The meeting was being held at an independent Christian Church, and I was surprised when the pastor informed me that he had invited a family of Mennonites to lead the worship each evening. He assured me that they were an outstanding group.

When it came time for the Sunday evening service to begin, the Mennonites had not yet arrived. The pastor was getting very nervous. He kept pacing around on the front porch of the church, looking hopefully up and down the street. At about five minutes after the hour, several pickup trucks arrived and the Mennonites jumped out carrying their instruments.

They were an interesting sight to behold. The men were dressed in dark-colored work clothes and wore vests. The women wore long dresses with long sleeves and had little bonnets on their heads. But the person who caught my eye was the stern-looking patriarch who led the clan. He had on overalls and a vest. He had a classic Mennonite beard and was wearing a wide-brimmed black hat. He looked like he was ready to preach hell fire.

I shuddered to think what kind of worship leaders these people might be. I figured we were in for a week of drab hymns sung like Gregorian chants.

Surprised by Joy

The patriarch gruffly apologized for being late. He explained that their milking chores had taken longer than expected. The women quickly set up their instruments, then the men stepped forward to sing. The patriarch took off his hat, cleared his throat and, in a deadpan fashion, said they were glad to be with us.

Then, he suddenly started patting his foot and snapping his fingers. "Ah one and ah two and ah three," he said rhythmically — and the whole group broke out in one of the liveliest renditions of "Old Buddha" that I have ever heard!

I was in stitches. They had turned out to be opposite of what I had expected. They were anything but drab. "Old Buddha" is one of the funniest Christian songs I have ever heard, but it has a powerful message about the folly of legalism and sectarianism. It was the last song in the world I would have expected this group to sing.

They went on that night and the rest of the week to bless us greatly with anointed leadership in worship. They were people who loved the Lord, and it came through in the worship they led. I have always wondered if the stern patriarch was putting us on that night. I don't think he was.

He reminded me of the Hasidic Jews of Israel. They take their religion very seriously. They are stern in countenance and drab in dress. But they know how to relax before the Lord and throw their whole being into the expression of joyous worship.

An Instrumental Surprise

The next year when I returned to that same church, they again had a worship treat in store for me. The pastor had invited one of the most gifted Christian songwriters and worship leaders in the country to come from Nashville, Tennessee, to both teach and lead worship. The day before the meeting was to begin, the fellow called and asked if he could bring his own piano player. The pastor agreed.

When the worship leader and his accompanist arrived, I experienced a real surprise. The pianist was none other than a young man by the name of Mark who had grown up in the same church that I had in Waco, Texas. He was several years younger than me, but I knew him well and recognized him instantly, even though I had not seen him in years.

The next day when I got up to preach, I told the congregation about our common roots in the same boyhood church. Then I made an observation: "Our presence here this morning is proof positive that God has a great sense of humor. You see, Mark and I grew up in a church that does not believe in prophecy or instrumental music. Yet, here am I preaching prophecy — and there Mark sits playing the piano. We have made a pact. I won't tell the folks back home what he's playing, if he won't tell them what I'm preaching!"

Hanging Loose

Some people strongly object to humor in the pulpit. They feel like it detracts from the sanctity of God's Word. I respect their view. I, too, cringe in response to preachers who think their major purpose is to make people laugh throughout their sermons.

But I do not object to using some humor to establish rapport with the audience. It helps them to realize that you are human like them and that, although you take your message seriously, you don't take yourself all that seriously.

Because I have an earned doctorate, I am forever being introduced as "Dr." Reagan. I don't like that It sounds stuffy, formal and religious.

I always respond to the pastor's introduction by thanking him for being kind and gracious, but then I shift gears and threaten him if he calls me "Dr." again. I usually say something like, "Brother, if you call me 'Dr.' one more time, I'm going to start referring to you as 'His Holiness the Right Reverend.'" That really isn't much of a threat since most pastors would welcome that kind of respect!

Debunking Titles

I sometimes follow up that comment with one of my favorite stories. I tell the folks that every time I'm called "Dr." it reminds me of the fellow who was invited to speak to the national church convention. When he received the convention's pre-publicity packet, he noticed that every other speaker that year had a doctorate except him. He not only did not have a doctorate, he had no master's or bachelor's degrees. In fact, he was a high school dropout with only one qualification to speak — he was full of the Spirit of God.

When he started filling out the background publicity

sheet that always comes with one of those packets, the devil got the best of him. He wrote down his name, paused for a moment, then put a comma and wrote, "M.D., D.D., L.L.D."

When he arrived at the convention, he quickly discovered that he was the talk of the town. Everywhere he went he overheard people talking about "the fellow with the three doctorates." They were all going to his session to hear him speak.

By the time he got up to speak, his conscience had gotten the best of him. "Ladies and gentlemen," he began, "I must start with a confession. Those letters after my name — M.D., D.D., L.L.D. — do not stand for what you think. What they really stand for is Mersy Doates, Dosey Doates and Little Lamsey Divies!"

Lone Star Stories

I am constantly kidded about being a Texan, particularly if I'm preaching in the rival state of Oklahoma. I bring some of this upon myself because during the football season I always exhort the congregation where I'm preaching to pray for the Dallas Cowboys to win that Sunday afternoon. That plea is often greeted with boos and hisses.

But I quickly explain that it is in their best interest to pray earnestly for a Cowboy victory because when the Cowboys lose on Sunday afternoon, I always preach hellfire and brimstone on Sunday evening! I generate a lot of prayers for the Cowboys that way.

Actually, I rarely tell Texas stories because I got into big trouble one time when I bragged about Texas from the pulpit. I was preaching about Paul, and I casually mentioned in passing that Paul was one of the greatest Texans who ever lived.

After the service, an irate lady came up and challenged me. "How dare you say Paul was a Texan! What proof do you have of that?"

I explained that I really didn't have any proof. I just assumed he was a Texan because he was such a great man.

"Well!" she said in disgust. "I can prove beyond a shadow of a doubt that he was not a Texan. Read Philippians 4:11."

That passage says, "I have learned to be content in whatever state I'm in." The woman was right. Paul was not a Texan, because no Texan could ever make such a statement!

At the next service I corrected my statement and shared the Biblical evidence for the correction. I asked the people to forgive me for misleading them. When that service ended another irate lady came up and said, "Paul may not have been a Texan but he was definitely a Southerner. Read 2 Corinthians 13:14."

That passage says, "The grace of the Lord Jesus Christ, and the love of God, and the fellowship of the Holy Spirit, be with y'all." No doubt about it. Paul was a Southerner.

A year later I was sharing all this with a congregation in Oklahoma. Another lady came up afterward and said, "I've got some really tough news for you. You see, Paul was really a Sooner!"

Now that was too much. I couldn't bear the thought of the great Apostle having Okie roots. I demanded Biblical proof. She told me to read Hebrews 13:19. It says, "I urge you all the more to do this, that I may be restored to you the sooner." That's a tough pill for a Texan to swallow. More than ever, I now believe that Paul did not write Hebrews.

Prophetic Chuckles

I find that people are often uptight about prophecy preachers coming to their church. They figure they will be subjected to a bombardment of doomsday preaching. I like to use humor from the prophetic scriptures to put these people at ease.

One of my favorites is 1 Corinthians 15:51. I urge each congregation to frame this scripture and hang it in their nursery. It contains a prophecy that is fulfilled during each service. The verse reads: "We shall not all sleep but we shall all be changed."

My meetings usually end on Wednesday night. I often like to begin my sermon that evening by sharing a story about Wednesday services.

When I was growing up in the church, our preachers had an obsession with what we called "Wednesday Evening Prayer Meeting." The preachers were always trying to build up the Wednesday night attendance with different gimmicks, usually to no avail.

They would almost always end up trying to motivate attendance by putting a guilt trip on us. This came in the form of a fiery sermon that left you with no doubt that you would spend eternity in Hell if you did not attend on Wednesday night. That was always effective. Wednesday night attendance would immediately shoot up, but it would begin to taper off after a few weeks.

With this background, you can appreciate one of the favorite stories of my heritage. It seems that a large group of our people were in line at the Pearly Gates, waiting to be interviewed by St. Peter. The line was very long that day, and our group was about half a mile back.

As we slowly approached the gate, we noticed something unusual. Every time a group would get to the gates, the leader would say something to St. Peter, St. Peter would respond, and the group would then go bananas! I mean they would put their hands up in the air and start dancing and shouting, "Hallelujah!"

We started getting nervous. These folks were acting like Pentecostals, and we sure didn't expect to spend eternity in Heaven with such unruly people. Finally, we could not stand the suspense any longer. We appointed one of our staid elders to go up to the front of the line and find out what was going on.

We watched him anxiously as he said something to St. Peter and St. Peter replied. All of a sudden, the elder stuck his hands up in the air and started dancing in the Spirit! We couldn't believe our eyes. He danced all the way back to where we were standing, all the time shouting, "Praise the

Lord!" at the top of his voice.

"What is it? What is it?" we called out.

"Oh! I've got incredibly good news," he shouted. "Guess what? Wednesday nights don't count!"

A Scripture for Everything

I use a lot of scripture when I preach. People often discover books that they didn't even know were in the Bible. This extensive use of scripture has prompted a lot of comments.

A lady came up to me one time and said I reminded her of a preacher she once knew who had a scripture for everything. She then gave a hilarious example of what she was talking about.

It seemed this particular preacher had gone to visit one of his flock — a lady who had just come home from the hospital. He knocked on the door of her house and waited. He heard a door open inside and the pitter-patter of feet as someone ran across the room. But no one came to the door. He continued to knock. He continued to hear noises inside. But he couldn't get anyone to the door.

Finally, he gave up and started walking back to his car. Just as he got to his car, it occurred to him that there must be a verse that would be appropriate for the occasion. He thought for a moment and then got an idea. He pulled out a calling card and wrote on the back of it, "Revelation 3:21." He went back to the house and stuck the card in the door. That verse says, "Behold, I stand at the door and knock; if anyone hears my voice and opens the door, I will come in to him and will dine with him and he with me."

Two days later the preacher received an envelope in the mail. Inside was the calling card he had left on the lady's door. On the back side, underneath his scripture reference, she had written, "Genesis 3:10." That verse says, "I heard the sound of thee in the garden, and I was afraid because I was naked; so I hid myself."

Teaching the Future 17

In addition to evangelistic meetings, I have held prophetic seminars all over the United States. These can be
tailored to any time period, but they normally extend over a
weekend.

I find that many people come to these seminars very
uptight because they suspect that my purpose is to convert
them to a particular prophetic viewpoint. That suspicion is
often based on past experiences with other prophecy teachers.

I don't know what it is, but there is something about the
nature of Bible prophecy that seems to bring out the dogma-
tism in people. Prophecy teachers as a whole tend to be some
of the most dogmatic people on the face of the earth. They
also tend to be both sensational and polemical in their style.

Thus, the typical prophecy teacher has an answer — the
one and only right answer — to every question. He tends to
be argumentative and debative, almost relishing a good verbal
duel. He often will spend most of his time attacking the
viewpoints he disagrees with, rather than presenting his own
view in a positive manner. He usually traffics in the sensational, being more concerned about the Anti-Christ than Jesus
Christ.

It is not at all unusual for prophecy teachers to run newspaper ads showing drawings of strange, multi-headed crea-
tures and featuring teaser questions like, "Does Jane Fonda's
name add up to 666?" It's no wonder that people often

shudder in horror when they hear a prophecy teacher is coming to their church!

Teaching Purposes

I try to cut though all this reservoir of ill will by stating up front that I have no desire to convert anyone to a particular prophetic viewpoint. I have a particular viewpoint, and I believe in it very strongly, but it doesn't bother me in the least if someone doesn't agree with it.

My first and foremost purpose is to get people interested in studying God's Prophetic Word. It constitutes one-third of the Bible, and I'm convinced that it is the most ignored portion of the Bible.

My second purpose is to draw people closer to Jesus through their study of prophecy. If prophecy is taught properly, it will automatically do this, "for the testimony of Jesus is the spirit of prophecy" (Revelation 19:10)

My third purpose is to convince people, regardless of their particular prophetic viewpoint, that Jesus is coming soon.

Differing Views

With respect to differences in viewpoints, I stress that what people believe about Bible prophecy has no impact whatsoever on where they are going to spend eternity. Heaven is going to be occupied by premillennialists, amillennialists, postmillennialists, and some people who don't know the difference between a millennium and a millipede.

One of my favorite prophecy stories is the one about the four little boys at Sunday school who were trying to impress each other with their Bible knowledge. "I'm a premillennialist," said one of them. "That's nothing," said the second, "I'm an amillennialist." "So what?" said the third. "I'm a postmillennialist."

The fourth boy didn't say anything. The others began to press him. "Come on, tell us what you are." "Well," he replied, "I guess I'm a panmillennialist." "What's that?" they asked. "A panmillennialist," he explained, "is a person who doesn't know what's going to happen in the end-times. All he knows is that God is in control, and therefore everything will pan out in the end."

This is not to say that what a person believes about prophecy is irrelevant. All truth is relevant, and we should seek the truth in all matters. The point is that what we believe about prophecy is not relevant to our justification. The only thing relevant there is what we believe about Jesus. But our prophetic beliefs are very relevant to our sanctification — to how we live in the present.

Impacting Behavior

I'm a classic example of what I'm talking about. For the first 30 years of my life I knew almost nothing about Bible prophecy. I was saved because I had accepted Jesus as my Lord and Savior. But my spiritual development was in neutral because of erroneous concepts and pure ignorance regarding things like the Holy Spirit and Bible prophecy.

Not once during that 30-year period did I ever yearn for the Lord to come. Not once did I pray "Maranatha!" (1 Corinthians 16:22). I was apathetic about the return of the Lord — and even fearful of it. After all, He might come on one of my bad days and catch me committing some sin!

My study of Bible prophecy had a transforming effect upon my life. It helped me to better understand the grace, mercy and love of God. It brought me to the realization that the Lord's return is my "Blessed Hope" and not my "Holy Terror."

It also convinced me that Jesus is coming soon. That conviction had a purifying effect because it motivated me to holiness. For the first time in my life, I accepted Jesus as my Lord as well as my Savior.

Understanding Prophecy

Another important point I try to make at the beginning of each seminar is that a person does not have to be a walking genius in order to understand Bible prophecy. Many people have the mistaken idea that a person must have a Ph.D. in hermeneutics or a doctorate in imagination in order to understand Bible prophecy.

This erroneous concept is due to several facts. One is the vocabulary. Prophecy teachers often sound like they are speaking non-stop in tongues! That's because they are constantly using words like "premillennial, postmillennial, amillennial, chiliast, antichiliast, pretribulation rapture, and posttribulation rapture." It's enough to scare anyone. I try to cut through all this technical verbiage by showing the meaning of these terms through simple diagrams.

I also emphasize that I believe the Bible was written by God for the common man to understand, with the help of the Holy Spirit. I've found that the key to understanding Bible prophecy is a very simple one: "If the plain sense makes sense, don't look for any other sense, lest you end up with nonsense." The problem with Bible prophecy is not that it is hard to understand. The problem is that it is hard to believe. If you will believe it, you will understand it.

Prophetic Ignorance

I find that most Christians know almost nothing about Bible prophecy. Since they themselves realize this, they often come to my seminars with a rather defensive attitude.

I try to put them at ease on this point by emphasizing the fact that I knew almost nothing about Bible prophecy until I was 30 years old. After attending church for that long, I was so prophetically ignorant that I thought the Rapture was a sensation you feel when your girlfriend kisses you! I would have identified Gog and Magog as the name of a comedy team. And I thought the Anti-Christ was a "denominational" preacher.

Maybe that's one of the reasons God called me to teach prophecy. I can really identify with those who have gone to church all their lives and still couldn't find the book of Habakkuk if their lives depended on it. I know how they feel.

I know the embarrassment of looking for the book of Heze-
kiah, only to discover that no such book exists.

Handling Questions

At my prophecy seminars, I always try to save at least
half the time for people to ask questions. I used to approach
this segment of the seminar with sweaty palms, but no longer.
I now look forward to it with delight, mainly because I never
cease to be amazed — and amused — at some of the questions people can come up with.

The three legitimate questions that are most frequently
asked are the following (listed in order of their frequency):

1) Where is the United States in Bible prophecy?
2) When will the Rapture occur?
3) Will we know each other in Heaven?

Some of the most unusual questions I can remember are
these:

1) Will we have the same pets in Heaven?
2) Will the Antichrist go through the Tribulation? (The
    normal question here is, "Will the church go through
    the Tribulation?")
3) Will the Illuminati fight at Armageddon?
4) Will I have to diet in my glorified body?
5) Will we recognize our enemies in Heaven?
6) How long will church services last in Heaven?
7) Is the 1,000-year reign during the Millennium simi-
    lar to the 40-day rain of Noah?
8) Will I have to learn how to play a harp in Heaven?
9) Is the Pope amillennial?
10) Will a pregnant, unsaved woman's baby be taken
    from her womb at the Rapture?
11) Will going to Hell be similar to being sucked into a
    black hole in space?
12) Will there be sports teams in Heaven?

Now you can understand why I used to get sweaty palms? But I've learned to roll with the punches, and I've also learned how to simply say, "I don't know."

Audience "Helpers"

One question that often comes up is, "What language will we speak in Heaven?" I always answer by saying that my best guess is Hebrew, and I give several scriptural references to back up the guess.

A Mexican-American friend of mine recently heard me give that answer, and he challenged it. "Oh no!" he protested. "We are going to speak Spanish in Heaven."

"Where did you get that crazy idea?" I asked.

"Right out of the Bible."

"Where?"

He smiled. "Haven't you ever heard of the 'Chicano Glory' of the Lord?" (He was referring, of course, to what the Jews call the "Shekinah Glory of God.")

At a seminar in Louisville, Kentucky, a person asked if I knew the prophetic significance of the word, "Selah." This is a word that is found in the margin of some Psalms (for example, Psalm 24). I patiently explained that no one knows for sure what the word means — that the best guess is that it was some sort of musical notation. I added that I did not believe it had any prophetic significance.

I was about to go on to the next question when a fellow spoke up and said he thought he knew what the word meant. He said he thought it was a cuss word that David used whenever he broke a harp string! It's always a joy to receive help from the audience when trying to answer the really tough questions.

One of the most irritating questions I ever received came during the taping of a television series before a live audience. The format was for me to teach for 25 minutes, break for a five-minute musical interlude, and then conclude with 25 minutes of questions from the audience.

We wanted to keep our editing costs to a minimum, so

we emphasized to the audience that they should keep their questions brief and relevant. We especially emphasized the relevant aspect since we wanted the questions to relate directly to the presentation.

On the night I spoke about the "Jew in Prophecy," the very first question from a lady in the audience was, "Do you speak in tongues?" The tape editor made a lot of money off us before we finished that series.

Prophetic Rumors

The only thing more weird than some of the questions asked at the seminars are some of the rumors that circulate among prophecy buffs. I'm absolutely convinced that most prophecy enthusiasts have very vivid imaginations. The thing that upsets me is the way otherwise normal people will jump upon prophecy rumors with enthusiasm and pass them along mindlessly to other people without ever bothering to check them out.

Some of the favorites that I keep running across include the following:

1) There is a "computer beast" in Belgium that contains the names and addresses of every person in the world.
2) The Ark of the Covenant has been found and is ready to be placed in a rebuilt Temple.
3) Henry Kissinger's name adds up to 666.
4) Bar codes will soon be tattooed on our hands.
5) Social security checks will have to be endorsed with the number 666.

On and on it goes, ad nauseam. My favorite is one that still pops up from time to time. It is the rumor that the building blocks for the new Temple have been cut, finished and numbered — and that one building block is stored in each Kmart in the U.S.!

Let's hope and pray God has a really good sense of humor.

Filling the Airwaves 18

When the ministry began we had no intention of going on the radio. Our outreach was to be through meetings, seminars, cassette tapes and publications. But the Lord had a different idea.

The ministry was hardly six weeks old when one of my trustees called and said I should get in touch with a farmer in Hereford, Texas, right away. The trustee had met the farmer at a Dallas religious gathering, and the farmer had asked that I contact him.

I called the man immediately. He told me that he had heard a taped sermon of mine on the Second Coming of Jesus.

"Are you broadcasting that message on the radio?" he asked.

"No sir."

"Why not?"

"We can't afford to."

"Why not?"

"Well, sir, this ministry is only six weeks old. We don't have any money or equipment to use for radio broadcasts."

"Well, I'm interested in putting you on the radio. Can you come see me?"

He didn't have to ask twice. I was on my way to Hereford the next day. I didn't even know where Hereford was located. I soon found out. It's a small town on the High Plains of the Texas Panhandle. As I traveled there, I marveled at the way God had brought us together. I was to marvel even more over the ways of the Lord after the meeting was over.

A Generous Man of Faith

The first thing I discovered on arrival was that this "farmer" happened to own one of the largest natural food companies in the entire country. Yet, he was a humble man of God with an office barely large enough for two people to sit in. We spent a couple of hours just talking about the Lord. Then he got down to brass tacks.

"Is radio expensive?" he asked.

"It costs $60 a day in Dallas," I replied.

"That's peanuts!" he observed.

"Well, sir," I said, "it may be peanuts to you but we don't have that kind of money."

He thought for a moment, and then he said, "I tell you what I'm going to do. I'm going to give you a check that will enable you to get on the radio in Dallas. It will be 'seed money.' If God wants you to continue on the radio, He will supply the additional money. But don't ever expect any more out of me. This is a one-time gift to start a new outreach. I'm giving it because God has convicted me that He wants your message on the radio."

He then wrote me a check for $4,000! I was speechless. He had never asked me what church I attended or what creed I affirmed. He had simply heard a message that had touched his heart, and he wanted to share it with others.

A New Outreach

Because of this man's faith and his love of the Lord, we launched a radio ministry in the summer of 1980, broadcasting over one station in Dallas. The program was called "Christ in Prophecy." It was aired daily, Monday through Friday, for 15 minutes.

For a year we broadcast only over the Dallas station. I focused on the teaching of Bible prophecy and emphasized my conviction that Jesus is coming soon.

Near the end of that first year, I began to move in a different direction regarding the program content. I began to speak out on national and international issues from a biblical perspective, stressing from time to time that many of these issues are signs of the soon return of the Lord.

What I was doing was blending my biblical knowledge with my professional training in national and international politics. The new format really clicked. People began to respond in dramatically increased numbers, and we began to consider the possibility of expanding the program to other stations.

Our mail made it clear that we were speaking to a real need — the need of Christians to relate their faith in meaningful terms to the world around them. Many letter writers confessed that they were bewildered by both national and world issues. I began to speak out on pornography, abortion, homosexuality, humanism, satanism and many other such controversial topics.

As I did so, both the interest and support level grew, and we began to expand to other stations. That meant making a lot of very difficult decisions. At what pace should we expand? Should we choose this station or that one?

Wise Counsel

I praise God for the wise trustees He has always blessed me with. From the beginning of our radio ministry, the trustees insisted upon two things: first, that we would never operate in the red; and second, that we would never use air time to beg for money. They stressed to me over and over that God would supply every need of the radio ministry if we would be faithful to Him, and if we would expand our outreach at his pace and not ours.

That meant expanding slowly and cautiously. It meant spending a lot of time in prayer, praying about every possible addition to our growing network of stations. It meant looking earnestly for signs of God's will in every situation. Sometimes those signs were subtle. At other times they were very dramatic.

A Clear Sign

One of the most dramatic episodes occurred when I called WXLN in Louisville, Kentucky. I asked to speak to the station manager, but he was not in. I was directed instead to a salesman. I introduced myself and told him I was interested in putting our program on his station. He started giving me his sales pitch. Suddenly, he stopped in mid-sentence and said, "What did you say your name is?" I repeated my name. He asked if we had ever met. I told him I didn't think so. "Well," he said, "your name sure is familiar." He went on with his sales pitch.

Then, again, very suddenly, he stopped his presentation and started shouting "Hallelujah! Hallelujah!"

I thought the poor fellow had lost it. "What's the matter?" I asked.

"Oh praise God!" he shouted. "I can't believe this."

"Believe What?"

"I knew your name sounded familiar," he said. "I just glanced at my prayer list and your name is on it."

"How could that be?" I asked.

"Weren't you on The 700 Club about two months ago?"

"Yes, I was."

"I thought so!" he replied. "I was sick that day and stayed home. I saw you interviewed, and God impressed upon my heart that I was to pray for you and your ministry. I've been doing that every day for almost two months. And today you call me!"

By that time I was shouting, "Hallelujah!" To me, it was certain confirmation that we were to put our program on his station.

More Signs

Not long after that I received a call from the manager of station KAJN in Crowley, Louisiana. He had heard our program over a Houston station, and he wanted it on his station. I wasn't interested. I wanted to reach as many people as possible and that meant spending our money on stations in large urban areas. Crowley is a little country town. I wasn't interested in broadcasting to chickens and cows.

But the Crowley manager was very persistent. He kept calling and calling. He just wouldn't take no for an answer. I asked the Lord for clear direction, and it came loud and clear.

First, I received a mailing honoring J. Vernon McGee's fortieth anniversary in Christian broadcasting. Here was one of the most honored men in Christian radio, broadcasting daily over more than 600 stations. A testimony from Dr. McGee was enclosed and a sentence in that testimony caught my eye. He said that of all the stations he was broadcasting over, that three were particularly effective — and one of those was KAJN in southern Louisiana.

Two days later I received the second sign. A lady living in Crowley called me and said that if I would put our program on KAJN, she and her husband would donate $250 a month! The program has been on KAJN since that time.

Not all the decisions have been that easy. There have been times when we have missed the Lord's leading. But overall, the Lord has blessed our program, and we have been able to keep it on the air continuously since 1980.

Expanding Cautiously

Hardly a week goes by now that we do not get at least two or three calls from stations wanting our program. The offers are always very enticing. The first month free. The second month at half price. The third month at two-thirds price. Four months before we have to pay the full rate. It is so easy to say yes and start running ahead of the Lord. It's really no wonder that so many radio and television ministries are so deeply mired in debt.

I remember a visit I had several years ago from a good friend who had just started a radio ministry. He asked how many stations I was broadcasting over.

"Oh, I think about 12 or 15," I said.
"What's the matter with your program?" he asked.
"What do you mean?"
"Haven't you been on the air for five years?"
"Yes."
"Well, I've been on for only six months and I'm already broadcasting on over 30 stations."

Of course he was. I could have been on 100 stations. But a day of reckoning comes when the bills start pouring in. Within a month that particular minister was not on any stations. He had run ahead of the Lord.

Financial Blessing

During the first five years of our radio ministry we ended every month with all our bills paid. That was a real miracle, particularly when you consider how we operate. Every day we offer something free on the program like a cassette tape or a publication. We tell people to send a donation, if they can, but we stress that it is not essential. The items really are free.

We might open 25 letters in a row requesting a cassette tape and not a one of them have anything in them except an apology for not being able to send a donation. Then, the 26th envelope will contain a check for $250 from someone we never heard of. That donation will pay for their request and all the others.

Financial Crisis

We never experienced any serious financial problems in our radio ministry until January of 1986 when the bottom fell out. It was like everyone forgot we existed for one month. The result was that when we got to the end of that month we did not have enough money to pay any of our radio bills.

I went into a period of soul searching. Was I personally out of God's will? Had the ministry moved out of the Lord's purpose? Were we running ahead of God? I prayed and sought the Lord, and in the process I became convicted that we were being put to a test. I felt like the test was related to two things.

Beyond a doubt it was related to a courageous decision the board had made the previous year. The board had stepped out in faith and voted unanimously that during 1987, the seventh year of the ministry, I was to take a Sabbatical rest from my travels. They asked me to stay home for one year and devote myself to study, prayer and writing.

At that time we were receiving at least $50,000 a year from love offerings at meetings and seminars. That income would have to come from other sources during the Sabbatical Year. No one knew where it would come from. They were just going to trust the Lord to supply.

I marveled at the board's faith and rejoiced over their courage. I knew God was calling the ministry to a year of preparation for greater service in His kingdom than I had ever imagined. I knew, too, that the decision would infuriate Satan.

For that reason, I could see Satan's handprint all over the financial crisis of January 1986. It was as if he were taunting us, trying to shake our faith in the Lord, with the hope that we would waver and surrender the commitment to the Sabbatical Year.

A Test of Commitment

I also saw that crisis as a second kind of test. I felt that the Lord was using it to see if we would be faithful to our dual commitment to never operate in the red and never use radio time to beg for money.

The board stood firm in all of its commitments. The trustees never wavered on their decision to use 1987 as a year of rest, even when the financial crisis worsened in the summer of 1986. And they never hedged on their other principles. We cut our number of stations more than in half to adjust to financial realities. There was no begging on the air. There were no desperate appeals. The stations were simply cut.

Cutting these stations was not easy to do. In fact, it hurt.

It was like losing dear friends you had visited with every day for years. Listeners were shocked and outraged. We were deluged with mail asking where we had gone. We sent out explanations of our policies. We were deluged with mail again, filled with apologies for taking us for granted and not supplying us with the gifts needed to keep us on the air.

It was a tough year, but God gave us the victory. We ended the year broadcasting on only a handful of stations, but all our bills were paid in full for the seventh calendar year in a row. In fact, by the end of that year we were beginning to add back some of the stations we had cut.

Encouraging Mail

The radio ministry has been a constant source of joy and encouragement to me. When I'm feeling the least bit down, all I have to do is pick up a batch of radio mail and start reading the marvelous letters that come in from listeners all over the country.

In response to a broadcast on racism, a black woman from Denver wrote: "Hallelujah! Thank you brother Reagan . . . I would like to inform you that I have adopted you as my 'Dad.' Would you be so kind as to send me a picture of you for my family photo album?"

A 14-year old girl in Sulphur, Louisiana, wrote a heart-touching request: "I listen to you on the radio every chance I get and it is a blessing. Please pray for my father, mother and brother. They do not go to church and they do not see the way of the Lord and how close it is to His coming."

A lady in Richmond, Kentucky, wrote words of encouragement: "I enjoy your program very much. I used to listen to Paul Harvey at 12:30 p.m. each day, but since I started listening to your program, I have not had the desire to listen to Paul again even though he has a very good program."

Exciting Testimonies

Especially thrilling are the testimonies about spiritual experiences. A lady in Stanford, Kentucky, wrote these words in response to a tape that was sent to her: "You are in part responsible for my accepting Christ, as I did so after listening to your tape, 'Jesus is Coming Soon.'"

From Lafayette, Louisiana, came these encouraging and motivating words:

> On my day off this week I turned on the radio and heard you discussing the Second Coming. I immediately felt the anointing of the Holy Spirit and fell to my knees in prayer and thankfulness to Jesus my Lord and Savior. Tears rolled down my cheeks and, for the first time, I could actually see the astounding light and absolute glory of Jesus descending from Heaven and being crowned King of the Universe.

> Brother Reagan, at that moment I received a joy in my spirit and in my whole body and mind that nothing and no one will ever be able to dim or take from me.

In response to a broadcast on homosexuality, I received a wonderful testimony from a man who had been delivered from this bondage:

> I listen to your program each time it is broadcast and I truly enjoy it . . . I especially enjoyed your talks on homosexuality. I am a former homosexual whom God has redeemed, and it is good to know that someone is on my side . . .

> I praise God that He has removed me from such a hideous problem and has put me back on a road of righteousness.

A Thrilling Reconciliation

I have devoted many broadcasts to the problem of abortion, which I consider to be the number one problem in America. In response to those broadcasts, I have received many powerful letters from women who have had abortions, and I have read many of these over the air, without identifying the authors.

The result of reading one such letter was to bring healing and reconciliation to a family in Sunset, Louisiana:

Greetings in the name of our Lord and Savior Jesus Christ. I'm writing to tell you about the blessing the Lord brought about in my life through your radio program.

I wrote to you before about the mistake I made in having an abortion. On June 19th you read my letter on your program. You may recall that I wrote that my parents did not know about my abortion. I have wanted to tell them about it for a long time, but I just couldn't bring myself to do it.

Since my mother and father listen to your program every day, I knew that more than likely they would hear my letter on your show. [We always notify people in advance as to what date we are going to use one of their letters on our program.] So I prayed to the Lord that either they would not hear your program that day or else they would hear it and it would help them understand. I just told God to have His will.

Well, my mother did hear the letter and knew it was from me. My parents were so understanding and forgiving. I feel so free now that it's out in the open. I know the Lord has forgiven me and I feel He will use me in helping other women and maybe somehow I can save the lives of some of the unborn babies that are being slaughtered every day.

Now, that's what I call a "blockbuster" letter! It's amazing the miracles God can perform through radio.

Laughing with Listeners

We receive a lot of humorous letters. One of my favorites came from a man in the hills of West Virginia who wrote: "I have a lot of trouble getting your telecast on my radio."

Another favorite came from a lady in Wichita, Kansas, who said she listened to the broadcast everyday with her four-year-old daughter: "I knew my daughter was a great fan of yours," she wrote, "but I never realized how much until last night. At the end of her bed time prayer, she said, 'And thank you God for Jesus, brought to us by Lamb and Lion Ministries.'"

One letter that really amused me was motivated by my constant appeals for Christians to do something about the problems of our society. I am always emphasizing that we are to be the salt of the earth, and that means we are to stand up and be counted for righteousness.

I urge people to pray for God to lay a burden on their hearts for some social problem and then to pray for God to tell them what to do about the problem.

A lady in a large metropolitan area wrote and said she had prayed and prayed for God to show her something to do. She said He had finally given her a great idea. She explained that her job was to test about 20 cars every day for one of the country's leading car rental companies. "As I drive each car along the test route," she wrote, "I set the buttons on the radio to each Christian station in our city. Everyone who rents one of our vehicles gets a car with a radio tuned only to Christian stations."

Ambivalent Responses

Sometimes people are a little ambivalent about the program. A lady in Beaumont, Texas, wrote: "I love your show. Actually, I thoroughly disliked it at first because I figured sooner or later you'd start on the 'end-time-Armageddon-scare-you-out-of-your-wits' stuff or else start getting really militant about denominational doctrine."

Another fellow from Owenton, Kentucky, expressed the same sort of ambivalence in more direct terms:

Lamb & Lion
Thrills me
Chills me

But most of all
Fills me
With the Spirit of Jesus.

Denominational Fuzziness

People are always writing to find out which church the ministry is affiliated with. They can't seem to believe that there really is such a thing as a nondenominational ministry.

One lady wrote a compliment in this regard that really blessed me: "I'm very happy to be able to say that after several months of listening, I still don't know what kind of church you belong to. Thank you for that! It proves to me that your interest in the Word of God is simply that, an interest in the relevancy of the Word to today and the future."

Recommending Churches

In the Dallas area, radio listeners are always calling to ask what church I pastor. When they are told that I do not pastor a church, they often ask if I will recommend a church to them. That is always difficult to do. I usually respond by asking what sort of church they are looking for.

One lady who called looking for a church said she wanted a "Charismatic" one and that it had to be located in Richardson, Texas. I told her I did not know one firsthand in that city that I could recommend. She insisted that I recommend one anyway. I suggested she go to an Assembly of God. She said she wanted a nondenominational church. She continued to insist that I give her a recommendation.

I finally remembered that I had attended a minister's luncheon recently where I had met the pastor of a new, independent, Charismatic church in Richardson. I gave her the name of the church.

That recommendation was to get me in big trouble. I learned never to recommend a church I have not personally attended.

A Nauseating Church

About two weeks later I returned to my office from a meeting tour. My office manager told me I had received a call from an irate woman who wanted me to call her right away. She was upset about a church I had recommended. I recognized her name and remembered which church I had sent her to. Before calling her, I called a minister friend who I knew was familiar with the church.

"Tell me about the new church in Richardson," I said.

"Oh, you mean the barf-bag church?" he replied.

"Barf-bag church! What do you mean by that?"

"They specialize in exorcising demons," he explained. "When you walk in they hand you a towel and a bag, and then during the service they try to get you to vomit up your demons."

I accused him of putting me on, but he insisted that the church really did practice the vomiting of demons. I nervously called the lady. The moment I identified myself, the woman started raving. "You're not going to believe what happened to me. When I walked in the door they handed me a towel and a bag . . ." The detailed description of the antics that followed still makes me nauseous.

Beasts on the Brain

I often put aside commentary on current events and spend a week or two on the radio just answering questions about Bible prophecy. The letters I get in response to the prophetic broadcasts are always stimulating, to say the least.

People are often prompted to share experiences they have had with some prophecy fanatic. A lady in Lawrenceburg, Kentucky, wrote about such an experience in response to a broadcast I made about the Jews in prophecy:

> I must admit that for many years I was ignorant of the Jew's continuing role in earthly history. Churches don't seem to talk about this very much ... I've only heard one preacher give comprehensive

lessons on Revelation; and he was so caught up in it all, the only thing he talked about was "beast this," and "beast that."

I began to have nightmares about weird-looking beasts of every color, size and form! I wasn't afraid of the end-times because I knew I was saved; but this brother had beasts on the brain, and he put them in my brain too.

The Personal Touch

As the radio ministry began to expand, I soon became burdened down by the flood of mail. I wanted to read each letter and respond personally to the many who wrote asking for prayer and counsel, but there are only so many minutes in each day. I asked the Lord for help, and He soon provided it.

I was able to hire a sensitive man of God to oversee the mail ministry. I continued to survey all the letters we received, but this man took over the responsibility of responding to those requesting prayer or counseling. It quickly proved to be one of the most effective aspects of our ministry, as attested by the following letter from a listener in Longmont, Colorado:

> Dear Mike: I received your letter today telling me that you would be praying for me to find God's direction in my life.
>
> I wanted to write and let you know that in all my years I have been writing and sending money to various ministries, this is the first time I have ever received a handwritten, direct reply . . .
>
> Praise God for your ministry. It really does my heart good to know that God still has servants out there who take a personal interest in people. I'm not putting other ministries down because I know that they are doing great things for the Lord. But this letter from you is like a breath of fresh air to my spirit.

Critical Mail

Not all the mail we receive is complimentary. We get our share of hate mail and crank letters — even poison pen letters that are unsigned but claim to be written in "the love of Jesus." I've been called every imaginable name, as well as a few that are unimaginable and unprintable. One letter was addressed: "To That Big Shot, Know-it-all, So-called Preacher."

One thing that always produces an avalanche of hate mail is any negative comment about the King James Version of the Bible. I have discovered that there are legions who are ready to fight to the death in defense of the Bible translation that was "good enough for Paul." Some people even strenuously object if you read from any version other than the King James.

Another topic that always produces a lot of critical mail is any reference to ill health. All I have to do to guarantee a bunch of negative letters is to mention that I'm suffering from hay fever or a cold. The friends of Job are quick to respond: "Of course you're suffering from hay fever. That's because you confessed that you have it. If you would confess that you don't have it, then it would go away."

A variation on the theme states: "I can't believe that a man of God would admit over the radio that he is ill. Don't you know that all illness is due to sin? If you will confess your secret sins, God will heal you." It's enough to make you really sick.

Misunderstandings

One particularly memorable negative letter was prompted by a misunderstanding of something I said. Each time we add a new station to our network, I always explain that we are a faith ministry. In part of that explanation I usually say, "I'm personally on a fixed salary that is determined and supplied by my board. That means that everything you contribute to the ministry is used for outreach."

Some man thought I said "fat" salary instead of "fixed"

salary. He wrote, "Praise God, I've finally found an honest radio evangelist who is willing to admit that he is on a fat salary!" I got him straightened out real fast.

Another misunderstanding of something I said led to a flood of mail. I advertised a free tape called "Sects and Denominations." For days we were literally knee-deep in letters requesting a copy of the tape about "Sex in the Denominations." I'm afraid our tape was a great disappointment.

A lot of these misunderstandings are due to the fact that I talk fast. I naturally speak at a rapid pace and talk even faster on the radio due to the time constraints. One person compared my radio delivery to the "speed of a machine gun shooting full blast."

Name Confusion

I always end each program by giving the name of the ministry and our mailing address. Because I'm talking so rapidly, many people have a difficult time understanding the name of the ministry.

The result is that we get letters addressed in very strange ways. Here are some of my favorites:

Lanolin Ministries
Land of Lions Ministries
Land of Limes Ministries
Lam 'N Lynn Ministries
Lame Loan Ministries
Leg of Lamb Ministries

The most frequent mistake is "Lemon and Lime Ministries." I guess people think we are in the fruit juice business. My all time favorite was the letter addressed to "Lame and Blind Ministries." I thought the fellow must be hard of hearing. He wasn't. He didn't like our program, and he had misstated our name on purpose as a clever sort of editorial comment.

For several years the ministry was located in a Dallas suburb called Plano. Everyone in Texas has heard of Plano because the town grew from 2,000 to 100,000 in 25 years and, during that growth spurt, the high school won the state championship in football in every division. But no one outside of Texas seems to have heard of Plano.

When we would give our mailing address on the radio, people would evidently do a double take on the name of the town because we got mail addressed to all sorts of strange places — like "Plane'O, Plain'O and Plain Old."

My favorite garbling of the name came from a lady in Illinois. We got the letter because the zip code was correct. Otherwise, we would never have seen it because she addressed it to "Playtex, Texas!" I guess she thought we were in the girdle business.

Matching a Face with a Voice

One thing that's fun about a radio ministry is traveling around the country and meeting listeners face to face. The Lord uses these encounters to keep me humble. The conversation usually goes like this:

"You mean you're the fellow on the radio?" the listener asks in obvious unbelief.

"Yes, I am. What's wrong?"

"Your voice sounds so much younger than you look!"

A variation on the theme came one time when a woman exclaimed: "But your voice sounds like you have a lot more hair!" I guess that means I have a hairy voice.

The funniest comment I ever received about my voice came in a letter from a student at Texas A&M. He wrote:

> I'm not sure how old you are but you sound at least middle-age. It does my heart much good knowing there are older men and women out there who are still hot for God. I hope and pray I get hotter as I get older.

Speaking to a Deep Need

The most memorable and touching experience to come out of the radio ministry occurred during a meeting I was holding at a large church in Lexington, Kentucky. A few months prior to the meeting, I had done a special week of radio broadcasts on the topic, "What Happens When You Die?" We had offered the material contained in those broadcasts on both cassette tape and in printed form.

The broadcasts evidently spoke to a real need because we received thousands of requests for the cassette and the brochure. Unknown to us, one of the persons who had written for copies of the brochure was the chaplain of the Lexington Police Department.

On the second or third night of the Lexington meeting, as the pastor of the church was about to dismiss the service, the police chaplain stepped forward, identified himself, and asked permission to say a few words to the church. He explained that he had been ministering to a police officer who was dying of cancer. He had tried to bring the officer to Christ, but with no success. One day as he started driving back to the office from the hospital he heard one of my broadcasts on the topic, "What Happens When You Die?" He stopped and called our office and asked my staff to send him some copies of the brochure immediately.

When he received the brochures, he took one to the dying officer. A few days later the officer told the chaplain he wanted to accept Jesus as his Savior. He did so and died shortly thereafter.

A Touching Memento

After telling this story, the police chaplain called me up and presented me with a framed watercolor painting done by one of Lexington's policemen. It shows a person lying wounded in a street with a policeman kneeling beside him, ministering to him. In the background, looking over the policeman's shoulder is Jesus. The picture is entitled, "His

Brother's Keeper: Christ Marks the Fall of a Sparrow."

There is an inscription on the picture that reads: "Dr. Reagan: Thank you for your letter and prayer for the salvation of our sergeant."

That picture hangs in my office. It is an everyday reminder to me of the effectiveness of radio in reaching people for Jesus.

Adventuring Abroad 19

In the summer of 1984 I was given an opportunity to go to Eastern Europe and spend several weeks preaching and teaching. As is always the case with such spiritual adventures, I ended up learning a lot more than I was able to teach.

As I prepared to depart, I started requesting that individuals and churches pray for me. The response was almost unanimous: "No, we're not going to pray for you. We are going to pray for your translators!" No one believed that any translator could keep up with my rapid-fire style of delivery. They were right.

Translation Frustrations

I learned quickly that working through a translator can be a most frustrating experience. I had to change my whole style of speaking. I had to speak slowly, distinctly and in simple, short sentences. I also had to avoid idiomatic expressions.

It was not at all unusual to be interrupted in the middle of a sentence by the translator who would stop me and ask what a particular word meant. While we were discussing the word with each other, the audience was waiting for the translation. By the time we would get settled on a translation of the word, I would have lost my train of thought. It was maddening.

I remember preaching a sermon from Habakkuk. It was entitled, "Tough Faith." I had been speaking for about 20 minutes and had used the phrase, "tough faith," at least 15 times, when the translator suddenly stopped me and asked, "What does the word, 'tough' mean?" I couldn't believe it. What had he been translating for 20 minutes? I never found out.

Of course, the whole translation process was further complicated by my Texas accent and colloquialisms. Some Eastern Europeans who prided themselves in their good English wondered aloud if I was really from an English-speaking country! "What do you mean," they would ask, "when you say you are 'fixin' to go to town? What does 'fixin' mean?" Needless to say, we had a lot of good laughs over me trying to explain "y'all," "sure-nuff," "yonder" and other weird Texan slang expressions.

But the Eastern Europeans were polite and patient. They were willing to sit through any inconvenience to hear a message from the Word of God, even one they might not fully agree with. For example, when I preached a rather long sermon on the Holy Spirit, the translator turned to me at the end, smiled, bowed and said, "That was very nice but we do not agree with you." He repeated his statement to the audience, but then he asked them to thank me for coming. They gave me a standing ovation. I thought to myself, "What a contrast to the States. There I would have been lynched for preaching a 'doctrinally unsound' sermon."

Dropping In Unannounced

My visit to Eastern Europe certainly impressed upon me the fact that we Americans take so many of our freedoms for granted. I was there under the auspices of a very experienced American missionary group, and we had to follow strict rules that they had developed through their years of experience with Communist repression.

One cardinal rule was never to notify any congregation in advance that we were coming. I thought this rule was rather strange at first, but I soon found out that it was essential. It was necessitated by the fact that almost every worship service was monitored by some member of the secret police.

If a minister said something the policeman considered "out of line," then the minister was called to the Communist Party headquarters the next day and interrogated.

Likewise, if a Westerner appeared as a guest speaker, the minister and all officers of the church were likely to be hauled in for interrogation. If it was discovered that they had officially invited the Westerner, their congregation might suffer reprisals. But if they could truthfully say that they did not know the Westerner was coming and that they invited him to speak only out of courtesy to a visitor, they would usually be left alone.

Incredible Openness

So, my guide and I would always arrive unannounced a few minutes before the service was scheduled to start. The moment I was introduced as an evangelist, I would be invited to speak, no questions asked. Their eagerness to have me speak always impressed me.

We went to all kinds of churches. Half of the time I didn't even know what kind of church I was in. But they were equally ignorant about me. All they knew about me was that I was an evangelist. That was enough for them. "Just preach the Word," they would say.

Again, I was impressed with the contrast between their attitude and that which exists here in the States. We are too concerned about doctrinal differences to invite any stranger to preach or teach. The person must first be put through a denominational inquisition to determine that he bleeds Presbyterian or Baptist or Methodist before he will be allowed to open his mouth in behalf of Christ.

The Christians under Communism in Eastern Europe understood who the enemy is. We don't. We have carefully constructed denominational walls to prevent ourselves from becoming contaminated by those who do not agree with us on every nuance of doctrine. We abuse our freedom by lobbing doctrinal hand grenades over the walls at each other.

Visitation Rules

Another rule we had to follow at all times was to be very careful about what we said out loud during unguarded moments. We were told to assume that all hotel rooms were bugged — and I'm talking about electronic devices and not bedbugs! We were therefore never to talk to one another in a hotel room about our contacts in Eastern Europe.

We never drove to a contact's residence. All cars in Europe have a decal on the back that identifies their country of origin. Our car had a decal from a Western country. If we parked that car in front of a contact's residence, a neighbor would immediately call the secret police because the police give rewards for such surveillance. So, we would try to park in a public area about half a mile from the contact's home and then walk.

As we walked, we were told to hold conversation to a minimum because, again, if someone heard us speaking in English, they might follow us to our contact's residence and then report our visit to the police.

Communist Repression

The Communist countries liked to brag about their freedom of religion. But it existed on paper only.

Ministers and churches were under constant watch. Churches could not broadcast services. Times and places of services could not be advertised in newspapers or anywhere else. Facilities could not be expanded without permission of the state. No one under the age of 18 could be baptized.

Police agents were always at each service taking notes. If a minister said anything the agent considered critical of the state, the minister might find himself either out of a job or reassigned to a small country church in the middle of no-where.

Because the worship services were monitored, very few men attended church. They feared they would lose their jobs or else lose any opportunity for promotion. Thus, most Eastern European churches under Communism were composed of elderly people, women and children. That, unfortunately, is still the case today. The men who got out of the habit of going to church have been slow to return.

One thing that fascinated me about the Eastern European churches was the "sea of white" that I saw every time I got up to preach. This was due to the fact that most of the churches practiced head covering for women. Since the churches were primarily composed of women, the typical view from one of their traditionally elevated pulpits was a sea of white, because you were looking down on the tops of heads that were covered with white scarves.

One thing the churches in Eastern Europe did not worry about was church attendance. The churches were packed to the rafters for every service. The people were hungry for the Word, and they never forgot that the next service might be the last one the state would tolerate.

Again, I was impressed with the contrast to our country. Here, because we take our freedom for granted, the church has grown fat and lazy, and ministers spend most of their waking hours trying to dream up gimmicks to promote church attendance.

Rumanian Opportunity

One of the highlights of my visit to Eastern Europe was the two weeks I spent on the outskirts of Vienna at a large chalet nestled in the foothills of the Alps. It was a storybook setting. The chalet had been converted into a training center for Eastern European preachers.

I spent two weeks at this place teaching Bible prophecy to a group of about 15 senior pastors from Rumania. The government of Rumania at that time was the most repressive one in all of Eastern Europe. For example, it was a capital offense to own an unregistered typewriter in Rumania!

The government tightly controlled all religious activity. There was only one Protestant seminary in the country. This seminary received on the average about 100 applications per year. The government would allow the seminary to accept only ten students. Since no person was allowed to pastor a church unless he was a seminary graduate, the government greatly curtailed church growth by only allowing ten ordinations per year. Most of the ministers I worked with were trying to pastor five to seven churches each, using a bicycle to travel between each one!

Communist Ruthlessness

The insidious attitude of the Rumanian government toward Christianity was illustrated in two events that took place about the time I was tutoring the Rumanian ministers.

The government discovered that one of the largest Baptist churches in the country had exceeded its building permit for a new addition by one meter. So, the government ordered the entire church to be bulldozed to the ground!

At the same time, the government was trying to get most-favored nation trade treatment from the U.S. To stifle congressional criticism of its religious repression, the Rumanian government announced that it was going to allow the importation of several thousand Bibles. Later, it was revealed that the Bibles had been sent to a paper mill and had been reprocessed into toilet paper!

Suspicions

The institute officials where I taught were actually shocked that the Rumanian government had agreed to allow 15 ministers to come for training. They were even more shocked when the ministers arrived with their wives! This was totally unprecedented. Although the institute always invited the wives, the Rumanian government would never allow them to come. The wives were, in effect, held as hostages to make certain that their husbands would return home.

The Rumanians themselves were astounded over their government's action. They had been informed only the day before their departure that they would be allowed to bring their wives along. Since they could not imagine the government allowing 15 couples to leave the country unattended, they naturally suspected that someone within their group was an informer. For that reason, it took almost a week before we were able to get the ministers to open up and say very much, and even then, they preferred to talk one-on-one in private.

A Shopping Spree

I'll never forget when we took all of the Rumanians to the one and only Western style shopping mall in Vienna. Each couple was given $100 to spend. They simply did not know what to do. There were too many goods and too many types of each item. They were not accustomed to making shopping decisions.

As one man put it, "When we go to buy shoes at home, there's only one style, only one color and, often, only one size."

Several of the ladies simply broke down and wept over the cornucopia of Western goods displayed before their eyes. One particularly distraught woman turned to me and said, "It's all a waste because the border guards will steal whatever we buy." Oh how we take America for granted!

Getting to Know One Another

The Rumanians loved to sing, and each meal with them in the institute's dining hall began with beautiful songs of praise to the Lord. I've never seen people savor coffee like they did. They would linger after each meal and sip the coffee with great relish until the dining hall lights were turned out. I discovered the reason for this was that coffee sold for $60 a pound in Rumania!

After two weeks of teaching them several hours a day, I got to know some of the ministers pretty well. Near the end of the second week we were sitting around one evening chatting with each other through a translator. One of the senior ministers said he wanted to ask a question but was afraid to do so because I might think he did not appreciate our hospitality. I urged him to go ahead and ask his question.

To say the least, his question caught me off guard.

"When," he asked, "are you folks going to serve us some wine or beer?"

I told him he would have to ask the institute's directors, but I said that I did not think they were going to be offered any wine or beer.

"Why not?" he asked incredulously.

I tried to explain that many Christians in America did not think it was a good Christian witness to drink alcoholic beverages. They looked at each other and shook their heads as if to say, "What ignorant people!"

The next night we were once again sitting around chatting and drinking coffee after a meal. Someone mentioned something about smoking, and I expressed my appreciation for the fact that none of them smoked.

They looked stunned. I asked what was the matter. They explained that smoking is a horrible sin and that no one can be saved who smokes.

"Now that's interesting," I observed. "Most of you call yourselves Baptists. Back in the States, many of our Baptists smoke, but they believe you will go to Hell if you drink wine or beer. You believe just the opposite. Isn't that funny?"

There was a long moment of silence. Then, one of the ministers said, "No, it's not funny. Your Baptists are wrong!"

A Spiritual Wrestling Match

When I left for Eastern Europe that summer I was in the midst of a spiritual struggle over sin in my life. The Holy Spirit was doing a mighty convicting work within me, and I was resisting His work.

The battle inside me continued all the time I was in Eastern Europe. I felt like Paul in Romans 7 where he wrote about his spiritual struggle. He said he knew what was the right thing to do, and he willed to do it, but he ended up doing the very thing he hated. I knew how Paul felt and, like him, I kept crying out, "What a wretched man I am!" (Romans

7:24).

After I finished my preaching tour in Eastern Europe, I returned to the institute's chalet on the outskirts of Vienna to rest for a few days before flying home. One morning I decided to take a rather strenuous hike. I climbed a steep, 2,000-foot hill behind the chalet and started walking through a thick forest. The forest was so dense that there was very little underbrush — just a thick covering of leaves on the ground. In fact, the forest was so dense that it filtered out almost all light, and I had the eerie feeling of walking in the night during daylight.

As this darkness enfolded me, so did a spiritual darkness. I suddenly became aware of an evil presence. Never before had I encountered such a satanic reality. I had difficulty breathing. I stopped walking and began taking deep breaths. I noticed an incredible stillness. There was no wind. No movement of leaves. Just deathly silence. A whisper would have sounded like a thunder clap.

Then I experienced the most intense spiritual struggle of my life. A voice began speaking to my spirit, "You're worthless. You're a sinner. You're hopeless. You will never change. You're an embarrassment to God. You've got to get out of the ministry."

Charge after charge was flung at me, all loaded with judgment and condemnation. I was overwhelmed by the vehement accusations. I fell to my knees and began to weep.

"It's true, Lord," I cried. "I am a sinner."

"I know," said the Lord. "Sinners are all I have to work through."

"But Lord, I am worthless."

"I know," the Lord replied, "but you're precious to me because you're one of my children."

"But you're hopeless," said the evil voice, "and you're going to bring down your ministry in shame."

"You're not hopeless," said the Lord. "Remember My love and the power of My Spirit."

Bathed with Scripture

With those words, a verse came to mind: "He who is within you is greater than he who is in the world" (1 John 4:4). I summoned up the Spirit within me, and by His power I began to rebuke the devil. Then I began to cry out to the Lord in the name of Jesus for deliverance.

"Oh, Lord," I cried, "I just want to serve You. If I can't do that with complete integrity, then I want You to take my life."

That's all I said, but it ended the struggle. The evil presence dissipated. My spirit was flooded with joy and peace. Scriptures began to race through my mind. "All things work together for good for those who love the Lord." "There is no condemnation for those who are in Christ Jesus." "Trust the Lord, for He is an everlasting Rock, and He will keep you in perfect peace."

The Peace beyond Understanding

I opened my eyes. It really was night time. The struggle had seemed to last only minutes. But I had been there for hours. A gentle breeze was blowing, refreshing my being, even as the Lord had refreshed my spirit.

That night, as I prepared for bed, I opened my Bible and read these words: "The eyes of the Lord move to and fro throughout the earth that He may strongly support those whose heart is completely His" (2 Chronicles 16:9).

Off to Africa

In the fall of 1985 the Lord opened another foreign door of opportunity for me. I was suddenly invited to go on a fact-finding mission to South Africa, together with a group of 20 other ministers. I quickly rearranged my schedule of meetings and, before I knew it, I was in Johannesburg, at the southern end of the world.

I had traveled throughout Asia, Europe and the Middle East, but this was my first real trip into Africa. I had been to

Cairo, but I had considered it more Middle Eastern in nature than African.

I was fascinated by the incredible beauty of South Africa. Cape Town, in particular, stole my heart. Never have I been so awed by the majesty of God's creative ability. At Cape Town the Lord outdid Himself!

But I was even more impressed by the people of that land. The variety is remarkable. There are Whites, Blacks, Coloreds (mixed races) and Indians. Then, there are varieties within these groups. The Indians are divided by religion. Most are Hindu, but significant numbers are Muslim and Christian. The Blacks are divided into 10 major tribes, each of which have a different language, culture and religion. Even the Whites are divided between the Afrikaans-speaking of Dutch descent and the English-speaking of British descent.

A National Spiritual Awakening

But something impressed me even more than the geography and the people. It was the openness of the people to the Gospel. Like the people of Eastern Europe, the people of South Africa were hungry for God's Word.

The people of that land, people of all colors, were reaching out to God with open hearts and childlike faith, and God was responding by pouring out His Spirit. All that the newspapers reported at the time was racial violence, but the real story of South Africa was that the country was ablaze with the fire of the Holy Spirit. Spiritual renewal was sweeping the land, and with it was coming a breakdown of racial barriers.

I first experienced this spiritual awakening in the coastal city of Durban. I was invited to speak to an Indian congregation that met in a back room at a factory. About 200 people were present. They stood for an hour and sang songs of praise, most of them scripture songs. Then I preached for an hour on the soon coming of Jesus.

When I finished my sermon, I didn't know what to do. I had forgotten to ask the pastor in advance if he wanted me to issue an altar call. I paused, looked at him, and asked what I should do. "Whatever you feel led of the Lord to do," he replied.

An Altar Stampede

I knew nothing of their traditions, and I didn't want to offend them in any way. I didn't know what to do, but I did feel led to offer a time of ministry. I explained to them what I meant by that term — that they were invited to come forward for prayer for any need that might exist in their lives. I had no idea how they might react.

We stood and started singing, and there was a stampede. People began to rush to the front. I was pressed up against the pulpit. I pulled myself free from their reaching hands and stepped up on the podium to get a better view of what was happening. I looked over their heads and saw no one. All 200 had come forward for prayer! For the next hour I prayed individually with these people for physical healing, jobs, the healing of marriages, and the forgiveness of sins.

When I returned to my hotel room completely exhausted, I sat there and wept over the contrast between that church and the typical American church. These people were like children, wanting all that their Heavenly Father has to offer.

Most Americans are so full of spiritual arrogance that they would not go forward for prayer if their lives depended on it — and that is often the case! I've seen people in American crusades who were under so much conviction that they would weep and shake all over, but they would hold on to the pew and refuse to budge, as if their feet were in concrete.

A Return Crusade

I returned to the States with a heart for South Africa. I wanted to return with a crusade team to preach the soon coming of Jesus to churches all across that country. I shared the vision with my staff, and they agreed that it was from the Lord. We began raising money to pay for the trip. God wondrously provided, and in August of 1986 ten of us departed Dallas for South Africa.

But Satan had other ideas. He was not the least bit excited about our trip. We were supposed to arrive in New York City at 6:15 p.m. and catch an 8 p.m. plane to South Africa. We touched down exactly at 6:15 p.m., but as we began to taxi toward the terminal, the pilot came on the intercom system and said, "Welcome to Harrisburg, Pennsylvania." My heart sank. There were only two flights a week to South Africa, and we were about to miss ours.

We sat on the ground in Harrisburg for two hours waiting for clearance to proceed to New York. A severe thunderstorm had knocked out the control tower computers, and all inbound New York traffic had been either grounded or rerouted. We finally arrived in New York at 9:30 p.m. Our plane to South Africa had already departed. We were taken to a run-down hotel where we spent two hours in the lobby with several hundred other stranded people trying to get rooms.

By midnight, when my wife and I finally reached our room, I was mentally, physically and emotionally drained. I didn't know what to do. I checked with the airlines and found there was only one other direct flight to South Africa that week. It was in three days and was overbooked. We were stranded. I cratered.

Encouraged by Prayer Warriors

But, praise God, we had with us in our group some ladies who were real prayer warriors. They never took their eyes off the Lord. While I sat in my room and felt sorry for myself, they gathered in another room and began to pray. They came out of that prayer meeting filled with conviction that it was the Lord's will for us to go to South Africa and, if we would trust in Him, He would find us a way to get there.

One of the ladies took me aside and said the Lord had given her a scriptural insight during the prayer meeting. She opened her Bible to Luke 8:22 and pointed out the story of the disciples who had been caught in a storm on the Sea of Galilee. As they fought to keep their boat afloat, Jesus slept.

Finally, they awoke the Lord and told Him they were about to perish. He rebuked the wind, and the storm calmed. He then turned to the disciples and said, "Where is your faith?"

I thanked her for the insight. It seemed to fit our situation perfectly, and it reassured me that the Lord would see us through if we would only lean on Him. Before she walked away, I said kiddingly, "Yes, the Lord got them across the lake, but don't forget what happened when they reached the other side."

"What's that?" she asked.

"They encountered a man who was filled with demons."

"Oh dear!" she said. "Let's hope that doesn't happen to us."

The next morning the airlines called and said they had arranged for us to fly to Johannesburg via London! The Lord had prevailed. It took us an extra day to get to Johannesburg and, when we arrived, we were dog-tired, but we got there, and the Lord mightily blessed our proclamation of His Word.

A Precious Memory

We preached from one end of the country to the other in all kinds of churches. It was a richly rewarding experience.

One of my sweetest memories is a service we conducted at a small church in the heart of Zululand. The service was held at the town hall and was attended by people of all races.

The town hall and all the rest of the buildings in the town were owned by the only business in the area, a sugar cane refining factory. It was a classic "company town." All the Zulus lived in company houses and worked in the refinery. Because a visiting evangelist was speaking that morning, the British manager of the refinery had come to the service even though he was not a professing Christian.

Most of the Zulus sat at the back because an interpreter translated my message for them. When I offered the time of ministry, the first person in line was a very elderly Zulu warrior who wanted prayer for chest pains. When I finished praying for him, I looked up and, to my astonishment, the next person in line was the British aristocrat who owned the town.

"I've got a bad heart," he said.

I prayed for God to heal his heart, both physically and spiritually. I'll never forget that picture of the British gentleman standing patiently in line behind the old Zulu warrior, waiting his turn for prayer. What a leveler the Gospel is!

The Reality of the Demonic

We began and ended our crusade tour in Johannesburg. When we returned to that city for the last three days of ministry, I discovered that the scripture the lady had shared with me in New York had been prophetic. Yes, we encountered a demon-possessed man.

We were invited to minister in a remarkable setting. We had run across an American mission that had bought an apartment house with 75 units. In each apartment was a person this mission had picked off the streets of Johannesburg. There were prostitutes, drug addicts, insane, mentally retarded and physically handicapped. Never had I tried to minister to such a menagerie of people.

I had with me a remarkable worship and praise group called River of Life, and I turned over the bulk of the last two services to them because I had observed at the first service that these people were really ministered to by music. The approach worked and we experienced a powerful movement of God's Spirit.

On the last day, the missionary who directed this unusual ministry called me and asked if I had much experience in exorcising demons. I told him no and asked why. He explained that he had a young man living at the complex who was demon-possessed and that he was having great difficulty trying to cast out the evil spirit. He asked if I would help that evening following the service. I told him about all I could do was pray. He said that would be helpful.

The Need for Exorcism

I had never participated in an exorcism, so I approached this experience with some degree of apprehension. I believed in the reality of demons and demon possession. I had done a lot of reading on the subject. I had even discussed it in some detail with an Indian minister in Durban. He had pointed out to me that exorcism had to be a major part of any Christian ministry in Africa because demon-possession is so common there. The Indian people open themselves to demonic spirits through Hinduism and its pantheistic emphasis. The Blacks are subject to demonic invasion because so many of them are involved in ancestor worship and the worship of snakes.

The subject for our exorcism turned out to be a young British man in his mid-twenties. The pastor told me that they had found him wandering the streets in a totally disheveled condition. He had acted insane, and they assumed he was suffering from some sort of mental breakdown until they took him to a worship service. He had reacted immediately and violently to the mention of the name Jesus. The pastor knew then that he was dealing with a spiritual problem and not a mental one.

The pastor explained that he and his associates had held several exorcism sessions with the man and, although the man had shown much improvement as a result of their love and prayers, they had not been successful in exorcising the evil spirit.

Confronting a Demon

The session began with the young man sitting on a couch. Four of us sat opposite him in chairs formed in a semicircle. He appeared calm and rational. The pastor asked him if he wanted the demon out. He said yes. The pastor assured him that the demon would come out sooner or later.

The pastor turned to me and said, "We don't know why this demon hasn't come out, but we do know one thing. The Lord is using this to draw all of us closer to Him. Forty of us are currently praying and fasting in this man's behalf."

The pastor then turned to the man and asked if he was ready to begin. He said he was. The pastor leaned forward and said in a voice of authority, "Demon, I command you in the name of Jesus to manifest yourself."

Immediately, the man began to convulse. His eyes rolled back and then closed. His body shook. His face began to distort grotesquely. His lips formed into a sneer, and then a horribly vile voice, guttural in nature, began to come forth. The voice uttered all sorts of obscenities and profanities.

"Stop it!" the pastor snapped. "In the name of Jesus, I command you to stop this nonsense and tell me your name."

For the next 30 minutes the pastor labored to get the demon's name. The demon would evade the question by changing the subject, or shouting blasphemies, or telling lies. From time to time we would just stop and pray for guidance and faith and courage.

At long last the demon told us his name. It was Ashron. When we asked what the name meant, the demon said, "Power."

Struggling with a Demon

The pastor turned to me and said, "That's why we've been having so much trouble. This is a particularly strong demon, probably the type Jesus said could only be cast out through much prayer and fasting."

The pastor then called the demon by name and commanded him to come out of the man in the name of Jesus. The demon began to give excuses. He said he couldn't find his way out, that the man didn't want him out, that the Lord really wanted him to stay inside. Evasions, lies and excuses continued.

The pastor changed the subject. He asked the demon to tell him what sin he was rooted in.

"Masturbation," was the reply. The pastor shook the young man, told him to open his eyes, and asked him if he was in bondage to the sin of masturbation. He said he had been, but that one of the staff members had prayed with him about it the previous week, and God had instantly released him from the bondage. The pastor said he wanted all of us to pray about the matter again. We did, and then the pastor commanded the demon to manifest himself.

Again, the pastor asked what sin the demon was rooted in. When he answered "Masturbation," the pastor called him a liar and commanded him to tell the truth. He then began giving frivolous answers like card playing and stealing cars.

By that time the session had lasted three hours. We were all exhausted and getting nowhere. The pastor decided to call it quits for the night.

Supernatural Reality

But before he did, he turned to me and said, "I want you to see something we've discovered."

He explained that in their exorcism sessions they had discovered that the supernatural world takes the symbolic language of the Bible very literally.

"Watch this," the pastor said. He picked up a Bible and held it in front of the young man. (Keep in mind that this man was sitting there with his eyes tightly closed and his face distorted). "In the name of Jesus, I come at you with the 'sword of the Spirit,'" the pastor shouted. He thrust the Bible at the man.

The man went wild. He started backing up on the couch, flailing his arms about and shouting hysterically, "No! No!"

After he had calmed down, the pastor picked up another book. Once again he shouted that he was coming at the demon with the "sword of the Spirit." He thrust the book, but nothing happened. The man just sat there calmly.

"What book is that?" I asked.

"I don't know," said the pastor. He looked at the title. "It's a volume of the *Millennial Harbinger* by Alexander Campbell. I guess the demons don't respect Campbell."

A Sad Revelation

The next day this pastor told me something very sad. He

said that although exorcism was one of their main ministries, they could not reveal that to any of their supporting congregations back in the States.

"They just wouldn't understand," he said, shaking his head sadly. "They would think we had lost our minds."

He's right. Most American Christians have rejected the supernatural so completely that they no more believe in the reality of demons than they believe in the man in the moon.

American Hypocrisy

One final note about South Africa. Every congregation we ministered to over there was integrated. The love of Jesus working in people's lives is breaking down the racial barriers within the Body of Christ.

I was so impressed with this that I made note of it in the last sermon I delivered in the country to a large congregation in Pretoria.

Here's what I said:

> I think it's ironic that we in the States spend so much time condemning you people as 'racists.' Every church I've ministered to in this country has been integrated. Yet, I often minister to churches in the States for six months in a row and never see anything except a sea of white faces.

> May God have mercy upon us for our hypocrisy.

Walking in the
Footsteps of Jesus   18

I made my first pilgrimage to Israel in 1979. It was a life-changing experience. It brought the Bible alive for me. It drew me closer to the Lord. Before I went, a minister friend who had already taken the trip told me that it would be worth three years of seminary. He was right.

As I stood on the Mount of Olives that first time and looked down over the majestic city of Jerusalem, I felt in my spirit that I truly was standing at the "center of the earth" (Ezekiel 5:5 and 38:12).

Here the Lord God Almighty had come in the flesh to pour out His blood on a cross for the sins of man. And right here He had ascended into Heaven with the promise that one day He would return to the same spot to rule from Mount Zion over all the nations of the world.

A Magnetic Mount

On that first trip I was drawn like a magnet to the Mount of Olives. Every time there was a lull in the group's schedule, I would hop a taxi and go to the Mount to meditate, pray, study scripture, or just sit and soak up the sights and sounds of the City of David.

On the last day of the tour, I got up at three in the morning and took a taxi to the Mount of Olives for one last visit. I wanted to see the sunrise, to see the city come to life before my eyes.

It was a cold morning. I sat in the Jewish cemetery on the side of the mount and shivered as I waited for the first glimmer of sunlight to break over the mount behind me and strike the golden dome on the Temple Mount.

I heard roosters crow.

Donkeys brayed.

Bells rang at a distance.

Slowly the city was awakening.

Then, the first ray of brilliant sunshine hit the Temple Mount.

It was morning.

In my soul I had become a Jerusalemite.

I have returned to Jerusalem many times since then, and the thrill of experiencing that wondrous city has never faded. It is new each time. There are always new discoveries to be made, new insights to be gleaned. I actually get homesick if I don't get over there at least once a year.

Annual Pilgrimages

Part of the ministry I founded a year later has been to share the experience of the Holy Land and Jerusalem with other people who are seeking a deeper walk with the Lord. I have taken one or two groups a year to the land of the Bible. Each time, my spirit has been enriched.

We usually fly directly to Tel Aviv, spend the first night there and then head north up the coast toward the beautiful port city of Haifa. Our first stop is always the ancient Roman port of Caesarea, where the first Gentile, Cornelius, accepted the Gospel. It is also the place where the Apostle Paul was imprisoned for two years.

Only a small portion of Caesarea has been excavated. One of the largest discoveries to date is a magnificent amphitheater that sits right on the coast, facing the Mediterranean Sea.

A Prophetic Discovery

I always take my groups to this amphitheater to conduct a devotional and sing some songs. One year, after we had finished the devotional, I turned the group loose to wander for 30 minutes among the excavated ruins. I decided to just sit and look out at the ocean and meditate. While I was doing so, I picked up my Bible and opened it. The passage it fell open to was Isaiah 11.

Verse 10 caught my eye. Isaiah is speaking about the end-times and he says that in those days "the root of Jesse" will stand as a "flag for the peoples" and the Jewish remnant will return to the land from "the four corners of the earth."

I looked up. Directly in front of me, about 100 yards away, there was a flagpole sticking in the sand near the water line. On it was the flag of Israel. I studied that flag for a moment, and then I began to rejoice. I suddenly realized that on that flag was the symbol of "the house of Jesse"   the star of David.

That flag is serving as a magnet to draw the Jewish remnant from the ends of the earth, just as Isaiah had predicted. That is the excitement of modern-day Israel. It is a place where ancient prophecies are being fulfilled daily, before one's very eyes.

The Glory of Galilee

One of the most breathtaking places of grandeur in all of Israel is the Sea of Galilee. It is one of the few places central to the life of Jesus that has not been spoiled by man. There are no gaudy cathedrals or sleazy shops, and the lake itself has been protected from pollution. It is easy to imagine it looking in the time of Jesus exactly as it looks today. And it is easy to understand why Jesus loved it so much that He centered His ministry in the seaside town of Capernaum.

One of the highlights of any visit to Israel is a cruise across the Sea of Galilee. I always have the boat stop in the middle of the lake and, to the rhythmic sound of the waves lapping against the sides, we sing hymns and conduct a devotional. The devotional, of course, always focuses upon the story of Jesus and Peter walking on the water.

I like to end that devotional by reading a powerful poem written by Carl Sandburg entitled "Epistle:"

Jesus loved the sunsets on Galilee.
Jesus loved the fishing boats forming
    silhouettes against the sunsets on Galilee.
Jesus loved the fisherman on the fishing boats
    forming silhouettes against the sunsets on
    Galilee.
When Jesus said: Goodby, goodby, I will come
    again:
Jesus meant that goodby for the sunsets, the
    fishing boats, the fisherman, the silhouettes
    all and any against the sunsets on Galilee:
    the goodby and the promise meant all or
    nothing.

Baptismal Rites

At the point where the Jordan River exits from the Sea of Galilee there is a beautiful baptismal site that was built by the Israeli government in the early '80s. That has always amused me a little — the thought of a Jewish government building a special place for Christian baptisms. I had the special privilege of baptizing my dad at this site shortly after it was constructed.

When I first started taking groups to Israel, no such baptismal facility existed. For centuries, pilgrims had been baptized in the Jordan as an expression of their faith, and most of those baptisms had taken place at the traditional site of the baptism of Jesus, a place near Jericho at the southern end of the Jordan River. But since the Six Day War in 1967, that place has no longer been accessible to Christian pilgrims because it is located in the "no-man's land" between Israel and Jordan. So the Christian baptismal site shifted north to the only place on the Jordan that was safe from sniper fire.

Gentile "Ducks"

The first time I went to Israel I was privileged to go with an experienced leader. He had a special place on the Jordan near the current permanent site where he always conducted his baptisms. When our bus arrived at that site, there were about 30 Jews using it for a picnic. Our leader, who had a heart for Jewish evangelism, jumped at the opportunity to witness to these people.

The leader and all those to be baptized went upstream about 50 yards to a thickly wooded area where they could not be seen by the picnickers. They stripped to their bathing suits, waded out into shoulder deep water and started walking downstream toward the picnic area — a line of about 20 Gentiles.

As this strange parade of Gentiles approached the picnic site, the Jews stopped all their activities and stared at the line of human ducks, wondering what was going on. Meanwhile, I had slipped up behind the unsuspecting crowd and, on a prearranged signal, when our leader raised his hand in the air, I started reading in a loud voice from Matthew 3 — the account of the baptism of Jesus.

The moment I finished reading, our leader baptized the first person in the name of Yeshua Hamashiach — Jesus the Messiah. He proceeded to baptize every person in the name of the Messiah of Israel. Everyone then waded up to the shore, introduced themselves to the Israelis, and gave each of them a pamphlet showing how Jesus fulfilled the prophecies of the Hebrew Scriptures.

Amazingly, none of the Israelis got angry. I think they were too stunned by it all to know how to react!

The Valley of Decision

Heading south from Galilee to Jerusalem, I always like to stop in the Valley of Jezreel, better known as the Valley of Armageddon (Revelation 16:16). We usually climb to the top of a steep hill which marks the site of the ancient fortress-city of Megiddo so that we can get a panoramic view of the whole valley.

This view is always awesome to me. It is the largest valley in all of Israel, and it appears so serene, for it is lush with agricultural production year-round. Yet, it will be the site of man's last battle, the site where the blood will run as deep as a horse's bridle for a distance of 200 miles (Revelation 14:20). As we stand looking out over this apocalyptic valley, I always like to read the Old Testament account of the war that will be fought there:

> Multitudes, multitudes in the valley of decision!
> For the day of the Lord is near in the valley
>   of decision.
> The sun and moon grow dark,
> And the stars lose their brightness.
> And the Lord roars from Zion
> And utters His voice from Jerusalem,
> And the heavens and the earth tremble.
> — Joel 3:14-16

The Gate to Prophecy

The climax of any pilgrimage to Israel is, of course, the city of Jerusalem and, for that reason, I always leave it for last. There are so many special places in that city, but there are three that I particularly love.

The first is the Eastern Gate. I can always hardly wait to see it. It is special to me for several reasons. For one thing, it is what got me interested in the study of Bible prophecy.

During the Six Day War in 1967 I read a newspaper account about the Jewish commando group that broke into the city. According to this account, the group first contemplated the idea of blowing open the Eastern Gate which had been sealed since the 16th Century. They knew that such an action would catch the Jordanians by surprise. But one of the members of the group was an Orthodox Jew who strenuously objected to dynamiting the gate.

He was quoted as saying, "That gate must remain closed until the Messiah returns."

He won the argument, and they proceeded to the Lion's Gate where the Jordanians were waiting for them. The Jews suffered heavy casualties, but they were finally able to break through the gate and take the old walled city of Jerusalem.

I was intrigued by that newspaper article. I wondered where in the world that Jewish soldier had gotten the idea that the Eastern Gate has to remain closed until the Messiah comes.

I turned to my Bible and, with the use of a concordance, I finally traced down his Biblical source to Ezekiel 43 and 44 where it is clearly prophesied that someday the Eastern Gate will be closed and that it will remain closed until the Messiah comes.

That passage drove me to the history books. I discovered that the Eastern Gate had been bricked up by command of Suliman the Magnificent when he rebuilt the walls of Jerusalem in the mid-1500s. Legends abound as to why he did that, but no one knows for certain the reason. All we know for sure is that it fulfilled the prophecy of Ezekiel, and the gate has remained closed since that time — for over 400 years.

By the time I made all these discoveries, the Holy Spirit had me hooked on Bible prophecy, and I have been a student of it ever since.

So you can understand my special feeling for the Eastern Gate. To me, it is proof positive that the Bible is the revealed Word of God and that God is faithful to keep all His promises. The gate excites me because I know that just as God closed it, someday He will open it when He sends His Son again.

A Wall for Prayer

Another very special place to me in Jerusalem is one on the opposite side of the Temple Mount from the Eastern Gate. It is what Christians refer to as the Wailing Wall. The Jews call it the Western Wall. (They use the term "wailing wall" to refer to the building that houses their internal revenue service!)

This site is the most sacred place on the earth to Jews. It is part of the massive wall that supports the Temple Mount. It is sacred because over the centuries it has been the only part of the Temple area that the occupying forces would allow the Jews to approach. The eastern wall of the Temple Mount cannot be accessed by the Jews because it has a Muslim cemetery all along in front of it.

The northern wall and most of the western wall have buildings built right up to them. The same has been true of the southern wall throughout most of history. Only one small section of the western wall, a section about 50 yards long has been historically accessible to the Jews and, until recently, houses were built up to within a few feet of it, creating a narrow, alley-like corridor where Jews could approach the wall and pray.

Today this area has been cleared of obstructions, and Jews come from all over the world to mourn the loss of their Temple, to pray for its restoration, and to celebrate special events like bar mitzvahs. Every time I approach that wall with a prayer cap on my head, I feel a little uneasy because I feel like I am intruding upon sacred ground that has been set aside for God's Chosen People.

I approach the wall with reverence and with tears. I weep for the veil that is over the eyes of the Jewish people (2 Corinthians 3:14). I pray for the salvation of the Jewish remnant (Romans 11:25-32). I also pray for the peace of Jerusalem as we are commanded to do in Psalm 122, knowing full well that when I do so I am really praying for the return of Jesus, because the Word reveals that Jerusalem will never enjoy peace until the Prince of Peace returns (Isaiah 62:1-5 and Zechariah 2:10-13).

The Place of the Skull

The third place I cherish in Jerusalem is the Garden Tomb. It is a site outside the old city, about two blocks north of the Damascus Gate.

It was discovered in the late 1800s by a British army officer, General Gordon, who was a prophetic scholar and an amateur archeologist. He felt that the traditional Catholic site of the Crucifixion, the Church of the Sepulcher, could not be authentic because it did not fulfill biblical typology which pointed to the Crucifixion occurring on some part of Mount Moriah, the place where Abraham offered Isaac. That Mount is in part occupied today by the Temple area, but an extension of it runs to the north and constitutes an area outside the old city that is historically known as Jeremiah's grotto.

It was in this area that the British general observed an unusual imprint in the side of a hill. The imprint had the form of a giant skull. Knowing that the Bible referred to the crucifixion site as "Golgotha" (the place of the skull), and recognizing that this site was part of Mount Moriah, General Gordon asserted a claim for it as the true place of the crucifixion of Jesus.

A Place of Peace

Scoffers challenged him to show them the tomb which the Bible says was located "near by" (John 19:41-42). Excavations were conducted and, sure enough, a first-century tomb of a rich man was found nearby.

The excavations also revealed that the area around the tomb had been a beautiful garden. An evangelical British group purchased the site and restored the natural beauty of the garden. They specified in the deed that no church or monument could ever be built on the site. The site is therefore unique, for it is one of the only places in Israel that is associated with the life of Christ where some monstrous church has not been built. It is a place of quiet beauty where you can go in the midst of a busy city and meditate and pray without distraction.

The only sound you will hear besides the chirping of the birds in the trees will be an occasional hymn sung by some group conducting a communion service. It is a place of peace in the Lord.

Dealing with Americans

Taking a pilgrimage group to Israel is an experience that will either develop within you the virtue of patience or else drive you crazy. You feel like a mother hen, constantly counting heads and worrying about the disposition of each person. At any given moment, someone in your group is likely to be lost, ill, unhappy, or generally disoriented.

The fact of the matter is that Americans are some of the world's worst tourists. We want everything to happen on time with the least possible inconvenience. The result is that we are always complaining about something — usually something inconsequential.

Fortunately, Israel has the finest guides in the world. They are highly trained, they are very professional, and they have twice the patience of Job.

They have to have a lot of patience working with Americans because the average American has little historical or geographical knowledge. The result is a constant barrage of inane questions — questions which would cause me to explode, but which they always handle with grace.

Let me give you a couple of examples. On one trip I conducted, a lady asked our guide, "Why are there so many Jewish-looking people in this country?"

I blushed for her and looked for a seat to climb under. But the guide never got the least bit ruffled.

He just answered politely, "It's because this is the land of the Jews."

"Oh, I see," said the lady, "that makes sense."

In another group I had a lady complain to the guide about the fact that we had been in Israel for almost two weeks and had not yet met the Ayatollah Khomeini! I was mortified. The guide never blinked an eye. "I'm sorry, ma'am," he said, "but the Ayatollah lives about 2,000 miles from here."

Tests of Patience

The Holy Land contains many layers of civilization —
Canaanite, Greek, Persian, Roman, Byzantine, Crusader,
Arab, etc. For the average American, this is all just too much
to absorb. After about two days of historical lectures, people's eyes start glazing over when the guide mentions any
aspect of history outside the New Testament context. One
guide I often use refers to this glassy-eyed state as "the
Historicals."

Perhaps the greatest test of patience comes from the short
American attention span.

I'll never forget an incident in this regard that occurred
on my first visit to Israel. We were en route to Masada and,
when we reached the Dead Sea, the guide had the bus driver
stop on the side of the road. The guide then proceeded to
deliver a detailed lecture on the Dead Sea — its length, width,
depth and mineral content. When he finished, he called for
questions. So help me, the very first question was, "What is
the name of this body of water here beside the bus?"

Free Spirits

Every group has its collective personality, but every
group seems to have at least one of several special types of
individuals. One is what I call "the independent cuss." He's
the one who simply cannot conform to any schedule. He's
always late to meals and always late to the bus. He never
stays with the group when visiting a site. He wanders off
when the guide is lecturing and then expects the guide to later
repeat the lecture just for him.

The most independent fellow I ever had travel with me
was a medical doctor from Kentucky. He nearly drove me
crazy trying to keep up with him. He could disappear faster
than any person I've ever known — and he never left a trace
as to his whereabouts. We left many a site without him, never
knowing whether we would ever see him again. I rejoiced all
the way home when that tour was over, mainly because he

actually showed up for the return flight.

You can imagine how appalled I was when he signed up for the very next trip. I just didn't know what I was going to do with him. On that trip we went first to Egypt and, sure enough, he disappeared on the first day in the heart of Cairo, one of the world's most congested cities. We looked for him for over an hour and finally found him standing outside the Cairo Museum engaged in a spirited debate with an Egyptian cab driver over who was the greatest — Sadat or Lincoln.

At that point I decided to turn him over to the Lord. I gave him his ticket home and told him he was free to do what he pleased as long as he showed up for the flight home. I hardly saw him again. I didn't worry about him anymore, and he had a ball. He even managed to spend a night in a Bedouin tent with some Bedouins he met on the side of the road. I figure he must have had a special flock of guardian angels.

The Murmurers

Another type you find in some groups is the complainer. I'm not talking about someone who complains occasionally. I'm talking about professional murmurers who are direct descendants of the ones who drove Moses up the wall. These are people who complain from sunrise to sunset about everything — the hotel room, the food, the weather, the water, the seat on the bus. You name it and they don't like it. These people can turn a whole group sour if you don't deal with them quickly and firmly.

All one of these complainers needs is a legitimate complaint, and they will freak out. This happened once in a group I was taking from Egypt to Israel. Admittedly, Egypt is not a tourist paradise. It is, however, a paradise for a complainer, and we had one in the group. By the time we reached the Egyptian border, this lady had everyone's nerves on edge, complaining about a million and one trifling things that did not amount to a hill of beans. Then it happened. She was handed a legitimate complaint on a golden platter.

An Egyptian Shakedown

We had finished checking through Egyptian customs. As we lined up to march across the border single file to the waiting Israeli bus, a very excited Egyptian grabbed me by the arm and started shouting, "Wait! Wait!"

That seemed to be the limit of his English vocabulary so I went back to an official I knew could speak English. He conferred with the man and then said that each of us would have to pay an exit tax of $5 each.

I protested and pointed out that our Egyptian travel agent (who had disappeared) had already paid the exit tax.

The two conferred again. "This is a special exit tax," the man announced.

It was special all right. It was nothing but a shakedown.

Our professional complainer started crowing. "This is outrageous!" she shouted. "Never in my life ..."

I pulled her aside and told her to keep quiet. I got our group in a huddle and explained the situation. I told them there was nothing we could do about it, so we might as well pay and be done with it. I told them I knew the price of the tour was supposed to cover all costs, including taxes and tips, but this was an unexpected cost, and I did not have enough extra money with me to cover it. So, I asked each of them to pay their own $5 fee.

Our complainer went into orbit. She had just never heard of anything so unreasonable. We all ignored her and paid our fee. It finally dawned on her that if she wanted out of the country she would have to pay up, so she did.

Incessant Complaining

When we arrived at the bus on the Israeli side, she was livid. You would have thought I had personally planned the shakedown. For miles she continued to complain at the top of her voice, heaping abuse on me and the Egyptians. Finally, one of the men in the group could take it no longer. He turned around in his seat and yelled back.

"Lady," he said, "you should be shouting Hallelujah rather than complaining."

"What do you mean?" she asked in surprise.

"Because we got the best of those Egyptians," he explained.

"How do you figure that?" she asked.

"Because they left a lot of money on the table. You see, lady, I would have been gladly willing to pay $150 to get out of that lousy country!"

That shut her up — for a little while. But when the trip was over, I received a letter still complaining about the $5.

"It's the principle of the thing," she wrote. I sent her a check for $5. She returned it. She just wanted to complain.

Serious Shoppers

A third category of pilgrim that is present in every group is the shopper. These are the people who couldn't care less about where Abraham slept or where Jesus preached or where Joseph is buried. They just want a bargain.

They start hyperventilating when they see a street vendor or spot an Arab shop. When they discover that any shop in Israel will accept either a credit card or a personal check, they think they've died and gone to Heaven.

The Arab shopkeepers are some of the world's best bargainers. They are never in a hurry. They like to begin with treats like coffee or fruit juices to make you beholden to them. Then they move in with the flattery, kissing the ladies on the cheeks and complimenting them on their beauty. All the time they are talking about their "Christian faith," explaining that they always give a special 50 percent discount to "brothers and sisters in the Lord." The 50 percent discount is, of course, off a 500 percent markup!

But most people go away thinking they've gotten a great bargain. Both sides end up happy, and I guess that's what is important.

Bargaining Laughs

One of the funniest bargaining scenes I ever witnessed took place in a shop on the outskirts of Bethlehem. A lady in my group was bargaining very hard for a ring, and she was using every ploy — feigning disinterest, walking away, waving money in her hand. My curiosity finally got the best of me. I walked over and asked how she was doing.

"Great!" she said. "I've really 'jewed' this guy down on his price."

The words were out of her mouth before she realized it. She whirled around to the sales clerk and said, "Please excuse me for using that term."

"That's all right, lady," he said smiling. "I'm an Arab!"

On another occasion, when a clerk quoted this same lady a price, she asked, "Is that in your money or real money?" Sales clerks in Israel also have to have a lot of patience.

Singing and Laughing

One of the neatest groups I ever took to Israel was one composed of 20 ministers. It was the first trip for each of them, and they were brimming over with excitement. The group loved to sing. I think they literally sang all the way over and back and, while we were in Israel, they sang almost non-stop every moment the guide was not talking.

The longest bus trip we take in Israel is the day we drive from Tiberias on the Sea of Galilee to Jerusalem. If we go down the Jordan Valley, as we often do, there is not much to see nor are there many historical sites to visit. Consequently the guide usually has little to say. For most groups, this is a day to catch up on sleep. But not the ministers. For them it was a day made to order for singing.

But after two hours, they were sung out. That's when one of the men got an inspired idea. He got the guide's microphone and announced to the group that we were going to have a joke-telling contest. There was only one rule. The joke had to be a true story about something funny that had really happened in our respective ministries.

The next hour I never laughed so hard in my life. Their stories proved beyond a shadow of a doubt that there is never a dull moment when you're serving the Lord. When all the stories had been told and we had regained our wits, we decided to vote to select the best story. The stories that placed first and second were both yarns about incredibly embarrassing moments.

A Nervous Deacon

The second-place story came from a Canadian pastor. He said that at his church they required a deacon to preside over each Sunday morning service, rotating this responsibility through the board of deacons. It seems that there was one deacon who was particularly vulnerable to stage fright. He was always nervously putting his foot in his mouth by misspeaking some announcement whenever he presided.

One morning when this deacon was scheduled to preside, the pastor discovered the district superintendent was going to be present. He asked the nervous deacon to work the superintendent into the service.

When it came time for the offering, the deacon announced, "We are privileged to have with us this morning our district superintendent, Dr. DuPree. I'd like to request that Dr. DuPray come pee over the offering." The tears rolled down my cheeks over that one!

An Embarrassed Missionary

But the grand-prize winner came from a missionary to Central America. He said that when he first felt the call to go into mission work, he made a tour of Latin America to survey mission possibilities. One of his first stops was in Buenos Aires, Argentina. Keep in mind that he knew almost no Spanish at the time.

On Sunday morning he got a taxi at his hotel and headed for church. The only problem was that he could not seem to communicate the address to the cab driver. They drove around aimlessly for a while, and all he saw resembling churches were Catholic Cathedrals. Finally, he spotted what appeared to be a Protestant Church building. He stopped the taxi and went in.

The service had already started, and the place was packed out. The usher took him to the third row from the front. There was only one person between him and the preacher, a young man sitting on the second row.

The service turned out to be formal in nature. The people kept standing up, sitting down, kneeling and then standing back up. Since the prospective missionary could not understand what was being said, he decided to watch the young man in front of him and do whatever he did.

At the end of the service the pastor returned to the pulpit and began making some statements. Suddenly, the young man stood up. Our friend immediately followed him. The church exploded with laughter.

The missionary turned and looked behind him. He and the young man were the only ones standing. He quickly sat down and prayed for the floor to open up and swallow him.

When the service dismissed, the missionary stayed in his seat, too embarrassed to move. He didn't know what he had done, but he knew it must have been something awful. Finally, the pastor came up and spoke to him in English.

"You don't speak Spanish, do you?" asked the pastor.

"That's right."

"Do you have any idea why you caused such a commotion?"

"No."

"Well," the pastor chuckled, "I announced that Sister Gonzalez had given birth yesterday to a baby boy. And I asked the proud father to stand."

An Unforgettable Anniversary

Another very special group was the one that contained my mom and dad, my wife and my oldest daughter. What a joy it was to share with these precious family members the glories of Israel.

I had been trying to get my wife to go with me for years, but she is a homebody who simply does not like to travel. But at long last I talked her into going, mainly because the trip was going to fall on our 25th wedding anniversary. So, reluctantly, she went. She loved it. What a blessing it was to celebrate 25 years together at a dinner in the city of Jerusalem!

But it was not quite as romantic as it sounds because we had a roommate — yes, a roommate! On the third day of that tour, one of the men had told me that he could not get any sleep because his 75-year-old father whom he was traveling with "snored like a B-52!"

I offered to let him room with my wife and me because the hotels always give the tour leader a suite. That meant we had a sitting room separate from our bedroom. He promptly moved in and slept on our couch for the duration of the tour — even on the evening of our 25th anniversary.

Special Memories

My heart is full of wonderful memories of the Holy Land. But two in particular stand out. Both events touched me deeply.

The first was a visit to the Garden Tomb. I had a group with me. I had been there many times, and I was not expecting anything special. I was spiritually off guard, and the Lord "snuck" up on me.

The usual procedure is to listen to a brief lecture by one of the caretakers, then walk through the garden, view the crucifixion site, step into the tomb, and conclude with a communion service.

The caretakers who deliver the lectures rotate about every three or four months. Most of them are evangelical preachers from European countries, mainly England. They are always most cordial, and they never hold up a group for very long.

They usually speak about five minutes explaining how

the site was found, emphasizing that they cannot prove its authenticity, and making the point that the only important thing to keep in mind is that the tomb of Jesus, wherever it is, is empty. I knew the talk by heart.

Words of Power

That particular day, the man who came out to speak to us was a young Dutchman. In physical appearance he was ugly. He was tall and very thin, almost skeletal. He was completely bald-headed and had large ears that stuck out. His nose looked like it had been broken several times. It wandered all over his face. When he started speaking, I was startled to hear a heavy lisp. I was even more startled by what he had to say.

Instead of the usual tourist prattle, he simply said, "I want to take a moment to share with you what Jesus has done for me in my life."

I don't remember what he said after that. All I know is that I was translated into the presence of Jesus, and my heart was touched by the power of the Lord's Spirit.

When he finished, we all just sat there dumbfounded by what we had experienced. A lady next to me, who was a member of another group, turned to me and said, "You know, for the first time I think I understand why the Apostle Paul was such a powerful evangelist. I think he must have been like this man, with no strength or beauty in himself. Yet, in his weakness, the power of God was displayed."

In three sentences that lady preached one of the most powerful sermons I had ever heard. All I could say was "Amen" and "Thank you, Lord."

A Museum of Death

The other memory that still plucks at my heartstrings occurred at one of the most dismal places in all the world, a place in Jerusalem called Yad Vashem. In English, we call it the Holocaust Museum. As its name indicates, it is a collection of historical artifacts which authenticate every aspect of one of Mankind's most horrible crimes.

If you have any sensitivity at all, it is a tough place to walk through. It is arranged in chronological order. The first room records, in graphic photographs, the rise of Hitler.

The next room shows the beginnings of the Nazi persecutions of the Jews. On and on it goes, step by bloody step. Jewish shops are closed. Jews are arrested and taunted in public. Cattle cars are filled with human cargoes destined for work camps and ovens. There are films of executions. The prison clothing of adults and children is displayed, along with gold bricks made of fillings extracted from corpses.

Nothing is left to the imagination. Yet, the imagination cannot comprehend such bestiality. It is overpowering. I have seen entire groups walk through without speaking a word. I have witnessed people fainting. Others have gone hysterical. Some almost run through, not wanting to see any of the horror.

When I take a group there, I never try to keep them together as a group. It is too personal a place. I just give them a general introduction outside and then turn them loose to move through at their own rate of speed. I normally allot an hour and a half for them to get back to the bus.

If they finish early, I urge them to walk down the Promenade of the Righteous, a beautiful garden area outside where trees have been planted in memory of the righteous Gentiles who risked their lives to save Jews from the Holocaust. One of those trees is dedicated to Corrie ten Boom.

Weeping with My Daughter

When I visited Yad Vashem with the group that included my family members, everything seemed to go well until it was time to depart. We counted heads, and my daughter, Ruth, 23 years old, was missing. I started searching for her, but I just couldn't find her anywhere — in the museum or outside. I went through the museum a second time but still did not see her.

As I was about to exit, I noticed a stairway was open that I had rarely seen open during regular tourist hours. I knew where it led because I had been there several times. It led to a long, narrow, dark room where individual records are stored concerning each person who perished in the Holocaust. This is a research facility that is rarely visited by tourists.

I went bounding up the stairs and peered into the dark room. At the far end I could make out the form of a person in the shadowy darkness. No one ever speaks above a whisper in this room, so I could not call out to see if it was Ruth.

I walked to the other end. It was Ruth. She was standing there holding onto a display stand with both hands. The stand had a dim light on it. The light illuminated a sample document under glass. It showed the photograph of a little girl ten years old. The document contained her vital statistics — place of birth, parents, home address, place of arrest, place of imprisonment, date and place of execution. It read in matter-of-fact style.

Ruth was weeping. I put my arm around her and hugged her.

"Daddy," she whispered, "how could this happen?"

I couldn't speak. We just stood there, arm in arm, weeping together, staring at the picture of a child who represented six million of God's Chosen People.

Growing in the Lord 21

God is in the change business. He wants to shape and mold us into the image of His Son. He does this through the power of His Spirit working within us. His Spirit uses the Word, our prayers and our experiences.

Growth is never easy because it demands change. We don't like to change. We get comfortable in our ruts, and we hunker down in them and refuse to climb out. Sometimes the Lord has to jar us loose by plowing the ruts with jolting experiences.

As I've revealed, I've had a lot of these experiences because I was too stubborn to let the Lord change me gently. I've experienced a lot of change and subsequent growth in my years of evangelistic work. I have a lot of growth yet in front of me. We all do.

The Lord also uses experiences to give us insights that help us to grow. Often we are too spiritually insensitive to pick up on the insights, and the experiences are wasted. Other times, experiences that might on the surface appear inconsequential will have a profound impact simply because we had our spiritual antenna in place and were ready to receive what God had to offer.

As I look back over the wealth of experiences God brought my way during the first seven years I served Him, there are two that stand out as foundational to the ministry I've been entrusted with. Both helped me to understand the importance of the message that Jesus is coming soon. One related that message to the unbeliever, the other to the believer. God used both experiences to motivate me to proclaim the message He had laid on my heart with urgency and fervor.

A Sudden Death

The experience that related my ministry to unbelievers occurred very shortly after the ministry was established. The setting was the Cajun country of Southern Louisiana.

I was holding a meeting at a fairly large church in Jennings, Louisiana. Following the Sunday evening service, I went to the door to greet people as they left. A young woman about 30 years old came up to me and enthusiastically thanked me for the message. She said she could hardly wait for the Monday evening service. I was speaking on the "Signs of the Times" that point to the soon return of Jesus. The Sunday message had caught her imagination, and she was excited.

"I have so many questions," she said, "but I'll have to hold them till later because I've got to rush to my job."

"Oh?" I responded. "What kind of job do you have on Sunday evening?"

"I run the skating rink," she answered, "and we've got a lot of church kids coming over to skate this evening. I've got to hurry and get the place opened."

I thanked her for her kind comments and urged her not to forget her questions. She left hurriedly.

About 10:30 that evening the phone rang at the house where I was staying. I heard my host, one of the congregation's elders, suddenly exclaim, "Oh no! Oh no!" He hung up the phone and yelled at me, "Get your coat. We've got to go to the hospital."

As we tore across town in his truck, he explained that the call had been about the young woman who managed the skating rink. She had been skating with the kids when she suddenly dropped to the floor. She had been rushed to the hospital. The situation looked critical.

The moment we walked into the hospital lobby, we knew she was dead. Groups of youngsters and friends from the church were gathered in small groups all over the lobby and down the main hallway. Some were praying. Some were singing softly. Some were just comforting one another with hugs of reassurance.

She had suffered a massive cerebral hemorrhage. She was only 32. Death had come instantaneously. The doctor said she was probably dead before she hit the floor.

Reacting in the Lord

Her older sister arrived and received the terrible news. She was known as a woman of great faith. We tried to console her but she kept consoling us, reminding us that her sister was now with the Lord. She went from group to group encouraging them with the victory her sister now enjoyed.

Then her brother arrived. He was a man of the world. He had treated his sisters harshly because of their religious convictions.

When he learned of his sister's death, he was overcome with grief and guilt. He fell to the floor in a clump and began to weep and moan loudly.

His sister rushed to him, grabbed him by the shoulders and literally lifted him off the floor. She slammed him up against the wall and held him there with her forearm. Looking directly into his eyes, she said, "Don't weep for your sister. Weep for yourself. She's in Heaven with the Lord. But if that were you in there on that table, you would be in Hell!"

I was taken aback by what appeared to be a brutal approach to a grieving person. But it must have had the right impact because within a year that brother had accepted the Lord.

Reacting Outside the Lord

I started moving up and down the hallway from group to group, praying with them and trying as best as I knew how to offer some consoling words. Suddenly, a side door flew open and in came two paramedics running and pushing a litter on wheels. On the stretcher was a man who looked to be 60. He was dressed in a tuxedo. They wheeled him into an emergency room.

A few minutes later a large entourage of "beautiful people" arrived, all dressed in tuxedos and evening gowns. They gathered outside the emergency room doors and waited for some word. I learned they had been partying at a night club and that the man had collapsed on the dance floor. They thought he had suffered a heart attack.

They were right. The doctor stepped into the hallway and delivered the grim news. The man was dead from a heart attack. They all stood there for a moment in a daze, and then they turned on each other like a pack of wild animals.

A daughter, dressed in a red evening dress, turned to an older woman and began to shout curses at her. The woman was her mother, the widow of the man who had just died. There was no consolation from daughter to mother. Only curses and accusations.

"It's all your fault," the daughter screamed. "You're the cause of his heart attack. You've never given him anything but grief."

"Look who's talking," the mother shouted back, "the biggest slut in Southern Louisiana." It was a horrible scene. Family members cursing and blaming each other.

A Startling Contrast

I was standing at a corner of the hallway. Down one corridor I saw people cursing and clawing at each other. Down the other corridor I saw people consoling and loving one another. I saw death down one hallway. I saw life down the other. I saw the glory of dying in the Lord. And I saw the grim reality of dying with no hope.

God used that moment to impress upon my heart the desperate need that a lost and dying world has for the good news of Jesus Christ. Hebrews 2:15 says that Jesus died that

He might "deliver all those who through fear of death are subject to lifelong bondage." Revelation 14:13 says, "Blessed are those who die in the Lord."

Trying to be "Jazzy"

The experience that related my ministry to believers took place at a mainline denominational church in Grand Prairie, Texas.

Grand Prairie is a metropolitan suburb located between Dallas and Ft. Worth. It is in an area that many refer to as "the buckle of the Bible Belt." This experience also took place in the early months of the ministry, shortly after our radio outreach had begun.

I got a call one day from a man who identified himself as a deacon of a particular church. He said some of the members there had heard my radio broadcasts and were interested in the possibility of my coming to their church on a Sunday evening to present a lesson on prophecy. He asked if I would be willing to do so. I said I would.

"There's one problem," he interjected. "We have a tough time trying to get any of our people to come on Sunday evening, so you need to give us a jazzy title."

"A jazzy title?"

"That's right. We need something jazzy to attract attention and build curiosity."

I thought for a moment, and a title suddenly popped into my mind.

"What about calling my talk, 'The Future of the Late Great Planet Earth?'"

"Hey!" he said. "That's jazzy. I like it. That's what we'll call it. Now, there's one more problem."

"What's that?" I asked.

"We have a pastor who's not too hot about Bible studies. He likes to have folk singers and book reviewers. We've got to run this past him. He may not approve it."

I told him to give me a ring as soon as he knew something for sure. To my surprise he called back the very next day. He was excited. The pastor had "enthusiastically" agreed for me to come. We set the date.

A Mistaken Invitation

When the evening arrived, I saw what the deacon meant about Sunday evening attendance. Only about 50 people showed up.

The pastor excused the light attendance to me by saying, "I don't blame them. This has been a beautiful day. I would have gone to the lake myself if I could have." It was a strange welcome for a guest speaker. The evening was to get even stranger.

The pastor called the service to order and began introducing me right off the bat. No songs or prayers. It was obvious he wanted to get the thing over with.

"We're honored to have with us Dr. David Reagan, an expert on Bible prophecy," he began. "Dr. Reagan is going to show us what a fool Hal Lindsey is . . ."

"What?" I thought to myself. "Did I hear this guy right?" I perked up and leaned forward to give him my undivided attention.

He droned on.

"There's been a lot of nonsense written recently by sensationalists like Hal Lindsey who try to scare everyone by saying that 'Jesus is coming soon.' That's a lot of nonsense and I'm glad to have Dr. Reagan here this evening to set the record straight."

I just couldn't believe what I was hearing. Was I dreaming? Had this man gone mad? Was this some sort of sick joke?

My search for some rational explanation was interrupted by applause. I was on, and I didn't know what to say. I mumbled around for a few moments in bewilderment thanking them for inviting me, and then stopped and looked directly at the pastor.

"Pastor," I said, "I'm awfully sorry but I'm afraid there has been a terrible mistake."

"What do you mean?" he asked.

"Well, I happen to be a strong supporter of Hal Lindsey's. I think most of what he's written is right on target."

"You're right!" the pastor responded. "There's been a terrible mistake."

He thought for a moment.

"But we don't want to be impolite," he added, "so you go right ahead with your message."

I sighed with relief and asked everyone to turn to Acts, chapter 2. I wanted to start out by showing them how Peter utilized prophecy in his sermon at Pentecost.

Lost Bibles

Now when I ask people to turn to a Bible passage, I'm used to hearing the pages rustle. That's music to a preacher's ears. As I turned to the passage, I didn't hear any rustling of pages. I looked up. Everyone was just sitting there passively, staring at me.

"How many of you have a Bible with you?" I asked.

Not one hand was raised.

"Okay, then, let's use the pew Bibles."

"We don't have any pew Bibles," a man yelled.

"Well, we can't study Bible prophecy without Bibles," I said, "so let's find some." I asked four of the men to go through the classrooms in the educational wing of the building and gather up some Bibles. While they looked, I led the group in a couple of praise songs.

The men returned empty-handed.

"We can't find any Bibles in this church," one of them said.

The pastor jumped up. "I think I have a few in my office." He returned with five Bibles. We divided the congregation into five groups and gave each group a Bible.

"Okay," I said, "now turn to Acts 2." The pages started rustling. It sounded good. I started reading from Acts 2. The pages continued to rustle. I looked up. Every group was still searching for Acts! Some were at the beginning of the Bible searching through Genesis.

I was thunderstruck. I had grown up in a church that idolized the book of Acts. It was about all we ever studied. I didn't know there were Christians anywhere who could not find Acts.

I departed from my prepared lesson and conducted a Bible drill to familiarize the people with the book they had in front of them. I explained the difference between the Old Testament and the New and then we surveyed the various divisions — History, Wisdom, Prophecy, etc. The people got excited.

A Banned Book

All of us turned to the newly discovered book of Acts, and I made my point about Peter's use of prophecy. Then I asked them to turn to Daniel.

The pastor jumped to his feet.

"Why the book of Daniel?" he asked.

"Because I want to show you a prophecy in that book about the First Coming of Jesus."

"But there is no prophecy in Daniel," the pastor said. "The book of Daniel is a fraud. It shouldn't even be in the Bible. It is history written like prophecy to make it sell better. It claims to have been written about 500 B.C., when in reality it was written about 100 years before Christ."

Now keep in mind that this pastor is standing in front of his congregation publicly heaping scorn and ridicule on one of the books of the Bible. I was biting my tongue, trying to refrain from giving him some sort of scathing, sarcastic reply.

He continued. "You can quote from any other book except Daniel. But I don't allow Daniel to be quoted in this church."

Then he got personal and said, "You obviously are not a seminary graduate because no seminary graduate would ever stoop to quote Daniel."

My blood was boiling. I wanted to say something cute like, "I'm not a cemetery graduate, if that's what you mean."

But I prayed for self-control, and the Spirit prevailed. I decided to challenge him, but I tried to do so as politely as possible.

Arguing for Daniel

"If Daniel was written only a hundred years before Christ, how do you explain its inclusion in the Septuagint?"

"What do you mean?" he asked.

"I mean the Septuagint was translated around 250 B.C. Daniel was included in that translation, so Daniel had to be written before that time."

"I don't believe that's when the Septuagint was translated," he responded.

"Okay, then how do you explain the fact that when Alexander the Great came to Jerusalem in 333 B.C., he decided to spare the city because the High Priest showed him where he was prophesied in Daniel?"

"Where did you come across that crazy story?" the pastor asked.

"It's in the writings of Josephus."

"Then it's nothing but legend," he snapped, "because Josephus never wrote anything except old wives' tales."

"Maybe I should just go home," I replied.

"Oh no," said the pastor, "you go right ahead with your presentation. Just don't quote from Daniel."

A Banned Verse

I should have stopped. But I tried to continue.

"Let's take a look at the very first prophecy in the Bible. Everyone turn to Genesis 3:15."

Instantly the pastor was back on his feet.

"Come on, Dr. Reagan," he said, "you're not going to start talking about myths like the virgin birth, are you?"

So it went, all evening long. A man responsible for the care and feeding of a flock of 300 people kept jumping up to ridicule the Word of God and the fundamental truths it reveals.

I wish I could say this was an isolated experience. It has not been. I've had several like it since that time.

God used that experience to open my eyes to the dreadful condition of the contemporary church. He showed me the apathy and apostasy that have sapped the church of its vitality and dynamism. He showed me the overwhelming need for revival and spiritual renewal.

He let me see the meaning of Paul's prophecy in 2 Timothy 3:5 where he wrote that in the end-times the church "will have the form of religion but will deny its power" (RSV). He also allowed me to witness the reality of a Laodicean church — the type of worldly, unbelieving and apathetic church which the book of Revelation indicates will characterize the end-times (Revelation 3:14ff).

God's Sense of Humor

Believe it or not, the Lord showed me something else in this experience. He once again revealed His great sense of humor. You may be wondering what in the world I could possibly see in such an experience that could be considered humorous.

It relates to how I was invited in the first place. Several months later I ran into the deacon who called me. I asked how he ever got the pastor to approve my invitation when he so obviously disagreed with my viewpoint.

"It was a remarkable coincidence!" he said.

He explained that the morning he went to the pastor's office to clear my invitation, the pastor was sitting at his desk reading a book. The book was entitled, "The Future of the Late Great Planet Earth." I had never heard of the book, yet that was exactly the "jazzy" title that the Spirit had led me to give my proposed talk.

The book contained a scathing denunciation of Hal Lindsey and his prophetic concepts. When the deacon told the pastor my proposed topic, the pastor assumed I had pulled the title from that book and that I agreed with the book!

The Lord has worked in equally hilarious ways many

times to open doors for me that would never have been opened otherwise. God has a great sense of humor, and the results are not "coincidences." They are "God-incidences."

Part III
The Message

"Living on Borrowed Time."

Knowing the Season   22

Forty years ago if you had asked me, "Can we know when the Lord will return?" I would have answered with an emphatic, dogmatic "No!"

But after many years of studying God's Prophetic Word, I have come to a different conclusion. Now, my answer would be "Yes and No." No, we cannot know the date of the Lord's return. We can't know the year or month or day. But, yes, we can know the season — and the exciting news is that we are living in that season!

Now by a "season" I don't mean a period of three months, nor do I mean a particularly short period of years. Keep in mind that Noah preached for 120 years that the people of his time were living in the season of the pouring out of God's wrath.

I'm sure that after preaching that message for five years, people wrote him off as a "one issue obsessionist." And I'm certain that after half a century of preaching the same message, people laughed and jeered and reminded him that he had been saying the same thing for 50 years. Some probably kept on laughing until they couldn't tread water anymore.

But Noah was right, and he got the last laugh. They truly were living in the season of God's wrath, and the wrath of God could have been poured out on them at any time after Noah issued his first warning.

Encountering Scoffers

I often encounter the same kind of scoffing among Christian people today when I talk about the soon coming of Jesus. Some laugh. Others write me off as nuts. Some get hostile. Others are just cantankerous.

One of the most common comments I receive is, "I've heard all that before." Once a crusty old farmer came up to me after a sermon on the signs of the times. He patted me on the shoulder in a condescending manner and said, "That was really nice, son, but I heard that stuff back in World War I when I was a kid."

"Praise God!" I responded. "You need to thank God for growing up under a Bible believing preacher."

The Significance of the Jews

What that man did not realize is that his boyhood preacher was right on target because we have been in the season of the Lord's return ever since the beginning of World War I. God worked through that war's evil to initiate His end-time program, for that war resulted in the land of Israel being transferred from a people who hated the Jews — the Turks — to a people who were sympathetic to the Jews — the British. The first thing the British did was to issue the Balfour Declaration in which they declared that Palestine should become a homeland for the Jews.

But the Jews did not return to that land in large numbers. They had become acculturated to their adopted nations. They had to be motivated to return to their ancestral land. That motivation came with the Holocaust of World War II. The Jews emerged from that nightmare saying, "Never again! Never again! We will have our own land and our own state. Never again will we submit ourselves to another Hitler." Millions began to stream back to Palestine from the ends of the earth.

Old Testament prophecy always presents the return of the Lord at a time when the Jews are back in the land. The Old

Testament prophets speak repeatedly of the fact that in the end-times the Jews will return in unbelief to their homeland, and the nation of Israel will be reestablished (See Ezekiel 37).

God has the wisdom and power to orchestrate all the evil of Man and Satan to the triumph of Jesus. He proved that by converting the Cross into a triumph. Likewise, God was able to work through the evil of World Wars I and II to bring about His own purposes. He used World War I to prepare the land of Israel for the Jews. He used Word War II to prepare the Jews for the land of Israel.

The Great Put-Down

The moment I start telling people that we can know the season of the Lord's return, I always get the same scripture thrown at me: "Jesus is coming like a thief in the night." I know exactly how those who use that scripture feel. I grew up in a church that put no emphasis on prophetic teaching concerning the Second Coming. Every time someone would ask a question about the return of the Lord, they would be put-down with the words, "Jesus is coming like a thief in the night."

Because that was the only prophetic scripture I knew, I drew the conclusion that there was nothing we could know about the timing of the Lord's return. He was going to sneak up on us like a thief and catch us unaware. Therefore, it was a waste of time to worry about when He would return. I put the whole matter out of my mind and became apathetic about the return of Jesus.

A Startling Discovery

You can imagine how shocked I was when I started studying Bible prophecy and one of the first discoveries which the Spirit led me to was the fact that this famous scripture about the Lord returning as a thief does not apply to Christians! The Bible says so point-blank.

Let's look at 1 Thessalonians, chapters 4 and 5. Chapter 4 ends with a detailed description of the Rapture of the

Church (verses 13-18). Chapter 5 begins with a statement about the timing of this end-time event: "Now as to the times and the epochs, brethren, you have no need of anything to be written to you. For you yourselves know full well that the day of the Lord will come just like a thief in the night" (verses 1 and 2).

There it is, the famous statement that the Lord will return like a thief.

But keep reading: "But you, brethren, are not in darkness, that the day should overtake you like a thief" (1 Thessalonians 5:4).

How could anything be clearer? Jesus is going to return like a thief in the night — that is, suddenly and unexpectedly — except for the "brethren."

This means that the return of Jesus will be a shocking surprise to the world — to those who have rejected Him. But it should be no surprise to those who have accepted Him in faith. He is not coming for Christians as a thief in the night.

The Spirit's Illumination

But how can Christians know the season of His return? The next two verses tell us: "For you are all sons of light and sons of day. We are not of night nor of darkness; so then let us not sleep as others do, but let us be alert and sober" (1 Thessalonians 5:5,6).

We can know the season of the Lord's return because we are "children of light."

What does this mean?

I think it is a reference to the indwelling Spirit of God. All true Christians are indwelt by the Spirit (Romans 8:14). The Spirit opens our eyes and enlightens our minds so that we can understand the mysteries of God's Word (1 Corinthians 2:6-12 and 1 John 2:27). In other words, if we will read the Word, and believe the Word, the Spirit will help us understand the Word, and through that understanding we can recognize the season of the Lord's return.

What I'm saying is that there is no excuse for the return

of the Lord to catch any Christian by surprise. Yet, tragically, many professing Christians will be caught by surprise, like a thief in the night, because they either do not read the Word or do not believe it or do not rely upon the Spirit to explain it.

God's Obligation

There's another reason we can know the season of the Lord's return. It's because God is obligated to reveal the season to us. That's right. God is obligated to let us know the season of His Son's return. You ask, "Why?" It's because of the nature of God's character.

Let me put it this way: God would violate His character if He were to send Jesus Christ back without any warning. Since God cannot violate His own character, He is obligated to warn us before Jesus returns.

This point raises a further question: "Why is God obligated to warn us of Jesus' return?" The answer is simple. It is because Jesus is returning in wrath, and the Bible teaches from beginning to end that God never pours out His wrath without warning because God does not wish that any should perish but that all should come to repentance.

Now, consider carefully the points I have just made:

1) Jesus is returning in wrath. He is coming to pour out the wrath of God upon those who have rejected the grace and mercy of God (1 Thessalonians 1:10).

2) God does not wish that any should perish but that all should come to repentance (2 Peter 3:9).

3) Therefore, God must warn before Jesus returns, just as He has always warned before He has poured out His wrath (2 Peter 2:4-10).

God warned through Abraham before He destroyed Sodom and Gomorrah. God warned through Noah before He poured out His wrath upon all the earth. God sent both Jonah and Nahum to warn the pagan city of Ninevah. And God sent prophet after prophet to warn both Israel and Judah.

Likewise, the Bible says God will warn all the earth through an angel before He pours out His final bowls of wrath at the end of the Tribulation period (Revelation 14:6-7). Since the entire Tribulation will be a time of wrath, God must warn before that period begins, and He is doing precisely that today. Let's consider how He is presenting those warnings.

Recognizing the Season   23

How can we recognize the season of the Lord's return? What are we to look for? The Bible tells us to be alert for "signs of the times."

It is a principle that applied to the First Coming of Jesus, and we can learn from its application there. Look at Matthew 16. The chapter begins with Jesus being tested by the Scribes and Pharisees. They asked Him to prove that He was the Messiah by performing a sign — or a miracle.

Jesus answered them sarcastically: "When it is evening, you say, 'It will be fair weather, for the sky is red.' And in the morning, 'There will be a storm today, for the sky is red and threatening.' Do you know how to discern the appearance of the sky but cannot discern the signs of the times?" (Matthew 16:2,3)

What Jesus is saying here is, "I don't understand you fellows. You can read the weather signs but you can't read the signs of the times!" What did Jesus mean by the term, "signs of the times"?

I think He was referring to Old Testament prophecies. There are more than 300 of those prophecies or signs, and they reveal every aspect of the nature and being of the Messiah. They tell that He will be born of the lineage of Abraham and David, that He will be born in Bethlehem of a virgin, that He will go into Egypt, that He will reside in Galilee, and that He will be a prophet, teacher and healer.

Now think about it — these Scribes and Pharisees had spent their lives studying these signs. They knew them by heart. Yet, they were so spiritually blind that they could not recognize the One who was fulfilling those signs before their eyes.

Signs of the Second Coming

Likewise, the Bible contains many signs about the Second Advent of the Messiah. In fact, there are many more prophecies about the Second Coming than there are about the First. There are over 500 prophecies in the Old Testament about the Second Coming of the Lord and, in the New Testament, one out of every 25 verses focuses on that event.

There are, in fact, so many signs given concerning the Second Coming of Jesus that it is hard to get a handle on them. I've tried to do so by sorting them into broad categories.

Here are the categories I've come up with:

1) The Signs of Nature — earthquakes, famines, pestilence and signs in the heavens.

2) The Signs of Society — immorality, lawlessness, violence, humanism, materialism, hedonism and despair.

3) The Spiritual Signs — There are negative ones like cults, satanism and the apostasy of the professing church. There are positive ones like the worldwide preaching of the Gospel, the pouring out of the Holy Spirit and prophetic illumination — that is, the understanding of Bible prophecy.

4) The Signs of Technology — These include biblical prophecies that can only be explained by the development of lasers, computers, aircraft and nuclear weapons.

5) The Signs of World Politics — the emergence of Russia and China as major world powers, the con-

solidation of Europe into a loose confederation of states, and the world armaments race.

6) The Signs of Israel — the regathering of the Jews, the re-establishment of the state of Israel, the revival of the Hebrew language, the reclamation of the land, and the reoccupation of the city of Jerusalem.

The specific signs within each of these broad categories are numerous. I've only named a few to give you a feel for each category.

The Olivet Discourse

One of the most comprehensive and detailed passages in the Bible regarding these signs of the Second Coming is one that Jesus Himself spoke during the last week of His life. It is often referred to as "The Olivet Discourse" because He delivered the speech to His disciples while they were sitting on the Mt. of Olives, looking down at the Temple Mount. The speech is recorded in Matthew 24, Mark 13 and Luke 21.

It is in reality a double prophecy, referring in part to the destruction of Jerusalem by the Romans in 70 A.D., but referring ultimately to the destruction Jerusalem will suffer right before the return of the Lord at the end of this age. This is something characteristic of Bible prophecies. They often have a prefillment in type before they experience their ultimate fulfillment.

History or Prophecy?

There can be no doubt that the Olivet Discourse was not fulfilled in 70 A.D. In Matthew 24 it is recorded that Jesus said the signs to be watched for would precede the greatest tribulation ever to be experienced by the Jewish people (verse 21). The destruction of Jerusalem in 70 A.D., as terrible as it was, with the loss of a million Jewish lives, was nothing compared to the Nazi Holocaust. The Holocaust will pale in comparison to what the Jews will suffer at the hands of the Anti-Christ during the Tribulation. The prophet Zechariah says that during that time two-thirds of the Jews will perish (Zechariah 13:8).

In Matthew 24:22 the Lord says that the signs will precede a period so terrible that His return will be the only thing that will prevent mankind from destroying itself. That was not true in 70 A.D. In fact, we are living in the only period of history where that prophecy could come literally true because of the development of nuclear weapons.

Also, Jesus says that the signs He outlines will precede a period that will climax with His return:

> But immediately after the tribulation of those days the sun will be darkened, and the moon will not give its light, and the stars will fall from the sky, and the powers of the heavens will be shaken, and then the sign of the Son of Man will appear in the sky, and then all the tribes of the earth will mourn, and they will see the Son of Man coming on the clouds of the sky with power and great glory. — Matthew 24:29-30

Notice, He says, "immediately." It has been almost 2,000 years since Titus destroyed Jerusalem. The Lord did not return then. The signs of Matthew 24 are yet to be fulfilled.

The Signs of Matthew 24

Let's look at those signs. I think it's significant that Jesus begins with a spiritual sign — the emergence of false Christs (verse 5). I think it is also significant that this is the only sign He repeats, and He repeats it twice, in verses 11 and 24. In the latter verse He warns of false Christs who will even be able to perform miracles. I think it is no coincidence that the world has experienced a literal epidemic of cultic groups since the mid-1800s and that today some of the cultic leaders are able to perform miracles by the power of Satan.

In verses 6 and 7 Jesus shifts to the signs of world politics. He speaks of wars and rumors of wars, of nation rising against nation and kingdom against kingdom (civil war).

We live in that age. The period since the end of World War II has been the most violent period of "peace" in the history of Man. World War II took 57 million lives. Over 60 million have died in wars (and civil wars) since that time. Some of the wars that have produced especially massive losses are the civil wars in Cambodia, Lebanon, Afghanistan and Yugoslavia — as well as the conflict between Iran and Iraq.

In verse 7 Jesus also mentions signs of nature — famines and earthquakes. Luke's account adds pestilence and signs in the heavens (Luke 21:11). There is probably no category of signs with less respect than the signs of nature. People respond, "But there have always been earthquakes and famines. What else is new?" But note what Jesus says in verse 8 of Matthew 24. He says the signs of nature will be like "birth pangs."

Now, I have never experienced birth pangs, so I asked my wife what this means. She said it was "obvious." She explained that when birth pangs begin they increase in frequency and intensity. In other words, the closer we get to the coming of the Lord, there will be more earthquakes and more intense ones. The same will be true of famine and pestilence and other signs of nature.

Spiritual Signs and Signs of Society

In verses 9 and 10 of Matthew 24, Jesus shifts back to spiritual signs — the persecution of believers and the apostasy of the church. Some will fall away because of persecution (verse 10). Others will depart from the faith because of the deception of false prophets (verse 11). And others will forsake the Lord because they will get caught up in the lawlessness of society (verse 12).

The Lord's mention of lawlessness in verse 12 is not His only reference to the signs of society, He focuses on this category in verses 37-39 where He says that society will evolve full circle and that in the end-times it will take on the characteristics of Noah's corrupt civilization. People will be living it up, their hearts hardened against God and their lives given to the pursuit of pleasure.

The Signs of Israel

Most important, the Lord emphasized the signs of Israel. He says that His return will take place at a time when the Jews are back in the land, their temple has been rebuilt, and their sacrificial system has been reinstituted (verses 15-20).

Although there is not one prophecy that must be fulfilled for the Lord to come for His Church, there are some that must be fulfilled before the Lord returns to reign. Two are mentioned in this passage — the rebuilding of the Temple and the reinstitution of the Mosaic system of sacrifice. The third prophecy mentioned here, the return of the Jews to the land, has been fulfilled in this century.

Matthew 24 is just one of many detailed passages in both the Old and New Testaments which outline signs we are to watch for, signs that will alert us to the Lord's return. If you will believe these and watch for them, the Lord's return will not catch you "like a thief in the night."

Understanding the
Urgency of the Season   24

God worked through World War I to initiate His end-time program. We have been in the season of the Lord's return ever since that time.

But there is an important point yet to be made. The signs of Israel indicate that we are near the end of the season, that Jesus is at the very gates of Heaven, and that we are living on borrowed time.

The signs of Israel are more important than all the rest of the signs put together. The reason for this is that the Jewish people are God's prophetic time clock. God always links major prophecies to events that will occur in the history of the Jewish nation.

The Timing of the First Coming

Let me give you two examples. There are two Old Testament prophecies which nail down the time period of the Lord's First Advent. Both relate that advent to events in Jewish history. The first of these prophecies is found in Genesis 49:10 where Jacob said to his son Judah, "The scepter shall not depart from Judah, nor the ruler's staff from between his feet, until Shiloh comes, and to him shall be the obedience of the peoples."

"Shiloh" is a recognized Messianic title. What this prophecy says is that Judah will not lose its ruling power before the Messiah comes.

Judah lost its ruling power in about 7 A.D. when the Romans removed the power of the Sanhedrin Council to apply the death penalty. Jewish history records that on that day the High Priest put on sack cloth and ashes and wept over the fact that "the scepter has passed from Judah and Shiloh has not come." But Shiloh had come, for Jesus had been born in 4 B.C., and He was to begin His ministry in 27 A.D.

The second Old Testament passage that uses Jewish historical events to set the season of the Lord's First Coming is found in Daniel 9:24-27. Here Daniel prophesies that the Messiah will be "cut off" after a period of 69 weeks of years, dating from the issuance of a command to rebuild Jerusalem. The command was issued by Artaxerxes in 457 B.C., and 69 weeks of years later (483 years), Jesus began His ministry (27 A.D.). He was to be "cut off" 3½ years later in 31 A.D.

The Timing of the Second Coming

If the Bible contains two such specific prophecies concerning the season of the Lord's First Coming, I think it is only logical to assume that there must be prophecies which narrow down the season of His Second Coming, particularly when you keep in mind the fact that He will return in wrath, necessitating God's warning.

I want to show you three such prophecies which link Jewish historical events to the return of Jesus. All three point to the period in which we are living. I'm going to start with the broadest and most general and conclude with the most specific.

Hosea's Word from the Lord

The first is found in Hosea 5 and 6. Here's the whole passage as it appears in the New American Standard Version:

> I will go away and return to My place
> Until they acknowledge their guilt and seek
>   my face;

In their affliction they will earnestly seek Me.
"Come let us return to the Lord.
For He has torn us but He will heal us;
He has wounded us but He will bandage us,
He will revive us after two days;
He will raise us up on the third day
That we may live before Him."

— Hosea 5:15-6:2

To summarize this passage, Hosea says a time will come when the Lord will return to His place — that is, Heaven. The Lord will remain there until "they" — the Jewish people confess their guilt and seek His face. We know from other Old Testament passages (for example, Zechariah 12:10) that the Jews will not turn to the Lord until the end of the Tribulation. They will have to have their hardened hearts pounded by the wrath of Man, Satan and God before they will repent.

The next clause affirms that the repentance will occur during the Tribulation. Hosea says the Jews will cry out to God "in their affliction" at a time when they have been "torn" and "wounded." Then the Lord will bind them up and revive them.

When will this take place? The passage gives the timing. It will occur "after two days." In 2 Peter 3:8 and Psalm 90:4 we are told that to the Lord, a thousand years is like a day. Is that the meaning here? I think so, because the next clause says that at the end of the two days, the Lord will "raise us up" to live before Him "on the third day." This appears to be a reference to the resurrection of Jewish believers that will take place at the end of the Tribulation (Daniel 12:1-2). Living before the Lord on the third day appears to be a reference to the 1,000-year reign of Jesus (Revelation 20:1-6).

So, Hosea is saying that the Jews, as a nation, will repent and accept Jesus as their Messiah at the end of a two-thousand-year period which will be followed by the millennial reign of Jesus. We are at the end of that 2,000-year period. We are living on borrowed time.

Jesus' Parable

The second timing prophecy is found in Matthew 24:32-36, in the middle of Jesus' Olivet Discourse. Have you ever noticed that prior to these verses everything He says in that speech is presented in matter-of-fact, one-two-three-form? He says this event will happen and then that event and then some other event. But when we get to verse 32, the Lord suddenly shifts gears and moves into mystery language. He suddenly inserts a parable:

> Now learn the parable from the fig tree: when its branch has already become tender and puts forth its leaves, you know that summer is near; even so you too, when you see all these things, recognize that He is near, right at the door. Truly I say to you, this generation will not pass away until all these things take place. — Matthew 24:32-34

Now why did the Lord shift to symbolic language in verse 32? Why did He interject this parable?

A lot of people have a mistaken idea about parables. They think Jesus used parables to make things simpler to understand. That was not always the case. Jesus sometimes used parables to make things harder to understand. He cloaked great insights in parables so that only those who have the Holy Spirit can understand (see Mark 4:10-12).

Accordingly, I believe Jesus shifted to the symbolic language of a parable at this point in His speech because He wanted to give believers a clue to the timing of His return. The clue is "the fig tree." This is one of several symbols of Israel that is used in Old Testament prophecy (see Hosea 9:10, Jeremiah 24:1-10 and Joel 1:7).

The Symbolism of the Fig Tree

But why the fig tree? Do you remember what had happened on the previous day? Jesus and His disciples were walking over the Mt. of Olives when Jesus suddenly stopped and put a curse on a barren fig tree. The tree withered (Matthew 21:18ff).

What was that all about? Jesus was using the fig tree as a symbol of Israel. Like the barren tree, Israel had no spiritual fruit. The Jews had rejected their Messiah. The curse on the tree and its withering was a symbolic prophecy of the wrath of God that would fall on the Jews.

Now, on the next day, Jesus says, "Remember the fig tree? Watch it. When it blooms again, all these things I've been talking about will take place."

For the past four hundred years prophetic scholars have pointed to this passage and have urged us to watch for the re-establishment of Israel. And for four hundred years most people, including Christians, have laughed and scoffed and ridiculed because they did not believe that the nation of Israel would ever exist again.

But the laughing stopped on May 14, 1948, when the independence of the state of Israel was proclaimed to the world. Israel, as prophesied, once more became a reality in the face of incredible odds. The rebirth of that nation is one of the surest signs that we are living on borrowed time.

The Meaning of a Generation

One note — when the nation of Israel was re-established in 1948, many people used the fig tree parable to draw an inappropriate conclusion. Since the Bible sometimes (but not always) identifies a generation as 40 years, many people jumped to the conclusion that the Lord had to come for His Church before the end of 1988.

The parable does not say the Lord will return within 40 years of Israel's rebirth. It says that the generation that sees the re-establishment of Israel is the generation that will see all the end-time events come to pass. "Generation" here is used generically, like we would use it in reference to the "Beat Generation" or the "Rock Generation." It simply refers to the people who will be living at that time.

I think the parable means that someone who was alive on May 14, 1948, will be alive when the Lord returns. That may be a person who was a six month old babe in 1948 and will be 70 years old when the Lord comes back.

The point is that the word "generation" does not tie the prophecy down to a fulfillment within a 40-year period. But it does narrow the period. And we are in that period. Again, we are living on borrowed time.

Jesus' Prophecy

The third prophecy that helps set the season of the Lord's return is the most specific of all. It is also the one that convinces me the most that we are definitely living in that season.

It is found in Luke's account of the Olivet Discourse (Luke 21:24):

> . . . they will fall by the edge of the sword and will be led captive into all the nations: and Jerusalem will be trampled under foot by the Gentiles until the times of the Gentiles be fulfilled"

In the first half of this prophecy, Jesus says that the Jews will be conquered and led captive among the nations. They were conquered in 70 A.D. by the Romans, and in the years that followed, they were dispersed over the face of the earth, just as Jesus prophesied.

Now, look at the second half of this prophecy. Jesus said Jerusalem will be trodden down by the Gentiles "until the times of the Gentiles are fulfilled." The Romans were the first Gentile nation to take Jerusalem following the pronouncement of the prophecy. They were followed by the Byzantines. The Byzantines were followed by the Arabs; the Arabs by the Crusaders; the Crusaders by the Mamelukes; the Mamelukes by the Turks; the Turks by the British; and the British by the Jordanians.

A Prophecy Fulfilled

Jerusalem was "trampled by the Gentiles" from 70 A.D. until 1967. On June 7, 1967, during the Six Day War, the old city of Jerusalem was conquered by the Israelis. The Jews regained control of their sacred City of David for the first time in 1,897 years.

On the day Jerusalem was retaken, the Jewish commandos rushed to the Wailing Wall to pray. As some shouted praises and other wept, Rabbi Shlomo Goren, the Chief Rabbi of the Israeli Army, came up to the wall in his army fatigues, blew a ram's horn and lifted his right hand, signaling for silence. He then said, "I proclaim to you the beginning of the Messianic Age."

The Orthodox Jews understand the significance of the season we are living in. They are watching for the appearance of the Messiah any moment. They will not be surprised by His coming. They will be surprised by the nail prints in His hands.

Overlap Periods

The Christian Age began with an overlap period. The Church was established in 31 A.D. on the Day of Pentecost. It wasn't until 40 years later that God set aside His Chosen People, the Jews, by allowing the Romans to conquer Jerusalem.

Since June of 1967 we have been in a similar overlap period. While God continues to work through His Church to spread the Gospel to all nations, He has once again started working through the Jewish people to accomplish His purposes in history. Just as the first overlap period ended with the removal of the Jews from their land, the second will end with the removal of the Church from the world.

The Age is drawing to a close. God is preparing to take the Church out of this world in the Rapture. When He does so, He will pick up where He left off with the Jews to accomplish all His purposes in history and to prepare the way for the reign of His Son.

Living in the Season   25

As you await the soon return of the Lord, what is your attitude toward this world? There's a gospel song by Albert Brumley that always challenges me to examine my attitude toward the world. The first verse goes as follows:

> This world is not my home,
> I'm just a passing through.
> My treasures are laid up
> Somewhere beyond the blue.
>
> The angels beckon me
> From heaven's open door,
> And I can't feel at home
> In this world anymore.

Do those words express your feeling about this world? What words would you use? Enthusiastic or uncomfortable? Enamored or alienated? Do you feel at home or do you feel like a stranger?

A Personal View

Let me ask your indulgence for a moment as I share my personal feeling about this world.

The word I would use is "hate." Yes, I hate this world. I hate it with a passion so strong and so intense that I find it difficult to express in words.

Now, let me hasten to clarify my feeling by stating that

I do not hate God's beautiful and marvelous creation.

I have been privileged to marvel over the majesty of the Alps. I have been awed by the rugged beauty of Alaska. I never cease to be amazed by the creative wonders of God in the great American Southwest. I have been blessed to see the incredible beauty of Cape Town, South Africa. And I have been overwhelmed time and time again by the stark and almost mystical barrenness of the Judean wilderness in Israel.

When I say that I "hate" this world, I'm not speaking of God's creation. I'm speaking, instead, of the evil world system that we live in.

Let me give you some examples of what I'm talking about:

- I hate a world where thousands of babies are murdered every day in their mother's wombs.

- I hate a world where young people in the prime of life have their lives destroyed by illicit drugs.

- I hate a world that coddles criminals and makes a mockery of justice.

- I hate a world that glorifies crime in its movies and television programs.

- I hate a world that applauds indecent and vulgar performers like Madonna.

- I hate a world where government tries to convert gambling from a vice to a virtue.

- I hate a world in which professional athletes are paid over a million dollars a year while hundreds of thousands sleep homeless in the streets every night.

- I hate a world where people judge and condemn one another on the basis of skin color.

- I hate a world that calls evil good by demanding that homosexuality be recognized as a legitimate, alternative lifestyle.

- I hate a world in which mothers are forced to work while their children grow up in impersonal day-care centers.

- I hate a world in which people die agonizing deaths from diseases like cancer and AIDS.

- I hate a world where families are torn apart by alcohol abuse.

- I hate a world where every night I see reports on the television news of child abuse, muggings, kidnapings, murders, terrorism, wars, and rumors of wars.

- I hate a world that uses the name of my God, Jesus, as a curse word.

I hope you understand now what I mean when I say, "I hate this world!"

Jesus' Viewpoint

But how I personally feel about this world is not important. The crucial point for you to consider is the biblical view. Let's look at it, and as we do so, compare the biblical view with your own.

Let's begin with the viewpoint that Jesus told us we should have. It is recorded in John 12:25 — "He who loves his life loses it; and he who hates his life in this world shall keep it to life eternal."

Those are strong words. They are the kind that cause us to wince and think, "Surely He didn't mean what He said." But the context indicates that Jesus meant exactly what He said. So, what about it? Do you hate your life in this world or do you love it?

The Viewpoint of the Apostles

The apostle Paul gave a very strong warning about getting comfortable with the world. In Romans 12:2 he wrote: "Do not be conformed to this world, but be transformed by the renewing of your mind." How do you measure up to this exhortation?

Are you conformed to the world? Have you adopted the world's way of dress? What about the world's way of speech or the world's love of money? Are your goals the goals of the world — power, success, fame, and riches?

The brother of Jesus expressed the matter in very pointed language. He said, "Do you not know that friendship with the world is hostility toward God? Therefore, whoever wishes to be a friend of the world makes himself an enemy of God" (James 4:4).

Are you a friend of the world? Are you comfortable with what the world has to offer in music, movies, television programs and best-selling books? Friendship with the world is hostility toward God!

In fact, James puts it even stronger than that, for at the beginning of the passage I previously quoted (James 4:4), he says that those who are friendly with the world are spiritual adulterers.

The apostle John makes the same point just as strongly in 1 John 2:15-16:

> Do not love the world, nor the things in the world. If anyone loves the world, the love of the Father is not in him. For all that is in the world, the lust of the flesh, and the lust of the eyes, and the boastful pride of life, is not from the Father, but is from the world.

There is no way to escape the sobering reality of these words. Do you love the world? If so, the love of the Father is not in you!

The Focus of Your Mind

Paul tells us how to guard against becoming comfortable with the world. In Colossians 3:2 he says, "Set your mind on the things above, not on the things that are on earth." In Philippians 4:8 he expresses the same admonition in these words:

> Finally, brethren, whatever is true, whatever is honorable, whatever is right, whatever is pure, whatever is lovely, whatever is of good repute, if there is any excellence and if anything worthy of praise, let your mind dwell on these things.

As these verses indicate, one of the keys to living a triumphant life in Christ — to living a joyous and victorious life in the midst of a world wallowing in despair — is to live with a conscious eternal perspective.

I have personally found this to be so important that I carry a reminder of it in my shirt pocket at all times. It is a small card that was sent to me in 1988 by the great prophetic preacher, Leonard Ravenhill. The card says, "Lord, keep me eternity conscious."

What does that mean? In the words of Peter, that means living as "aliens and strangers" in this world (1 Peter 2:11). Similarly, in the words of the writer of Hebrews, it means living as "strangers and exiles" on this earth (Hebrews 11:13). Paul put it this way: "Do not set your minds on earthly things, for our citizenship is in heaven" (Philippians 3:19-20).

The great Christian writer, C.S. Lewis, explained that to live with an eternal perspective means "living as commandos operating behind the enemy lines, preparing the way for the coming of the Commander-in-Chief."

What is Your Attitude?

Are you focused on this world? Are you attached to it, or do you have a sense of the fact that you are only passing through, heading for an eternal home?

    This life is transitory. This life is only a prelude to eternity. The song writer, Tillit S. Teddlie put it all in perspective when he wrote:

> Earth holds no treasures
> But perish with using,
> However precious they be;
> Yet there's a country
> To which I am going:
> Heaven holds all to me.
>
> Why should I long
> For the world with its sorrows,
> When in that home o'er the sea,
> Millions are singing
> The wonderful story?
> Heaven holds all to me.
>
> Heaven holds all to me,
> Brighter its glory will be;
> Joy without measure
> Will be my treasure:
> Heaven holds all to me.

    There is a more contemporary song that sums up the whole essence of what it means to live with an eternal perspective:

> Turn your eyes upon Jesus,
> Look full in His wonderful face,
> And the things of earth
> Will grow strangely dim
> In the light of His glory and grace.

Responding to the Season 26

The message of the soon coming of Jesus is like a two-edged sword. It cuts both ways. It is both good news and bad.

For those who have never accepted Jesus as their Lord and Savior, the news of His soon return is bad indeed. For them, Jesus will return as their "Holy Terror," for He is coming to pour out the incredible wrath of God upon those who have rejected God's grace and mercy.

This is the paradox of Jesus. He is both God's grace and wrath. He came the first time as a suffering lamb to die for the sins of Mankind. He is returning as a conquering lion to take retribution on those who have rejected His sacrifice.

A Closely Guarded Secret

The return of Jesus in wrath is one of the best kept secrets in Christendom. The Church has long proclaimed, as it should, the love that God expressed in Jesus. But the Church has neglected to teach that Jesus will return in wrath. It is not a pleasant message. Satan does not want it proclaimed. He has succeeded in cowering the Church into timidity. The result is that the world is ignorant of the coming wrath, as are most Christians.

Satan has convinced most people that God is a "Cosmic Teddy Bear," that He is a warm, cuddly figure who is full of only love. They imagine that when they stand before Him, He will put His arm around them and wink at their sins and ignore the fact that they never accepted the gift of love that He gave in His Son.

God is full of love. But God is also holy and righteous. He cannot countenance sin. Because of His love, He has provided Mankind with a sin covering — the blood of His Son, Jesus. Because of His righteousness, He must deal with those who reject that covering. He will do so when He sends His Son back to this earth.

The Biblical View of the Second Coming

The Bible says that Jesus is coming "to judge and make war" (Revelation 19:11).

The Bible says that the politicians of the world will get on their knees and cry out for the rocks and mountains to fall upon them, so fierce will be the wrath of Jesus (Revelation 6:15-17).

The Bible says that on the day of the Lord's return the blood of those who have sinned against God will be poured out like dust (Zephaniah 1:17).

The Bible says the Day of the Lord will be one of "trouble and distress, destruction and desolation, darkness and gloom," a day when sinners will stagger about like blind men (Zephaniah 1:15,17).

The Bible says that sinners will be thrown into "the great wine press of the wrath of God" — and their very life will be squeezed out of them (Revelation 14:9).

The Bible says, "The Lord is good, a stronghold in the day of trouble and He knows those who take refuge in Him." But the same passage also says, "A jealous and avenging God is the Lord, the Lord is avenging and wrathful. The Lord takes vengeance on His adversaries, and He reserves wrath for His enemies. The Lord is slow to anger and great in power, and the Lord will by no means leave the guilty unpunished" (Zephaniah 1:7, 2-3).

The Message for Unbelievers

God does not wish that any should perish (2 Peter 3:9), but God demands repentance (Joel 2:12-13) and the acceptance of the grace that He has expressed through Jesus Christ (Romans 10:9).

If you have never accepted Jesus as your Lord and Savior, you need to get on your knees before God, confess your sins, and ask Jesus to come into your heart that you might be born again and have the hope of eternal life (John 3:3,16). If you do this, then you need to seek out a fellowship of believers where you can witness your faith in Jesus through baptism and where you can be discipled in the Lord.

The message of the season for the sinner is "flee from the wrath that is to come" by fleeing into the loving arms of Jesus Christ — *now!*

The Message for Believers

There is also a message in the Second Coming of Jesus for those of us who have accepted Him and have been born again. God is calling us to commitment and holiness.

With regard to commitment, the Church today is full of Christians who have accepted Jesus as Savior but have never accepted Him as Lord. The reason is simple. To accept Him as Savior is free. His saving grace is a gift of God.

But to accept Him as Lord requires a price. It means putting your hand to the plow and never looking back (Luke 9:62). It means becoming a disciple of the Lord and not just a cheerleader. It means making Jesus the Lord of everything in your life — the books you read, the movies you see, the music you listen to, the TV programs you watch, the hobbies you spend time on, the thoughts you cultivate, and the job you work at.

The Call to Holiness

This Lordship of Jesus is tied inextricably to the second thing God is calling believers to. He is calling us to holiness. Jesus is coming for His Bride, the Church. He wants a Bride that is clean and pure — one that is in the world but not of the world; one that is the salt of the earth, standing for righteousness.

The Church today is full of secular Christians whose Christianity is a cultural thing rather than a radical lifestyle separated from the world. Too many Christians are walking with one foot in the Church and the other in the country club. The only way the world even knows that most of them are Christians is the fact that they go to church on Sunday mornings. The rest of the week they live like pagans — cheating on their wives, cheating their business partners, cheating their customers, and cheating the government on their income tax.

God is calling Christians to stop playing church. He wants us to stop filling our lives with garbage. He wants to fill us, instead, with His Spirit.

The Biblical Call to Believers

The Bible says to believers: "The night is almost gone and the day is at hand. Let us therefore lay aside the deeds of darkness and put on the armor of light. Let us behave properly as in the day, not in carousing and drunkenness, not in sexual promiscuity and sensuality, not in strife and jealousy. But put on the Lord Jesus Christ and make no provision for the flesh in regard to lusts" (Romans 13:12-14).

The Bible says that believers are "to deny ungodliness and worldly desires and to live sensibly, righteously and godly in the present age" as they await the return of the Lord (Titus 2:12).

The Bible says to believers who are awaiting Christ:

"Gird your minds for action, keep sober in spirit, fix your hope completely on the grace to be brought to you at the revelation of Jesus Christ. As obedient children, do not be conformed to the former lusts which were yours in your ignorance, but like the Holy One who called you, be holy yourselves also in all your behavior; because it is written, 'You shall be holy, for I am holy'" (1 Peter 1:13-15).

Believer, have you accepted Jesus as Lord? Have you committed your life to holiness? All of it? Have you presented your body as a living sacrifice, holy and acceptable to God? (Romans 12:1) If not, you too need to repent. You need to call upon God to fill you with His Spirit so that Jesus can be the Lord of all your life (Luke 11:13).

Good News!

I want to close with some incredibly good news. It is the news that for those who put their trust in Jesus as the Christ, the Anointed One of God, the return of Jesus will be a blessed day, not a day of fear and darkness and terror.

For to those of us who have been born again, Jesus is our "Blessed Hope" (Titus 2:13), for He is returning "to deliver us from the wrath that is to come" (1 Thessalonians 1:10).

— Hallelujah and Maranatha! —

Postscript
1994

Looking Back
Over Seven Years   27

In the seven years since this book was first published, God has continued to shape both me and the ministry He has entrusted to me. In the process, I have come to appreciate even more the Lord's incredible faithfulness, His overwhelming sovereignty, His infinite love, and His awesome power. And through my growing appreciation of these qualities, I have come to trust the Lord more than ever before.

The Lord's Faithfulness

During the early years of the ministry, as I took my first baby steps of faith, I was constantly astounded by the miracles that God performed to meet the needs of the ministry. For a while it seemed like I experienced a "miracle a day." And each time, I found that I could hardly wait for an opportunity to share with others how exciting — even thrilling — the faith walk could be.

During the last seven years, as the ministry has stabilized and matured and the outreach has settled into a daily routine, the constant excitement of those early years has faded. It has been like the transition from the passionate love of romance to the steady, rock-solid and calm love that characterizes a mature marriage.

The enthrallment with God's dramatic responses to special needs has been replaced by a sense of wonderment over His quiet, daily faithfulness in supplying the basic needs of the ministry. I have come to the point where I can see and appreciate the Lord's provision in the mundane things of life, and not just the spectacular.

I know now what it means to sense the Lord's presence, as Elijah did, in a "gentle breeze" as opposed to a gale wind, a mighty earthquake or a roaring fire (1 Kings 19:11-13).

A Touching Testimony

This increasing awareness of God's faithfulness in small things was driven home to me in a very dramatic way by a testimony I was blessed to hear a few years ago. The testimony was given by James Watts who served as President Reagan's Secretary of the Interior.

He told how he had grown up going to church and thought he was a good Christian, but had never come to know the Lord. He explained that the churches he had attended had been more concerned about liturgy than relationships. In fact, he said that he had never experienced a single altar call in all his years of church attendance.

He was almost 40 years old when that experience came. The occasion was an invitation to attend a Full Gospel Businessmen's meeting. "I wouldn't have gone, if I had known what the meeting was all about," he said. But he didn't, so he went. The meeting ended with an altar call, and he responded and met the Lord personally for the first time.

Understandably, he was filled with excitement over what he had experienced. He began to read the Word day and night. In the process he became even more intimately acquainted with a personal, powerful and caring God. His excitement over the Lord increased.

He finally felt compelled to leave his dead church. He ended up at a church that featured personal testimonies on Sunday evenings. "I loved those times," said Watts. "I could hardly wait for each Sunday evening to arrive so that I could share some spectacular thing that I had experienced in the Lord the week before."

He told how he would rush forward to share the story of how he had witnessed to a drunk bum on the street, how that man had responded by accepting the Lord, and how he had been instantly, miraculously, delivered from alcoholism.

"Then," said Watts, "when I would finish with my dramatic story, Sister Johnson would get up and simply say, 'Twenty years ago I accepted the Lord, and I praise His name, for He has kept me for 20 years.'" Watts said he would just hang his head in shame for Sister Johnson because she had no better testimony than that.

"The next week I would rush forward again," said Watts, "to share the story of a dramatic healing of someone I had prayed for on their death bed. And again, Sister Johnson would follow by simply thanking the Lord for 'keeping her' for 20 years. Again, I was embarrassed for the poor lady."

Then, Watts paused for a few moments and stared at the podium. When he looked back up at the audience, there were tears in his eyes. He concluded with these words:

Folks, all that happened 20 years ago when I first encountered the Lord. Since that time I have grown a lot spiritually. And as I stand before you tonight I want to say that the greatest miracle God has performed in my life since then is that He has "kept me" for the past 20 years!

Sister Johnson had been right all along, but it took mature spiritual eyes to see her point and to understand it.

Look around you and stand amazed at the steady, quiet, unobtrusive ways in which the Lord daily ministers to your needs — and then thank Him with a grateful heart.

The Sovereignty of God

A second quality of the Lord's nature that has been impressed upon me repeatedly in recent years is His sovereignty. He is in control of all things whether we recognize it or not, and we cannot serve Him effectively unless we are yielded to His sovereign control. When we try to help Him

out, as did Abraham when he sired Ishmael, we always end
up in trouble.

This is a particularly difficult lesson to learn when you
have a message that is as urgent as the one Lamb & Lion
Ministries has been raised up to proclaim; namely, "Jesus is
coming soon!" You naturally want to trumpet that message to
as many people as possible as quickly as possible, and the
tendency is to end up running ahead of the Lord.

A Costly Lesson

My most jolting experience in this regard occurred when
I decided that we needed to go all out to develop an outreach
to Hispanics.

The idea made so much sense to me. After all, our location in the area of Dallas, Texas put us right on the doorstep
of several hundred million Spanish-speaking people in
Central and South America.

At great expense we hired an evangelist from Mexico and
set him up to broadcast and publish our message in Spanish.
But over the next year, everything that could go wrong
seemed to do exactly that. Every effort we made with this
new outreach seemed to end in utter frustration.

Meanwhile, every other thing we were doing in the
ministry was being greatly blessed. Consequently, it became
painfully apparent that it simply was not the Lord's will for
Lamb & Lion to reach out to Hispanic peoples, regardless of
how logical it might appear on the surface. We decided to
close the outreach down completely.

An Open Door

Before we could get the Hispanic outreach shut down, the
Lord dramatically opened a new door of opportunity for us to
minister in Eastern Europe!

I received a call from a Polish exile living in Toronto. He
explained that he had a ministry of raising support for Polish
churches. He said he had been driving across the U.S. visiting
churches and had stopped at one in Fort Wayne, Indiana

where I had recently held a meeting.

The pastor had given him a set of tapes containing the sermons I had presented on "The Signs of the Times." He had listened to them, and he was excited by the message about the Lord's soon return. "I want that message proclaimed throughout Poland," he said. "Will you come?"

I accepted his invitation, and it has since resulted in several trips to Poland, Belarus, and Russia. We have conducted prophecy conferences in many cities throughout the former Soviet empire, including major metropolitan areas like Warsaw, Minsk, Moscow, and St. Petersburg.

Other trips to various Eastern European capitals are planned. And our books on prophecy have been translated and published in Russian and Polish, with other foreign editions, like Hungarian, in the works.

I now know how the Apostle Paul felt when he ardently desired to share the Gospel with his fellow Jews, and the Lord said, "No, you are going to preach to the Gentiles." Then, when he went forth to the Gentile nations, he desired to go to Asia, but "was forbidden by the Holy Spirit" to do so (Acts 16:6). Instead, he was given a vision in which a man called out to him saying, "Come over to Macedonia and help us" (Acts 16:9).

God is sovereign. He has His own plans, His own methods, and His own time table. Even when the message is urgent and burning on your heart, I have learned that you must wait on the Lord to call and direct.

The Love of God

Zacharias, the father of John the Baptist, prophesied about the birth of Jesus, referring to His coming as an expression of "the tender mercy of our God" (Luke 1:78). What a beautiful expression — and how true it is, not only in the gift of His precious Son, but in the gifts of love which He ministers to us daily.

When I wrote the first edition of this book, I had just emerged from several years of experiencing the Lord's chastisement. The Word says that "the Lord disciplines those whom He loves" (Hebrews 12:5-7), and I had concluded that He loved me very much! He had clobbered me with several two-by-fours to get my attention, and I was still reeling from the experiences.

But, as painful as these experiences were, I was thankful for them, for the Lord used them to save me from myself. As I look back on them now, I can identify with the psalmist who wrote, "Before I was afflicted, I went astray, but now I keep Your word . . . It is good for me that I was afflicted, that I may learn Your statutes" (Psalm 119:67,71).

In the intervening years, I have experienced the love of the Lord beyond adequate words to express. This love has been manifested in many ways, but primarily through relationships. I have learned that as I take my eyes off myself and focus on the Lord, He opens my life to rich relationships with those around me because I am no longer relating to them on a selfish basis of what they can do for me.

A Special Support Group

As I have moved into the center of God's will for my life, He has surrounded me with loving people who constantly encourage me — my family, my staff members, the ministry's trustees, and a remarkable group of people called Prophecy Partners.

This latter group was founded in the latter part of 1986 as we prepared the ministry for my first Sabbatical. The trustees and staff had been concerned about how we could make up for the shortfall in income that would occur in 1987 when I would not be holding any meetings or seminars. It was a legitimate concern, so we lifted it up to the Lord in prayer.

His response was to give us the idea of establishing a Prophecy Partner Program. We issued an appeal for people to make a monthly financial commitment to the ministry for one year. We asked them to aim at a goal of one dollar a day or $30 per month, with a minimum commitment of $15 per month. In return, we promised to send them a special report each month on the ministry's activities, together with a teaching tape or publication.

The Lord anointed the appeal, and we began that Sabbatical year with approximately 100 new and enthusiastic Prophecy Partners. Today, seven years later, we are approaching 1,000 Prophecy Partners!

What a blessing they are to me and the ministry as they pray for us, encourage us, and support us financially. I consider each one of them to be a very special and unique expression of God's love for me and Lamb & Lion Ministries.

Blessings beyond Measure

The Lord has showered me with His love in many other ways, particularly through some memorable experiences — one of which I would like to share with you.

In 1988 I was invited by the International Christian Embassy in Jerusalem to come to Israel at my own expense to speak at a celebration of the nation's 40th anniversary of its independence. The gracious invitation alone was an overwhelming expression of the Lord's love. But He added blessing on top of blessing.

When I shared the invitation with a Jewish friend who owned a travel agency, he responded by giving me a first class round trip ticket to Tel Aviv! I was absolutely astonished, particularly since I had never flown first class anywhere, much less half way around the world. Later, the same man called and informed me that he had arranged for me to stay at Jerusalem's newest five-star hotel for half price.

The conference proved to be a blessed event. I was given the opportunity to meet Christian leaders from all over the world, as well as many Israeli political and religious leaders.

A Special Person

One meeting the Lord arranged that was particularly significant to me was the opportunity to talk briefly with Rabbi Shlomo Goren. He had been the chief rabbi of the

Israeli army when it reconquered the city of Jerusalem in 1967. In that capacity he had led the first prayer at the Wailing Wall. Now, he was the Chief Ashkenazi Rabbi of the whole nation.

The occasion for our meeting came because he arrived late at the conference on the morning he was to speak. He was so late, in fact, that the conference organizers gave up on him and asked the next speaker on the program to move up and fill his place. That speaker had hardly started when the rabbi suddenly appeared.

For some reason known only to the Lord, the conference director asked me to step into the hallway and keep the rabbi company while he waited to speak. I was awed and dumbstruck. Here was a living legend in front of me. What was I to say? I was too anxious at the moment to even appreciate the blessing of the opportunity.

Somehow or other we finally got a conversation going, and the part I remember most vividly was when I asked what he intended to speak about.

He looked at me with a twinkle in his eye and said, "I intend to shock this assembly of Christians with what I have prepared."

"Oh?" I responded. "How's that?"

"Well," he said, pausing for dramatic effect, "I plan to tell you people why I believe the Messiah is returning soon."

My heart leaped with joy. In fact, I could hardly contain myself. "We might not be as shocked as you think," I replied. And then I added a thought that I could hardly believe I actually expressed in words: "As a matter of fact, you may be the one who turns out to be shocked the most because I believe the Messiah is going to have nail prints in His hands."

His reply caught me completely off-guard. He looked me right in the eye and said, "I might not be as shocked as you think."

I didn't get a chance to follow up on that incredible reply, because at that moment he was called to speak.

A Special Meal

The final blessing of the conference came on the last evening. Because I was one of the featured speakers, I was informed that I had been invited to be a guest at a state banquet to be held in the Chagall Room of the Knesset (the parliament building of Israel). The featured speaker was Yitzak Rabin, who at that time was the Defense Minister of Israel.

The blessing of that glorious evening was almost more than I could bear. I just couldn't believe I was sitting there in that historic room celebrating with Jewish leaders the miracle of the rebirth of Israel.

When I got back to my room that night, I could not go to sleep. My soul was just too full of blessings that I needed to savor. I finally got out of bed, turned on the light, and opened my Bible to do some reading. When I looked at the page where the Bible had fallen open, my eyes filled with tears, and I began to praise God.

The passage was from the Song of Solomon, chapter 2, verse 4: "He has brought me to his banquet hall, and His banner over me is love."

The Power of God

In addition to God's faithfulness, sovereignty and love, He has continued to impress me with His power. What awesome events He has wrought since 1987! Most are hard to believe even now.

To put it mildly, the Lord has been shaking the nations. He is clearly orchestrating all the evil of Man toward the triumph of His Son — a triumph that will occur very soon when Jesus returns to claim the dominion over the world which He won on the Cross.

Who could have dreamed seven years ago that within a few years the Berlin Wall would come down, Eastern Europe would be liberated, the Soviet Union would collapse, Germany would be reunified, and the resurgence of Islam would propel 500,000 American troops into the Middle East? And who would have dared to predict that Israel would sign a treaty with the PLO that would go so far as to give Yasser Arafat Israeli territory?

The rapidity of these events and their radical nature is breathtaking, to say the least. They clearly illustrate how unstable the world is. They underscore the possibility of the impossible. They reveal that Man is not in control.

The End-Time Scenario

As I look back on these events, I see them clearly pointing to an accelerated timetable for the Lord's return. They are speeding the fulfillment of prophecies which the Bible says will characterize the end-times.

For example, the prophet Daniel said that Europe would come back together in the end-times to form a revived Roman Empire, out of which the Antichrist would arise (Daniel 7). Ezekiel prophesied that Israel would be living in peace when the land is invaded by Russia (Ezekiel 38). And Paul stated that at a time when the world would be shouting, "Peace and safety!" destruction would come "suddenly" (1 Thessalonians 5:3).

All the pieces of this end-time scenario are coming into place. Due to the disintegration of the Soviet empire, the world is chanting, "Peace and safety!" Europe is uniting. Israel and the Arabs are talking peace. Russia is consumed with anti-Semitism and is destabilized and desperate.

The Missing Piece of the Puzzle

The one thing that does not fit the Bible's end-time picture is the super power status of the United States. America is nowhere mentioned specifically in Bible prophecy. Most likely this is because we will not be a major player.

How could that be? At the moment it does not seem possible. But look once more at what has happened in the past seven years, and then hold your breath. America could be here today dominating the world, and be gone tomorrow, reduced to a poverty-stricken, third-world status.

On the surface we are rich and powerful. On the surface, we hold the world in our hands.

But beneath the veneer is a moral rot that is eating away the soul of the nation. America is in revolt against God. We are consumed in pride and materialism. We are living it up, compiling the greatest debt in history. And in the process, we are constructing a house of cards that could collapse any moment.

The Russian Example

The Lord impressed His impending judgment of this nation on my heart when I went to Russia the first time in the early 1990s. "David," He said, "hold Russia up to America as a mirror to show Americans what I can do overnight to a great world power."

What did I see? A dispirited people standing in bread lines. An economy in shambles. A government in gridlock. A society racked with immorality and violence. A currency that was worthless. It was almost impossible to believe that this nation had been the strongest military power in the world only two years before.

And then the Lord reminded me of a principle in His Word: "To those to whom much is given, much is expected" (Luke 12:48). And with those words I realized that the judgment of God upon America would be far worse than what He had placed upon Russia.

Think of it — we have no excuse before the Lord. We are a people saturated with Bibles, churches, ministries, Christian radio and television stations, Christian publishing houses, Christian music producers, and Christian schools. The Russians had none of these spiritual blessings.

Their rebellion against God pales compared to ours. Our revolt against the Lord continues to intensify domestically, while internationally, we continue to serve as the moral polluter of planet earth through our export of violent and immoral movies, videos and books.

God will not be mocked. America's day of reckoning is on the horizon. And when America falls, the world will be on the threshold of the Tribulation.

Reasons for Rejoicing

The only way I can keep a joyful heart in the midst of such ominous world developments is to constantly remind myself of two things.

The first is that God is in control. Psalm 2 says that while all the political leaders of the world conspire against the Lord, His Word, and His Son, He "sits in the heavens and laughs" — not because He does not care, but because He has it all under control!

The second reason I can rejoice is because all these events clearly point to the fact that we are in the end times, right on the threshold of the Tribulation. And since I believe the Bible teaches that Jesus is going to return for His Church before the Tribulation begins, I am expecting the Lord to appear any moment.

I can rejoice in that imminent prospect because I have been washed in the blood of Jesus, I've been born again, and I'm empowered with the Lord's Spirit. My sins have been forgiven and forgotten. I have been sealed for eternal life with God, and the return of Jesus is therefore my "Blessed Hope" (Titus 2:3).

A Plea

Is Jesus your hope? The Bible says that every person is under either the grace of God or the wrath of God (John 3:36). There is no in-between. There is no second chance after death. What you do about Jesus now will determine your eternal destiny.

God does not wish that any should perish (2 Peter 3:9). That's why He sent His Son to die for our sins. He has provided all that we need in Jesus to be reconciled to Him. If you have never received Jesus as your Savior, I pray you will do so now by repenting of your sins and asking Jesus to become the Lord of your life.

Salvation is a gift of God's grace. There is nothing you can do to earn it. But you must reach out in faith and receive the gift.

If you will do that, your life will take on new meaning now, your soul will be filled with hope, and the return of Jesus will be your "Blessed Hope" and not your "Holy Terror."

I pray You will decide for life and hope by choosing Jesus.

Epilogue
2015

Celebrating Milestones   28

All of us have milestones in our lives. I'm speaking of significant dates that mark life-changing experiences. Most are positive in nature, like a birthday, a marriage, or the birth of a child. Some are tragic, like the date of a crippling accident or a diagnosis of cancer or the death of a family member.

I have two dear friends whose most important milestones each year are the dates of their salvation experiences. One lived homeless on the streets for 20 years. The other had lived in the fast lane, making big bucks as a stock broker. But he lost it all in the 1987 stock market crash, and in the dark, depressed days that followed, he came to the end of himself and cried out to the Lord, experiencing a Road to Damascus conversion.

The Most Important Milestone

Actually, for all of us who are believers, the day of our salvation should be the most significant milestone of our lives.

For some, that day was a dramatic breakthrough that left them radically changed. But for many of us who were born and raised in a Christian family — like myself — it is hard to remember just when we placed our faith in Jesus because it was a part of our way of life as far back as we can remember. About all we can do is point to the date of our baptism.

A Milestone for Lamb & Lion

2015 is a milestone year for Lamb & Lion Ministries. It marks the 35th anniversary of our founding on April 1, 1980.

It's hard to believe that it has been 28 years since I wrote this book, and 21 years since I revised it for a second edition. That means that more than half the 35 years of the ministry's existence has passed during the intervening time.

As I explained in the preface, I wrote this book back in 1987 during a Sabbatical year in which I stayed at home and focused on study, writing and doing radio broadcasts. I gave up holding meetings at churches, even though that had been the ministry's major source of income up to that time.

It was a great step of faith on the part of our Board of Trustees, who mandated the Sabbatical year of rest for me. God greatly blessed their faith by providing all our financial needs.

The Lord also made it the most productive year of my life as I produced a 12 hour verse-by-verse audio commentary on the book of Revelation, put together the *Christ in Prophecy Study Guide*, produced a video about Israel in Bible prophecy, and published the first edition of this book. Whew! I get tired today just thinking about it!

God's Blessings

In 1987 we had three staff members in addition to me, and our annual budget was $337,000. Today (2015) we have 17 staff members and an annual budget of $2.9 million. We launched our Prophecy Partner program in 1987 to help sustain us during my Sabbatical year. By 1994 when I produced the first revision of this book, we had a little over 900 Partners. Today we have over 2,500 and are praying to secure 3,000 as soon as possible.

In 1987 we were broadcasting our radio program over about 15 to 20 regional stations. Today, we are airing our TV program over eight national Christian networks which have access to more than 110 million homes in America.

Needless to say, the Lord has blessed us beyond anything I could ever have imagined in 1980 when I stepped out in faith, gave up my academic career and established Lamb & Lion Ministries.

Key Celebrations

The year 2000 was a very significant one to me in many ways. It marked the 20th anniversary of the ministry. It was also the 50th anniversary of my baptism at age 12, back in 1950. And it was the 40th anniversary of my marriage.

In 2005 we celebrated the ministry's 25th anniversary with a special banquet attended by almost 500 people. Our featured speaker was my Bible prophecy mentor, Tim LaHaye, the author of the best-selling "Left Behind" novels. The theme of the banquet was "A Celebration of God's Faithfulness."

In 2010 we celebrated our 30th anniversary with another banquet that featured Ed Hindson as our special speaker. Ed is a member of the faculty at Liberty University. He is a renowned author of books about Bible prophecy, and he is one of America's most dynamic speakers concerning the truths of God's Prophetic Word.

As we enter this 35th year of the ministry, we are looking forward to another celebration that will feature a presentation by Robert Jeffress, the Pastor of First Baptist Church in Dallas.

A Regret

In the midst of all these celebrations, I have always had a major regret. That, of course, is the fact that when the Lord called me into His service, I ran in selfishness instead of yielding in joy. In the process, I threw away 20 years when I could have been serving the Lord in full-time ministry.

Thus, instead of celebrating the 35th anniversary of Lamb & Lion in 2015, I could be rejoicing over the ministry's 55th year.

But I do rejoice over the fact that when I ran, the Lord did not give up on me. He did not wash His hands of me.

Instead, he pursued me in His loving-kindness, and when I reached the point where I was so low that the only way I could look was up, He was there, ready to forgive and forget and move on with the plans He had for me.

Looking to the Future

As I look to the future, I will be yearning every moment for the greatest milestone of all — the return of Jesus to reign in glory and majesty with a rod of iron from Mount Zion in Jerusalem. I am ready for the world to be flooded with peace, righteousness and justice, as the waters cover the seas.

It is my earnest prayer that none of us at Lamb & Lion will be around to celebrate the ministry's 40th anniversary in 2020 because I hope the Rapture of the Church will occur before that time.

Maranatha!

Experiencing the
Impact of Technology　　　29

When I established Lamb & Lion Ministries in 1980, the Internet as we know it today did not exist. As a result, it was extremely difficult to become known. What a difference the Internet has made! Today, if you have anything worthwhile to say, you can become known overnight — both nationally and internationally.

But not so in 1980. I labored for 10 years trying to establish a name for the ministry, and even then, its impact was confined to a small group of churches.

I first heard about the Internet in 1995 when one of the ministry's trustees called and told me about it. He urged me to inform myself about it immediately and to get the ministry connected to it.

Discovering the Internet

And so, in response to his plea, one of my staff members and I signed up to attend an all-day seminar at a local Holiday Inn. When that day ended, I was mesmerized by what I had learned. I had discovered that for a small monthly fee, I could sit down at my computer and send instant messages called "email" to persons all across America and around the world! Further, I could create something called a "website" where I could store information about the ministry and where I could archive articles about Bible prophecy — and that website could be accessed by people all over the world!

At that time there were 16 million Internet users. Today that number has increased exponentially to 2.8 billion! The Internet has proved to be an electronic marvel that has tied our world together more closely than ever before, making it possible to communicate the Gospel to more people than anyone had ever dreamed would be possible.

For several years we used our website primarily to advertise our ministry and to provide articles on all aspects of Bible prophecy. It was mainly a research site. But I wanted it to become an interactive site where people could exchange opinions and ask questions. I also wanted it to be a site that was daily proclaiming Jesus as the only hope for this world.

Calling a Web Minister

I realized I did not have the time or expertise to develop such a site. So, in 2007 I put an advertisement in our magazine for a webmaster. I soon received a call from a fellow named Nathan Jones who was serving on the IT staff of one of our nation's largest churches.

Nathan explained to me that most webmasters working at churches were highly frustrated because their pastors had no vision for using the Internet to reach the world for Jesus. Instead, they were only interested in a website that provided basic information about the church: its staff, programs and worship times — and a map showing how to find the church.

As I talked with Nathan, I realized the Lord had led me to a very special person. He was an expert in web design, he had a vision for using the Internet to proclaim the Gospel and he had an in-depth knowledge of Bible prophecy. I was astounded.

Nathan joined our staff, and since that time, he has developed **www.lamblion.com** into one of the most useful Bible prophecy websites that can be found anywhere on the Internet. He spends eight hours a day answering questions and exchanging arguments with Atheists, advocates of false religions, and members of cults.

The Lamb & Lion Website

Today the Lamb & Lion website continues to be a repository of hundreds of articles about every aspect of Bible prophecy — all of which can be easily accessed through the use of the site's high speed search engine.

Additionally, the site provides many videos that can be live streamed, including our TV programs. Copies of our magazine are also available for downloading, and there is a blog for the exchange of ideas.

Thoughts About Technology

Isn't technology wonderful? Yes it is. But at the same time it is daunting.

The same technology that has made it possible for us to generate electricity with nuclear power is the same technol ogy that has produced horrible weapons of mass destruction. Likewise, the Internet has provided us with a wonderful tool to reach millions of people all over the world with the Gospel. But that same Internet is a highway of pornography.

It reminds me of the early days of television back in the 1950s. The major networks provided a great variety of whole-some programs based on Judeo-Christian values. And television still provides an outlet for Christian programming. But the medium quickly lost its moral compass and began to belch out immoral, blasphemous and violent programs that are undermining the moral foundation of our nation.

Technology is morally neutral. It can be used for good or evil. As we are in the process of abandoning our nation's Christian heritage, we are ending up with powerful technology in the hands of moral pygmies.

Making the Transition to Television 30

For 22 years, from 1980 to 2002, we produced a daily 15 minute radio program called "Christ in Prophecy." I used the program to present a commentary on national and international events from a biblical perspective.

In the late 1990s, as the 20th Century came to an end, members of both the ministry's staff and its trustees began to urge me to consider developing a television program. I strongly resisted this suggestion for three years.

My resistance was based on two considerations. First, I knew that television was a bottomless pit of expenditures, and I did not want to end up spending time on TV begging for money. Second, I understood that there is a crucial difference in radio and television. With radio, the focus is on the message, but with TV the focus tends to shift from the message to the messenger, resulting in overblown egos. The financial challenge of TV was overwhelming to me, and the ego problems were something I wanted no part of.

A Key Decision

But after three years of constant urging, I finally decided the Lord was speaking to me through my staff members and trustees, and I made the major decision to give up radio and shift our media outreach to television. We could not do both.

The great expense of TV production and broadcasting prohibited any continuation of our radio program. And so, in September of 2002, we ended our radio program after a total of 5,810 broadcasts.

That decision really upset a lot of our radio listeners. We received protests from all over the nation. The most memorable was one that said: "I can't begin to put into words how upset I am about your decision to end your radio program. All I can think of to say is that I feel like my dog just died." I wasn't sure whether that was a compliment or not, but I took it as one.

Preparing for Television

Earlier in 1999 we had produced two TV pilot programs, and during that process, we had discovered that renting a production studio and crew would be too costly because it would not leave us with any funds to pay for broadcasting. It became clear that we would have to build our own television studio and purchase our own equipment. In short, we were looking at having to raise hundreds of thousands of dollars. Borrowing the money was not an option since our trustees did not believe in going into debt for anything.

It seemed like an impossible task, but I had already learned that with God, nothing is impossible (Luke 1:37). One of our trustees stepped forward and offered to provide us with a huge metal building at his cost. One of our Prophecy Partners supplied the $25,000 needed for the foundation.

We poured the foundation in 2000, photographed it, and then ran the photo in our magazine, announcing that we needed about $30,000 for the next step in the construction process.

A Financial Miracle

And then the Lord intervened with a miracle. I was invited to speak for four Wednesday nights in a row at one of America's largest churches — Southeast Christian Church in Louisville, Kentucky. This is a church whose sanctuary, together with all its balconies, will hold over 8,000 people. I was told that the Wednesday night services were strictly for teaching. There were to be no invitations at the end of my messages and there would be no offerings taken.

On the first Wednesday evening, the pastor, Bob Russell, came to me and apologized for the small crowd that he expected to be present. He explained that there were several major conflicting events going on in town and that we would probably have only 2,000 present, instead of their usual 4,000. I was astonished. I had never heard of a pastor apologizing for an audience of "only" 2,000! Well, as it turned out, there were 4,000 there that evening because we had a large radio listening audience in that area, and many people came from other churches.

The next week we had over 5,000 present. The third Wednesday night there were almost 7,000 in attendance. When I arrived for the fourth and final service, I told the pastor that the Lord had impressed upon my heart that we should offer an invitation and take up an offering. The pastor readily agreed to the invitation, but he was reluctant about the offering. He explained that no one would be expecting an offering and would not be prepared for one. He also explained that organizing one at the last moment would not be possible because it would take too many volunteers. He said the most he could do was to have the ushers stand at the exit doors with offering plates to take donations as people left.

We had 8,000 present that evening, and a host of people came forward in response to the invitation I offered at the end of my teaching. I flew home the next morning exhilarated and exhausted. I decided to take off the rest of the day and all day Friday to rest.

Friday afternoon I got a call from our Director of Finance. "Are you sitting down?" he asked. I said I was. "Good," he replied, "I just got a call from the church in Louisville. Guess what the offering for our ministry came to."

I thought for a moment and figured it probably came to a dollar a person, so I answered, "How about $8,000?"

"No," he replied. "How about $28,000?"

I was dumbfounded.

But that's not all the story. The next Monday morning we had a meeting with our building contractor. He presented us with a long list of all the costs for the next phase of our TV studio construction. When we got to the bottom of the list, we turned the page, and there at the top of page 2 was the total — exactly $28,000!

I was left with the distinct impression that it truly was God's will for us to proceed full steam ahead with the development of a TV program.

Finishing the TV Studio

Over the months that followed, the money for the studio and the equipment literally poured in faster than we could spend it. For the first time ever, the Lord was running ahead of us!

Meanwhile we discovered a TV station in another state that was going out of business. Our Director of Finance, George Collich, rented a large truck and headed to the city where the station was located. He returned the next day with a truck full of equipment that he had bought at one-tenth the original price, including a large news set he got for almost nothing — a set that would have cost $50,000 new.

Securing a Broadcast Network

We sent our pilot TV program to the largest network in our area — Daystar. I had been interviewed on that network several times by its founders, Marcus and Joni Lamb. It was a fledgling network at the time, but it was expanding rapidly. Little did we realize it was destined to become one of the largest Christian networks in the world.

We were informed that there were more than ten programs competing for the time slot that was available. We went to prayer and waited and waited. And then one day, about three months later, we received the news that our program had been accepted. We have been broadcasting on Daystar ever since.

Expanding to a Second Network

After broadcasting on Daystar for a year, we began praying for God to make it possible for us to start airing our program on the Inspiration Network. We prayed about this off and on for a year. Then, one weekend morning during my personal prayer time, the Lord impressed upon me that the time had come for the Lamb & Lion staff to pray earnestly and daily for the funds that would be needed to launch our program on the Inspiration Network.

I announced this to my staff the following Monday morning, and we began our intense prayer vigil. It did not last long. On the following Friday morning, immediately following our prayer session, I received a phone call from a man in Houston. He said he would like to see our program expanded to other networks, like the Inspiration Network. He asked how much that would cost. I told him it would cost about $150,000. He said he would send a check right away!

I sat there stunned. Finally, I got my wits about me and called for a staff meeting. I announced to them the amazing news, and they joined me in praising the Lord for answering our prayers. That's when it suddenly dawned on me that I had no idea whether or not the Inspiration Network even had a time slot available for our program.

I raced back to my office, called the Inspiration Network, and asked to speak to the person in charge of programming. I was connected to a vice president by the name of Tom Hohman. I introduced myself and then started explaining why I had called.

But before I could finish my first sentence, Mr. Hohman interrupted me and said, "Oh, I know who you are, and I am familiar with your program. Are you calling in response to my letter?"

"What letter?" I asked.

He then explained that he had sent me a letter two days before in which he invited us to place our program on his network!

That's what I call a "God-incidence" of confirmation. And if that was not enough, he went on to say, "My wife loves Bible prophecy, and she has been using your materials for the past three years to teach her Sunday School class." Isn't it amazing how God works?

The Challenge of Television

Television production and broadcast have proved to be every bit as expensive as I had thought they would be. But the Lord has faithfully supplied all our financial needs without my having to plead for money.

Just consider, for example, the cost of producing a single TV program as it compares to the production of a radio program. During our radio days, I used to go into our recording studio on Thursday morning and record all five programs for the next week in about three hours' time, operating all the equipment myself.

In contrast, one TV program requires hours of preparation and a crew of seven people to videotape it. We must have three camera operators, a person working the teleprompter, an audio engineer, a switcher and a director.

After the program is shot, it usually requires an average of 20 hours of editing, and while it is being edited, a staff member has to transcribe it and encode it for closed captions.

The Blessing of Television

The time, energy, effort and expenses are challenging, but the payback has been overwhelming in terms of viewer response. It has dwarfed the response we used to receive from radio listeners.

We have now been broadcasting our TV program, "Christ in Prophecy," for 12 years. It can currently be seen on eight national Christian networks, seven regional networks, and seven Internet websites. Through the broadcast networks we have access to 110 million homes in America. And through the Daystar and Church Channel satellites, our program can be viewed in every nation in the world. It is even broadcast by Daystar on cable in Israel!

Our Television Focus

While I was in the process of praying about switching from radio to television, the Lord began to impress a very important message on my heart. He indicated to me that I was to focus our TV programs on Bible prophecy and the message of the Lord's soon return. I was not to spend any more time, as I had done for years on the radio, presenting biblical commentaries on national and international events.

There was only one other area where I felt like the Lord was giving me a green light — and that was apologetics, or the defense of the fundamentals of the faith.

I have tried hard to keep the focus of our programs on prophecy and apologetics, but it has not been easy. I am constantly receiving requests from friends, staff members, trustees and the general public to interview interesting people who have nothing to say about prophecy or apologetics. It is often hard to say no because the people truly have a wonderful Christian witness to share. But I have tried to hold the line, and the Lord has blessed that decision.

Program Preparation

Another key to the success of our TV program is rooted in the preparation that is made for the videotaping of each program.

I literally spend hours on the scripts. Nothing is left to chance. If I am going to interview a person, I find out about that person's background, and I try to read any articles or books written by the person. If the program is going to feature a group discussion, I prepare in-depth questions and suggest major points that should be made. If I am going to do a biblical teaching on a particular subject, I write the script out in detail and deliver it with the aid of a teleprompter.

And, of course, all the shooting we do in Israel is carefully planned out in advance. However, in recent years we have stopped using cue cards during our Israel shoots. Instead, we carefully think through each scene, and then we shoot it with me speaking off the top of my head. This technique has given the programs a sense of spontaneity that makes them more vibrant and interesting. But what I actually say on camera is anything but spontaneous!

The reason I spend so much time preparing for each program is rooted in my experience of being interviewed on Christian TV programs during the 1980s and 1990s. I was always appalled at the lack of preparation. I would be ushered onto the set, and the host would turn to me and say, "What do you want to talk about?" That was the total extent of the preparation, and the programs produced in that manner came across as shoddy.

When representing the Lord God Almighty, we should always strive to do our very best.

Producing Video Programs 31

In addition to the launch of our TV program in the Fall of 2002, our studio and equipment enabled us to start producing video programs that can be used in learning and teaching Bible prophecy.

Our First Video Album

Up to that time, we had produced only one video album called "Israel in Bible Prophecy." We had shot it in 1987 in Israel, using an American director and an Israeli film crew. It had proved to be very costly, mainly because the Israeli crew kept arriving late to work. One day the excuse was car trouble, the next day it was equipment problems and the next day it was due to a member of the crew being ill. What we later discovered was that the crew was pulling a "slow-down" in order to get more days of work out of us!

In that video, I taught about seven prophecies that were being fulfilled in Israel during the 20th Century. The video proved to be very popular.

Thirteen years later in 2000 I decided to reshoot this video, using our own video crew. I also decided to change the format by taking our Financial Director's two sons with me — Trey and Preston Collich — and having them ask me questions as we visited prophetic sites. At that time Trey was 16 years old and Preston was 14.

The shoot took about a week, and on the last day, we were shooting in an orchard. I told the director that I was going to pull a surprise on the boys and for him to keep the cameras rolling throughout the surprise.

I positioned myself next to one of the trees in the orchard and then motioned for the boys to enter the scene. They walked up to me, and Preston asked, "Dr. Reagan, how are they able to grow trees like these in what appears to be a desert?"

I exploded in response. I yelled, "Why do you keep asking me all these dumb questions? You are driving me nuts!"

Poor Preston nearly had a heart attack. But after he realized I was only kidding, we all had a good laugh, and we needed it after all the hard work we had done.

Continuing to Shoot in Israel

Once we acquired our own video staff and equipment, we started making regular trips to Israel to shoot both TV programs and video albums. I have many wonderful memories from those trips. One of the funniest was the time I waded out into the Jordan River to film a scene. We had to shoot the scene over and over several times to get it right. And all the while, I was slowing sinking deeper and deeper into the muddy bottom. When we finally got the scene right, I could not move! I was stuck in mud up to the mid-calves of my legs. They had to find a rope and tie it around me in order to pull me out.

Doing location shooting can drive you crazy in short order. I remember when we were doing extensive shooting inside the Old City of Jerusalem. It seemed like every time we would get a scene set up, a Muslim Imam would start his call to prayer, a ceremony that takes at least 15 minutes (but seems like an hour!). The prayers are broadcast over loud speaker systems, so all filming had to be suspended. When the prayer was finally over, the sun had moved, and we had to move the camera and all the equipment to a new spot to get the best shot.

And then there were the street urchins who would come

and stand directly in front of the camera and refuse to move unless we gave them a dollar. And once we gave in to their demands, the word would spread like wildfire, and other urchins would come running to collect their dollars.

But all the headaches of location shooting paid off with the production of many fascinating TV programs and video albums:

A Pilgrimage to the Holy Land — A tour of the most important sites related to the life of Christ and end time prophecies.

Jerusalem Through Spiritual Eyes — Provides a walk down the Via Dolorosa, a survey of the gates of the Old City and the tombs of Jerusalem, and a close-up look at the Garden Tomb where Jesus may have been buried.

The Galilee of Jesus — Gives a sweeping overview of the ministry of Jesus in the Galilee. Focuses on His life in Nazareth, His miracles in the Galilee, and the site of His transfiguration.

Profiles in Righteousness — Presents the stories of three biblical persons who were considered righteous in the eyes of God: King David of Israel, the prophet Elijah, and the Roman soldier Cornelius.

The Mountains of Jerusalem — Focuses on the four mountains of Jerusalem: the Mount of Olives, the Temple Mount, Mount Zion and Mount Herzl. The viewer is given a tour of each mountain and is shown the sites related to Jesus and to His Second Coming.

Insights from Jerusalem — Contains three programs. One is about the prophetic significance of the Eastern Gate. The second tells the remarkable story of Eliezer Ben Yehuda, the man who revived the Hebrew language from the dead. The third presents a fascinating walk through the Old City of Jerusalem.

Sermons from the Holy Land — Excerpts from nine sermons preached at their related sites in Israel.

Teaching Videos

Our television studio enabled us to start shooting in-house teaching videos on a great variety of subjects. Some of the more significant ones, from my viewpoint, are the following:

Revelation Revealed — A fast-paced, chapter by chapter overview of the entire book of Revelation.

A Prophetic Manifesto — A visual presentation of my booklet by the same name.

Heaven: Its Nature and Meaning — A response to the most frequently asked questions about Heaven.

The Reality of Hell — A confirmation of the existence of Hell and a presentation of the Conditional View of what Hell is all about.

The Fundamentals of Bible Prophecy — A teaching kit containing video and audio programs sufficient for six class sessions. Includes a teacher's manual and student study guides.

The Seven Churches of Revelation — Another teaching kit similar to the one about the fundamentals of Bible prophecy.

Preaching Videos

Many of our video albums consist of presentations I have made at major conferences, either our own, or conferences sponsored by others. Some of those that fall into this category are as follows:

The Middle East Crisis in Biblical Perspective — The biblical basis and meaning of the Arab-Israeli conflict, and the biblical case for Israel's legitimate claim to the land.

God and the Weather — Addresses a series of difficult questions related to God and the weather. Also, it considers whether or not natural cataclysms are increasing, and, if so, whether or not they are a sign of the Lord's soon return.

The Exponential Curve — Shows how all of life in the 20th Century was on the exponential curve, in fulfillment of end time Bible prophecy.

What Happens When You Die? — Presents what the Bible has to say about the fate of both believers and unbelievers.

Psalm 2: The King is Coming! — A verse-by-verse exposition of one of the Bible's greatest end time prophecies.

Wars of the End Times — A sweeping overview of nine wars that are prophesied for the end times.

Pre-Trib Interviews

Each year in December the Pre-Trib Study group, composed of teachers, preachers and scholars who believe in a Pre-Tribulation Rapture, holds a three day conference in the Dallas area.

I always take advantage of this gathering of Bible prophecy experts to interview them regarding certain subjects. We convert these interviews into TV programs, and we produce video albums from them. Here are a couple of the albums we have produced that feature these interviews:

The Antichrist — Eleven Bible prophecy experts talk about what the Bible reveals about the Antichrist and his worldwide rule during the Tribulation.

The Daniel Forum — Sixteen Bible prophecy specialists respond to a variety of questions about the book of Daniel.

Special Guest Interviews

When we do two or more TV interviews with a special guest, we often combine those interviews into a video album. We have produced many of these. Here are a few examples:

Ron Carlson — Albums about cults and false world religions.

James Walker — Hot topics on the religious scene primarily related to the growing apostasy in the Church.

Mike Gendron — The crucial and important differences between Catholicism and Evangelical Christianity.

Ron Rhodes — Responding to tough questions about the Bible.

Eric Barger — Apostate movements afflicting the Church and principles for defending the faith.

Caryl Matrisciana — The impact of Hinduism on Western culture and Christianity.

Robert Jeffress — Proclaiming and defending the absolute truths of the Bible.

Jobe Martin — The truth about Creation and the utter bankruptcy of Evolution.

Carl Gallups — The existence of God and the truth about Creation.

Mark Gabriel — The story of his escape from the darkness of Islam.

Charles Ryrie — The integrity of the Bible and guidelines for interpreting it.

Jim Fleming — The importance of biblical archaeology and the biblical viewpoint on key archaeological issues.

Warren Smith — The impact of the New Age Movement on Christianity.

Conference Albums

Since 2009 we have been producing a yearly video album featuring the presentations made at our annual Bible conference. The ones we have produced thus far are:

2009: Spiritual Apostasy in the End Times — Presentations about apostasy, cults, alternate religions, universalism and absolute truth.

2010: Defending the Faith — A focus on the fundamental truths of the Christian faith and how to defend them.

2011: Christianity Under Attack — Reflections on the challenges of Islam, the government, apostasy, evolution and atheism.

2012: Israel in the End Times — Various issues related to Israel in end time prophecy.

2013: Living on Borrowed Time — Survey of the Signs of the Times, with particular emphasis on Israel, technology, apostasy, the revival of the Roman Empire and the disintegration of America.

2014: America's Spiritual Crisis — Why our nation is falling apart, and what can be done about it, if anything.

A Unique Album

There is a humorous video we have produced that is designed to be a Gospel witnessing tool. It is titled, "The Strange World of Church Signs."

In this video I present over 200 church signs in 20 categories. Most are hilarious. Some are weird. A few are very profound. All are fascinating. A few are downright unbelievable.

One thing is for sure — the presentation will capture the attention of any viewer, even unbelievers. It was designed that way because it ends on a very serious note, with a survey of the Signs of the Times that point to the soon return of Jesus. It is a great Christian witnessing tool.

As the ministry matured over the years, I felt called of God to invest more of my time in writing..

I responded to this call first of all by expanding our four page monthly newsletter into a bi-monthly 20 page magazine. This enabled me to write longer and more in-depth articles that could be later expanded and included as chapters in books.

The Importance of the Printed Word

One of the ministry's trustees, Dr. James Hugg, had urged me repeatedly from the beginning of the ministry to write books. He often reminded me of the example of C. S. Lewis.

During World War II, Lewis was invited by the BBC to present a series of short radio messages about the essence of Christianity. The idea was to provide a source of biblical inspiration and encouragement to the war-besieged British people.

Perhaps as many as 500,000 to a million people heard the broadcasts. But after the war, they were combined into a book called *Mere Christianity* which became the number one best selling Christian book of the 20th Century, impacting millions of lives all over the world. "Never underestimate the power of the printed word," Dr. Hugg constantly reminded me.

As reported earlier, in the seventh year of the ministry,

in 1987, I wrote my first two books — this one and the *Christ in Prophecy Study Guide*. Both have remained in print since that time — a second edition of this book being printed in 1994 and a second edition of the Study Guide in 2001.

A Book for Children

In 1992 I wrote a book about end time prophecy for preschool and elementary children called *Jesus is Coming Again!* It is beautifully illustrated in full color from beginning to end, and it has remained popular to this day. Incidentally, that was the hardest book I have ever written. That's because it is not easy to provide an overview of end time events for children that is simple for them to read and which does not scare them to death.

I was able to handle the scary part by focusing on the good news for believers that is contained in end time prophecy. The wording was a whole different matter. After I finished the first draft, I submitted it to my wife, who was a first grade teacher at the time. She read it and then said, "Honey, this is a pretty good first draft, but you still have a long way to go." With her wonderful help, I was able to get the language down to preschool and elementary school level.

Years later, a lady from Galveston, Texas called me and said she wanted to thank me personally for the children's book. She said it had been invaluable to her in her teaching. I asked if she was a preschool or elementary Sunday School teacher. To my surprise, she said, "No, I'm the women's chaplain at the county jail."

I asked her to explain, and she did. She said that the average reading level of a woman in jail in Texas is 4th grade. "Because of that," she said, "I have to find simple illustrated books about the Bible." She added, "I have used your children's book to lead many women to the Lord."

My First Prophecy Book

My first overview book concerning all aspects of Bible prophecy was published in 1993. It was titled, *The Master*

Plan: Making Sense of the Controversies Surrounding Bible Prophecy Today. It took off like a rocket and was ultimately translated and published in six languages before it was replaced in 2005 by a greatly expanded version (from 243 pages to 415 pages). The new version was titled, *God's Plan for the Ages: The Blueprint of Bible Prophecy.*

The revised edition has gone through several printings and has received a number of accolades, including one by Bible prophecy teacher, Jack Van Impe. He ordered 5,000 copies for his supporters and told them:

> Recently I finished reading an amazing book. I was blessed beyond measure. It's that good. That important.
>
> *God's Plan for the Ages* by Dr. David Reagan offers a sweeping, panoramic view of prophetic events unlike anything I have ever studied, even after having read more than 11,000 books!

Anticipating the 21st Century

As the 21st Century approached, I felt impelled to write a book about the two major challenges I felt Christians were going to face in the new century: the disintegration of society and apostasy in the Church. The book was called, *Living for Christ in the End Times.* It remains in print to this day.

Of all the books I have written, this one is my personal favorite. I think it's because it gave me an opportunity to lay out my theological position on a great number of issues, such as worship, miracles, prayer, faith and hope.

Understanding Revelation

I think my most successful book, in terms of impact and widespread distribution, has been *Wrath & Glory*, published in 2001. It is my commentary on the book of Revelation. The title I gave it is based on the fact that the Scriptures reveal that when Jesus returns to this earth, He will first pour out the wrath of God on those who have rejected God's grace and mercy, and then He will begin to reign in glory and majesty over all the earth from Jerusalem.

Shortly after this book was published, my oldest daughter, Ruth, called and said she had just finished reading it. "I don't want to hurt your feelings," she said, "but I understood every bit of it." I laughed and explained to her that she had just given me the greatest compliment possible.

"You see," I explained, "I never write for scholars. All my writing is aimed at the person in the pew and the person who knows nothing about Christianity or Bible prophecy." What my daughter did not understand is that I want to reach the masses, both in and out of the Church. I will leave it to others to write for scholars.

The United States in Prophecy

In 2003, I decided to put my 20 years of teaching national and international politics to work by combining that knowledge with the Scriptures to write a book about what Bible prophecy says about the future of the United States and the nations of the world.

I titled it, *America the Beautiful? The United States in Bible Prophecy*. We have since issued two subsequent editions of the book (in 2006 and 2009) to bring it up to date with regard to national and international events.

Greater Concentration on Writing

In 2010, I decided to put more emphasis on writing, with the goal of producing at least one book per year. After all, I was 72 years old, and my days left on this earth were diminishing rapidly.

That year I took my controversial teachings about Heaven and Hell and put them together in a book titled, *Eternity: Heaven or Hell?* Basically, the book incorporated all my writings over the years about what happens when you die.

In 2011, I produced a book called, *Jesus: The Lamb & The Lion*. The title, like the name of the ministry I serve, was based on the two great symbolic images of the Messiah that can be found in Old Testament prophecy: the "Suffering Lamb" (the First Coming) and the "Conquering Lion" (the Second Coming).

Prophecy Forums

In 2012, I put together a book about the Antichrist. It was titled, *The Man of Lawlessness: The Antichrist in the Tribulation.* While working on the book, I came up with a new idea. I decided to send out a list of questions to 22 Bible prophecy teachers, preachers and scholars. I summarized their fascinating responses and put them together as a 60 page section of the book. I called it a "Prophecy Forum."

The idea worked so well that I decided the following year, in 2013, to incorporate another prophecy forum in my next book about the Signs of the Times. It was called *Living on Borrowed Time: The Imminent Return of Jesus.* This was the book I had dreamed of writing for years because it incorporated all aspects of the basic message I had been called to preach.

A Manifesto

In that same year, 2013, I suddenly felt a strong prompting of the Holy Spirit to write a manifesto. The best definition I have ever found of a manifesto is the following by Zach Sumner:

> A manifesto is defined as a declaration of one's beliefs, opinions, motives, and intentions. It is simply a document that an organization or person writes that declares what is important to them.
>
> A manifesto functions as both a statement of principles and a bold . . . call to action. By causing people to evaluate the gap between those principles and their current reality, the manifesto challenges assumptions, fosters commitment and provokes change.

What I proceeded to put together was a brief 40 page booklet concerning the impending collapse of our society and the increasing apostasy in the Church. It was a very hard-hitting, stern message designed to wake up people to the urgency of the hour and to call them to action. I named the booklet *A Prophetic Manifesto*.

One of our Prophecy Partners enabled us to send out 17,000 copies to pastors all across America. And since that time, the Manifesto has gone through six printings, producing over 60,000 copies. It has been an amazing process, with lots of incredible feedback. The highlight for me came the morning I arrived at my office and noticed the voice mail light blinking on my phone. It turned out to be a message from Jack Hayford complimenting me on the booklet.

My Latest Book

In 2014, I published my first "heavy" book. I call it that because it dealt with two very unbiblical theologies: Replacement Theology and Dual Covenant Theology. It was titled, *The Jewish People: Rejected or Beloved?* Even though it dealt with heavy topics, it was still written in a down-to-earth, easy-to-understand style for the average person.

In the book, I characterized Replacement Theology as an "evil" one because it has resulted in almost 2,000 years of deadly persecution of the Jewish people, culminating in the Holocaust. The theology argues that God has washed His hands of the Jewish people and replaced them with the Church because they murdered Jesus. Yet, despite its unbiblical nature and its horrible heritage, it is a theological position that continues to characterize most of Christendom, both Catholic and Protestant.

I characterized Dual Covenant Theology as a "tragic" one because it results in loving the Jewish people right into Hell. It is a theology that states the Jewish people do not need Jesus because they can be saved by obeying the Torah. Its advocates therefore take the position that the Gospel does not need to be shared with the Jews.

A Future Book

I am currently working on an overview of the Jewish people in prophecy — past, present and future. I hope the Lord will allow me to finish it, unless, of course, He wants to interrupt it with the Rapture — in which case I will be delighted to leave it unfinished!

Developing
New Forms of Ministry   33

Another major change in my ministry since I wrote the first edition of this book began in the late 1990s when I discovered PowerPoint, a slide show presentation program officially launched by Microsoft in 1990, together with Windows 3.

I have always been a visually-oriented person, and I had discovered during my 20 years as a college professor that learning and retention could both be greatly enhanced through the use of visual aids. So, as the new century dawned, I radically changed my method of preaching to incorporate PowerPoint slides. And, as with all new technologies, it was not an easy change.

The Challenge of PowerPoint

I was accustomed to using bare bone sermon outlines and to interjecting unscripted thoughts while relying primarily on the Scripture text, preaching in an expository style. But when you have a PowerPoint presentation, you must stick with a detailed sermon outline, while striving to make the delivery as fresh as possible — to the point that it sounds spontaneous. That is not an easy task.

And to make matters more complicated, I had to put up with other people advancing my slides because in the early years of PowerPoint very few churches had the capacity for me to operate my PowerPoint presentation from my laptop computer at the pulpit. And I quickly discovered that very few people could concentrate intensely enough to advance the slides at the proper time, even when they had a detailed script in front of them.

There was also the problem of moving PowerPoint presentations from one computer to another. Often the host church would have a different version of the PowerPoint program, and their version would change my fonts and transitions. It was maddening.

A Frustrating Experience

I vividly remember an experience I had at a large church in Lexington, Kentucky. They had no cable running from their computer to the pulpit, so I could not use my laptop. Instead, I had to load my PowerPoint presentation on their computer. I was presented with an eager 16 year old young man who was delighted to have the opportunity to run my PowerPoint slides. I went over the sermon outline with him in detail, and he seemed to understand everything. All the slide changes were clearly marked on a script I provided him.

But halfway through the sermon, I noticed people pointing at the screen behind me and giggling. Others just looked confused. I turned and looked at the screen and discovered that the PowerPoint presentation was six slides behind where I was at in my script. I looked up at the control booth, and the boy was talking on his cell phone!

Unfortunately, the technical problems continue to this day. I never know for sure what I am getting into, despite the fact that I outline all the technical necessities in advance. The worst situations are those churches who "guarantee" that I can load my presentation on their computer and operate it from the pulpit using a remote control. Invariably, it ends up that the remote control will work only if you stand on a chair on a particular side of the pulpit platform and hold the remote over your head while standing on one leg!

But all the effort seems well worth it. The greatest evidence is the number of young people who come forward after the service to express their appreciation for the sermon. When you have elementary school children and teenagers thanking you, it makes all the difficulties fade away.

Hosting Bible Conferences

Another new aspect of our ministry that has developed in recent years is the hosting of large Bible conferences.

We tried doing this early in the history of the ministry — back in the 1980s — but the time and money we put into the conferences did not prove to be worth the cost and effort. No matter who we invited to speak or how much money we spent on advertising, we did well if we could attract a hundred people.

It was before the days of the Internet and before our ministry was well known. So, we shelved this form of outreach until the turn of the century.

The Revival of the Concept

While speaking at a church in Kentucky in the year 2000, one of our Prophecy Partners suggested that we start holding an annual Prophecy Partner conference. I liked the idea, and we held the first one in 2001 at our new television studio. We had to limit participation to the first 50 people who signed up, and we always had a full house.

Because our seating was so limited, we decided in 2008 to move the conference to a local church that would seat about 300. It was packed out. So, the next year we moved it to a larger church and had about 450.

At this point we decided to convert the occasion into a general Bible conference that would be held annually at a conference center. Once again, the Lord filled the seats in 2010, with over 800 present.

Our Conferences Today

Since that time, we have held a conference each year with

800 to 1,000 in attendance. People come from all over the States. We always begin with a major concert on Friday evening featuring outstanding Christian artists like Dallas Holm, Marty Goetz, Ted Pearce and Janet Paschal. The concert is followed by our first speaker, and five more speakers continue all day Saturday.

These are not necessarily Bible prophecy conferences. Some have been. Others have focused on apologetics. And some have been concerned with the deterioration of American society.

In 2013 we began live-streaming the conference over the Internet, and 6,000 people from all over the world tuned in. The next year we had 10,000 Internet guests.

We videotape all the presentations and put them together in video albums. We also use excerpts from the presentations to produce television programs.

Publishing a Magazine

For years I dreamed of publishing a magazine. We had published a monthly newsletter ever since the ministry began, usually running four pages in length. It mainly consisted of one very brief article followed by news about the ministry.

In 1998 I finally decided to take the plunge. We converted the four page monthly newsletter into a 20 page bi-monthly magazine. It required an enormous amount of work, but the finished product proved to be very popular.

We usually feature a major, in-depth article about some aspect of Bible prophecy, followed by some guest articles, a page devoted to the Signs of the Times, and a page devoted to "Food for Thought." The last few pages of each issue are usually devoted to news about the ministry and its Bible study resources.

At first, we printed the cover in full color and the interior in black and white, but in 2009 we started publishing the entire magazine in full color.

A Major Change

Until 2009 we supplied both the newsletter and the magazine free of charge. By January of 2009 we had a total of 30,000 subscribers to the magazine, and it was costing us nearly $30,000 each time we printed and mailed an issue. We made the difficult decision that we simply could not afford to continue supplying the magazine free of charge.

Our Web Minister had been urging us to supply a digital copy of the magazine free of charge via email. I had resisted the idea because, as I told him, "I like to hold the magazine in my hands and underline it as I read it."

He would always laugh at this statement and tell me that I was revealing my age. "All younger people today prefer to read digital versions of magazines and newspapers on their laptops or smart phones."

So, in 2009, we started charging for a hard copy of the magazine sent through the mail, while supplying a digital copy free of charge through the Internet. Today, 35,000 people receive each copy of our magazine, and 30,000 of those receive the digital form by email. Our Web Minister knew what he was talking about!

All the full color covers of our magazines since 2009 are available for downloading on our website and can be used in PowerPoint presentations. Complete copies of our magazines are also posted on our website, beginning with the issue of November-December 2000.

Personally, there is no part of our ministry that I enjoy more than preparing our bi-monthly magazine. It takes a tremendous amount of work, but the enthusiastic feedback we receive from the readers makes the effort more than worthwhile.

Continuing
Involvement in Missions   34

Our involvement in mission work in foreign countries has continued but has changed in nature over the years.

Initially, it consisted of trips to foreign countries to conduct prophecy conferences for pastors. My colleagues and I have held conferences in Poland, Russia, Belarus, the Ukraine, the Czech Republic, Austria, Mexico, South Africa, India, England, the Philippines, Canada and mainland China.

But as the years passed and I grew older, I found the long airplane trips to remote parts of the world to be too physically exhausting, and so we began to change the nature of our missions outreach. Instead of traveling abroad to hold conferences, we began to supply significant financial support to both foreign missions and to indigenous foreign evangelists.

Mission Experiences

But before I tell you about the nature and extent of our new missions program, let me share a few of my mission experiences with you.

One of my funniest mission memories relates to an outreach in Canada. I was working at my computer one day when I got a call from a man who identified himself as an elder of a Mennonite church in La Crete, Canada. He said he was calling because his church had decided to host their very first prophecy conference, and they wanted me to be one of the speakers.

While he was talking, I typed the name of his town in my computer, and when a map came up showing its location, I was very surprised. It was located about as far north as you could go in the province of Alberta.

"Sir," I interjected, "the map on my computer shows that your town is located almost at the North Pole! How in the world am I supposed to get there?"

Without a moment of hesitation, he replied: "Oh, it's very easy. You take a plane from Dallas to Denver, change planes and fly to Edmonton. We will have one of our members meet you there. He will take you to a nearby river, and the two of you will paddle a canoe 350 miles north. At that point you will transfer to a dog sled for the remaining 60 miles."

There was a long pause as I absorbed what he had just told me.

Then, he started laughing. "It's really not all that bad. There is a small commuter plane that flies from Edmonton to our area, to an airport in a place called High Level."

I learned later that their favorite saying in that area is, "This is not the end of the earth, but we can see it from here."

A Terrifying Surprise

I arrived at the High Level airport in early April 2011. There was still some snow on the ground, but not much. The other two speakers had already arrived, and the three of us got into a large pickup truck driven by one of the church's elders.

As we drove out of the parking lot he said, "There are two ways to drive from here to La Crete, the short way and the long way. I'm going to take the long way because I want to show you a special bridge."

We drove for almost an hour, and I kept looking for the bridge. Finally, at one high point in the road, I looked down and saw a huge river.

"That's the Peace River," the driver said. "We will be at the special bridge in a moment."

And sure enough, in about five minutes we came around a bend in the road, and there was the massive river in front of us. But there was no bridge. He drove right up to the edge of the river and stopped.

"Where's the bridge?" I asked.

"Right in front of you," he responded. "It's an ice bridge, and we are going to drive across it."

All the blood drained from my head, and I turned white as snow. Before I could say a word, he hit the accelerator, and we started across the bridge. When we got to the middle, there was about ten inches of water standing.

"I've never seen this much water standing in the middle like this," the driver observed. And then he added, "You, know, I'm really surprised this bridge is still open this time of year."

To say the least it was a nerve-racking experience.

When I got back home and told my wife about it, she found the story hard to believe. So, I took her to my computer and typed the following words into Google: "ice bridge, La Crete, Canada." The first picture that came up showed an eighteen wheeler truck with its cabin in the air and its rear end through the ice!

Incidentally, the conference in La Crete turned out to be a great blessing. The people were very hospitable, and they were really hungry for God's Word. The church seated 350, and it was almost full for each service, and the services went from 9am to 10pm!

We were informed that the Mennonites have historically been strongly Amillennial. We were also told that nearly all Mennonite churches teach Replacement Theology. Our host church was, in fact, the only one in the area that was Premillennial.

China

I experienced some other jolting surprises on a mission trip to China in 2005. I had been invited by the missionary we support there, Paul Liu, to teach the book of Revelation to seminary students.

In preparing for the trip, I encountered my first surprise when I discovered that it is illegal to preach the book of Revelation in mainland China because it teaches that Jesus will one day return and reign over all the nations of the world. The Chinese government considers that to be a treasonous idea. But, I also discovered it is okay to teach the book to seminary students.

My second surprise occurred when I arrived in Shanghai. You see, I almost got shanghaied! The fellow who was supposed to meet me at the airport did not show up, and a very friendly Chinese man who spoke perfect English grabbed my big bag and took off running to what he called his "private taxi." I chased him down and retrieved my bag and got a regular taxi while he continued to harass me.

Then, as we were driving out of the airport, I got my third surprise. The very first billboard I saw was one advertising a Hooters' restaurant!

England

In the year 2000 I had one of my most memorable experiences ministering abroad. I was invited by The Prophetic Witness Movement International to come to Great Britain and spend several weeks preaching Bible prophecy. I considered this a great honor since the Prophetic Witness Movement is the oldest continuing Bible prophecy ministry in the world. It was formed in Britain in 1917, in response to the issuance of the Balfour Declaration which declared that Palestine was to be designated a homeland for the Jewish people. Its founders considered that Declaration to be the beginning of the end of the end times. They dedicated their organization to the proclamation of the Lord's soon return.

I began my visit by preaching at churches in London. From there we traveled to the English Channel, and I spoke at several cities located along the coast. Next, we went to Wales where I was blessed by some of the most beautiful singing I had ever heard. Our next stop was in Scotland. I spoke at several churches there, and the people seemed to understand me, and seemed to respond with enthusiasm, but I could never understand a word they said! I would just smile and nod my head in response to what they said to me, not having any idea what I might be agreeing to!

Our final stop was in Belfast, Northern Ireland where I met a remarkable man named Kenneth Humphries. More about him later.

I very much enjoyed meeting the people, all of whom were very cordial and hospitable. I learned quickly that the greatest compliment you could receive in response to a sermon was the phrase, "That was lovely," with the word lovely being pronounced, "luvley."

Disillusionment

Despite all the positive things I experienced, I returned home with a heavy heart for two reasons. First, I had discovered that the Church of England was spiritually dead. And because of that, the nation had become secularized to the point of rejecting its Christian heritage. Only seven percent of its people attend church anymore. And this was the nation that served as the world's center of Christianity in the 18th and 19th Centuries. It was the British who sent out missionaries all over the world and translated the Bible into many languages. It was also Anglican priests who wrote some of our greatest hymns.

The second reason for my heavy heart was the nature of most of the churches where I spoke. They turned out to be super legalistic. I was told in no uncertain terms that I could not quote from any version of the Bible except the King James — not even the New King James. I was told that I could not mention Billy Graham because he was considered to be a Catholic compromiser. And I was warned that any mention of the Holy Spirit would be dangerous since I might be considered to be a Charismatic or a Pentecostal.

Several of the churches where I spoke had a large sign at the entrance that read: "No women allowed in this church without a head covering." I asked one pastor what he would do if a woman just walked in off the street and sat down to hear a sermon. He responded that she would be told immediately that she had to either cover her head or leave!

An Exciting Discovery

I returned home to a very large stack of mail, and in that stack I found a manila envelope containing a musical audio album titled, "Revival in Belfast." I thought to myself, "Fat chance!" and tossed the album aside.

Several weeks later, I ran across the album again and decided to listen to it, and I was enthralled. I love to worship, and I love great worship music. This album turned out to contain some of the most anointed worship music I have ever heard, all of which was written by a man named Robin Mark. I decided I had to meet him personally and experience one of his worship services.

About a year later, one of my staff members and I paid our own way to travel to Belfast for a worship conference being sponsored by the church where Robin Mark served as worship leader. It was a glorious experience. I discovered that in the midst of all the spiritual deadness and legalism that characterizes the churches of England today, there are pockets of true revival.

One thing in particular that intrigued me about our visit to the Belfast church is that I discovered it was located in the neighborhood where C. S. Lewis was born and raised. We visited all the sites related to his life, and while doing so, it dawned on me that this same area that had produced one of Christendom's greatest authors 100 years ago had now produced one of its most anointed musicians.

Aiding a Ministry

While visiting in Belfast, I once again encountered Kenneth Humphries and got to know him better. I discovered that he started out life working as a baker before he decided to commit himself to the ministry. He became a Baptist pastor and functioned in that capacity for a number of years before he decided to establish a Bible prophecy ministry called Treasured Truth.

He was having difficulty financing the ministry because British Christians do not believe in giving to any ministry except a church. I was so impressed with Ken's passion to preach the Lord's soon return that I decided we would start helping him financially.

I became even more convinced of the necessity of helping him when he told me that 95% of the Baptist churches in the Belfast area had been Premillennial in their eschatology when he was a child, and that they were now 95% Amillennial. Like the Church of England, they had bought into the spiritualization of the Scriptures.

We continue to support Ken's ministry to this day. He is one of the most passionate preachers I have ever heard, and I am pleased to report that he is making real progress in reviving the Pre-Tribulational, Premillennial view of end time prophecy.

Changing our Focus

Since the turn of the century, we have shifted the focus of our missions outreach from foreign mission trips to the support of established missions and indigenous evangelists.

In 2014 we supplied over $300,000 in aid to all the foreign and domestic missions that we support. We are currently supplying regular monthly support to 20 such groups, 9 here in the United States and 11 in foreign countries, including Northern Ireland, Mexico, Nicaragua, the Philippines, Pakistan, India, China, Nigeria, South Africa and two in Israel.

Nigeria

Our most significant aid in recent years has gone to a tribe of Christians in Nigeria who have traced their ancestry back to the Jews. Their leader, Standfast Oyinna, is a great man of God who has led his people through incredible suffering.

They have been targets of that "religion of peace" called Islam. The militant Muslims of the terrorist group called Boko Haram have burned their village to the ground on two occasions, slaughtering people pell-mell and throwing children down wells while they were still alive.

Through the extensive support that the Lord has provided through our ministry, Standfast (I love that name!) has been able to supply clothes, food and shelter to his people and to hundreds of refugees from other areas.

Foreign Publications

A remarkable evangelist in Pakistan named Nazir Gill has translated and published our major Bible prophecy books in a number of different languages, including Urdu, Farsi and Arabic. Another wonderful evangelist in India by the name of John Ishmael has published our books in Telugu and Nepali. John also publishes an abbreviated Indian version of our *Lamplighter* magazine. The Chinese evangelist we support, Paul Liu, has published *Wrath & Glory* in Chinese and is distributing it among seminaries in mainland China.

Several years ago God led us to a young man in Nicaragua named Donald Dolmus. He turned out to be a very serious student of Bible prophecy with a zeal to proclaim the Lord's soon return. We have been providing him with major monthly support to enable him to conduct weekend meetings and conferences. He also translates our materials into Spanish and posts them on his website (www.endefensadelafe.org) where they are accessed by Spanish-speaking people all over the world.

Thanking God

All of us at Lamb & Lion Ministries feel so blessed to be used by the Lord as a channel of His blessings to other ministries. Our earnest prayer is that He will continue to use us for this purpose.

Replicating Our Ministry 35

In the early 1990s I decided that I wanted to start replicating our ministry by encouraging qualified men to step out in faith and commit their lives to the proclamation of the Lord's soon return. These are the "domestic missions" I referred to in the last chapter.

Lion of Judah Ministries

The first opportunity came in 1993 when a staff member and I traveled to Lexington, Kentucky to conduct an all day Saturday prophecy conference. When I got up to make my opening presentation, I noticed that the first two rows were packed with the most enthusiastic people I had ever seen at one of our conferences. Each person had two or more Bibles, and all of them were leaning forward in anticipation, with pens in their hands and tablets on their laps. They proceeded to take copious notes.

At the first break, I decided I had to get to know these people better. I quickly discovered that they were all from a Bible study class at a megachurch in Nashville, Tennessee. I asked if their teacher was present. They said he was, and they introduced me to him. His name was Gary Fisher.

Gary proved to be an amiable man with a great enthusiasm for Bible prophecy. I discovered that his enthusiasm for God's Prophetic Word was due to the fact that he had been saved by reading Hal Lindsey's book, *The Late Great Planet*

Earth.

I decided to keep in touch with Gary. I was impressed with his ability to get so many people fired up about prophecy. I recognized that he had been gifted by the Spirit as a teacher of the Scriptures.

At the time I met Gary, he was working for the Tandy Corporation. I discovered that he felt called of God to establish a Bible prophecy ministry, but — like I had done — he was running from the Lord. So, I began to encourage him to step out in faith, surrender his job, and commit himself to full time ministry.

He did that in 1994, forming a ministry called Lion of Judah. And we assisted him by supplying him with substantial financial support and by recommending him as a teacher and preacher.

Since that time, we have assisted with the establishment of seven other ministries, six here in the States and one in Northern Ireland. In each case, we have helped them get known to the public, and we have provided them with financial help which we gradually taper off over the years as they get established and build their own base of support.

According to Prophecy Ministries

Let me give you another example. I don't exactly remember when I first met Don Perkins, but I have never been the same since. He is an ebullient Black man who radiates the joy of Jesus. He has a great passion for the Lord's return, and he is on fire with the desire to communicate that truth to as many people as possible.

For several years he worked for a huge international ministry in Louisiana before he moved to San Diego to work for another similar ministry. At both, he used his weekends to teach and preach Bible prophecy at churches, schools and conferences. All the time he yearned to go into full time ministry.

One day as he was expressing to me his desire to establish a Bible prophecy ministry, I sensed the time had arrived for him to take that step of faith. So, I grabbed his hands and told him I wanted to pray for him. I prayed, "Lord, Don is finding it hard to take the step of faith you are calling him to, so I pray you will kick him out of his nest by making his current job miserable."

Don looked at me in astonishment. "I've never heard a prayer like that before," he said.

A couple of weeks later he called. "Dr. Reagan," he said, "you're not going to believe this, but your prayer has been answered." He went on to explain that he had a new boss, and the boss had just informed him that he would no longer be allowed any free time on weekends because he had to be available at all times.

Don resigned his job, stepped out in faith in October of 1998, and founded a ministry called According to Prophecy. He is the only Black evangelist in America that we know of who is devoted to the full time proclamation of the Lord's soon return.

Crown & Sickle Ministries

Don McGee is from the Cajun country of southern Louisiana. He's not a Cajun, but he can talk like one, and he can tell Cajun jokes that will keep you laughing all day.

I first met Don back in the early 1980s when we roomed together at a motel while attending the board meeting of a college in Winchester, Kentucky. Don had been on the board several years. I was new to it.

We set a wake-up call for the morning we were leaving, and the desk clerk at the motel forgot to call us. When we woke up late, we immediately realized that we were going to have to really hurry in order to get to the airport in time to catch our flights back home.

We threw our clothes in our suitcases, jumped in our rental car, pulled out on the Interstate and started driving to the airport in Lexington. I was driving, and I was "putting the pedal to the metal."

As we were breezing along, I turned to Don and said,

"You've never told me what you do for a living."

"I'm a Louisiana state trooper," Don replied.

I gulped and hit the brake to slow down to the speed limit.

"Don't worry," said Don, "I know the secret handshake."

I got a big laugh out of that experience, and yes, we did make it to the airport on time. More importantly, we became close friends.

Don is a no-nonsense Vietnam War veteran. He says he can prove that teenagers don't have good sense because when he graduated from high school he went down to the military recruiting office and said, "I will join if you can guarantee me I will go to Vietnam."

He said the recruiting officer replied, "Son, I think we can absolutely guarantee that."

After his military service, Don became a Louisiana State Trooper and even served as a bodyguard to the Governor. Later, he decided to enter the ministry full time and became the pastor of a church.

Don will readily admit that he was never cut out to be a pastor. His no-nonsense approach to life gave him little patience with complainers. He loved to preach, but he had little patience for the pastoral duties. Finally, he became so frustrated that he decided to quit.

That's when he came to me for counsel, and I urged him to step out in faith and form a Bible prophecy ministry. He did exactly that in November of 2002, and he has been going full steam ever since. He calls his ministry Crown and Sickle, based on Revelation 14:14 & 17.

A Cause for Rejoicing

What a joy it has been for all of us at Lamb & Lion to assist so many Bible prophecy ministries get started! I pray the Lord will continue to multiply them as the day of the Rapture draws near.

Receiving Financial Miracles 36

Financial miracles have characterized Lamb & Lion Ministries from the beginning. I have already mentioned several related to the beginning of our television ministry. I could write many more pages about them, but I will mention only a few that have occurred since the second edition of this book in 1994.

Some Timely Visitors

One of the most memorable occurred around 2004. Our financial director came to me in mid-November and said, "Dave, you had better start praying earnestly because it looks like we are going to have a tough time making the payroll at the end of the month."

That had never happened before. I was completely surprised by the situation. I immediately brought it to the attention of the whole staff, and we started praying.

At the end of the month, after all the pay checks had been written, I was informed that we had a grand total of only $7.50 left in the bank! We praised God for enabling us to pay all our bills, and we continued to pray for financial relief.

A few days later, in early December, one of the members of our mail room staff stuck her head in my office and said, "There's a couple here who would like to meet you personally."

I sat down with them and talked with them for about 30

minutes. They turned out to be a retired dentist and his wife. They had found our TV program and had called and requested a VHS copy of every program we had produced. They asked the staff to box the programs, and they would come by to pick them up. I discovered that the dentist was an avid fan of Bible prophecy.

As they prepared to leave, the man turned to his wife and said, "I feel like we should make a donation. How about 25?" She nodded her approval. He wrote the check, folded it and handed it to me. I walked them out to their car and dropped the check on my secretary's desk as I headed back to my office.

A moment later, my secretary appeared and asked, "Did you take a look at this check?"

I told her I had not, but I added, "He said it was for $25."

"No!" she responded. "It is for $25,000!"

I was dumbfounded. I wrote a special letter of thanks, but we never heard from them again. The whole experience is what I call "the Lord's perfect timing."

A Fascinating Last Will and Testament

More recently, in the year 2012, we were praying for funds to expand our TV outreach, when I received a letter from a Chicago law firm informing me that the ministry had been named as a beneficiary in a will. A copy of the will was enclosed with the letter. I was not familiar with the man who had died.

His will proved to be absolutely fascinating. It began by stating that he had no living relatives. He specified that a sum of $30,000 was to be given to each of his three best friends. He then directed that the bulk of his estate was to be divided among a dozen Catholic charities and super-liberal organizations like the ACLU. Finally, he stated that he would like several thousand dollars to be set aside for a party in his memory at a local bar, with drinks on the house!

By this point, I was throughly confused, wondering what this last will and testament could possibly have to do with our ministry. Then I turned the page, and there was a new will dated three years later.

He still provided for the three friends. But he said to forget about the party. He then specified that his estate was to be divided among three ministries — two Messianic ministries and ours. Our portion came to $104,000.

I realized that I was holding proof of a miracle in my hands. Not only had our prayers been answered, but here was a man whose life had been totally transformed in three years time by his encounter with Jesus. All his values had been radically changed. I still get goose bumps when I think about it!

Helping Tornado Victims

I must mention one other amazing financial miracle. I had a weekend meeting scheduled at Union Valley Baptist Church in Beebe, Arkansas. A staff member and his wife drove me to the meeting.

When we arrived, we discovered that a very powerful tornado had totally destroyed the small town of Vilonia, located about ten miles west of the church where I would be speaking.

While I worked on my sermons, one of the members of the church drove my staff member and his wife over to the site of the devastated town. They brought back photos that I found shocking. About the only thing left of churches, homes and businesses were foundations.

I spoke several times that weekend to standing-room-only crowds, and the Lord really blessed the outreach. The pastor had told me in advance that he would take up one offering for our ministry after the last service on Sunday evening.

As I spoke that evening, the images of the tornado's devastation kept racing through my mind. My heart was heavy with compassion for the victims. When it came time for the offering, I asked permission to speak. I told the people that I had decided to dedicate the entire offering to the tornado victims. I asked the church to distribute the funds as they saw fit.

The next morning as we were driving back home, my cell phone rang. It was my daughter, Rachel, who serves as the Chief Operating Officer of our ministry. "Dad," she said, "you are not going to believe this. We have been opening the mail, and we just opened a letter from a couple in Canadian, Texas, and there was a check in it for $40,000!"

You cannot outgive the Lord.

Dealing with Criticism   37

When I founded Lamb & Lion Ministries in 1980, I knew my teachings about the end times would generate some very hostile responses. After all, I was going to be teaching the Premillennial View and a Pre-Tribulation Rapture. The vast majority of the Christian world, both Catholic and Protestant, is Amillennial and does not believe in a Rapture that is separate from the Second Coming.

In thinking about how I would handle criticism, particularly the personal type of vicious and sarcastic criticism that so often characterizes Christians who consider themselves to be "watchmen on the walls," I decided right at the start that I would never respond in kind, and, in fact, I would never respond at all. I decided to leave it up to the Lord to protect my reputation and the integrity of the ministry.

The Early Critics

At first, the critics were few and far apart. They consisted in the most part of people who challenged me to debate them.

I had been a champion debater in college, and I was very familiar with all the debate techniques. Furthermore, I had grown up in a denomination that specialized in debating, in an effort to prove that all others were wrong.

I had long before concluded that religious debating was carnal by its very nature and was a waste of time. So, I turned down all debate challenges and then learned to wait for the challengers to denounce me as "yellow," chicken-livered," and "cowardly."

The Vicious Critics

After we got on the Internet in 1995, the criticisms began to build exponentially. We were no longer under the radar.

That's when I discovered that even among Evangelicals there are critics who are as ruthless as a junkyard dog. And even though I never wasted my time responding to each critic, I finally decided in 2013 to write a general response that we printed in our magazine. It was titled, "A Plea for Grace." It is reproduced below.

A Magazine Article About Criticism

I have had some favorable things to say recently about Oral Roberts and his ministry — both in our magazine and on one of our television programs. Those statements have prompted a number of negative responses from people who questioned whether or not anything good should be said about the man. One lady denounced him as an "apostate" and said she wanted nothing more to do with me or this ministry.

So, I thought I would share some thoughts with you about evaluating ministries.

First, let's keep in mind that there are no perfect ministries. All of them, including Lamb & Lion, are headed up by people and are composed of people, and people are flawed.

I would urge you, therefore, to look for the good — for that which lines up with the Scriptures — and either ignore or criticize responsibly what does not. Otherwise, you are going to miss some spiritual blessings.

Let me give you some examples from my personal perspective.

Examples of Ministries I Admire
but Disagree With

I have always greatly admired the incredible courage that Martin Luther showed when he stood up to the Roman Catholic Church, the most powerful institution of the Middle

Ages and one that did not hesitate to burn its critics alive at the stake. I am thankful that he pointed Christendom to God's true plan of salvation of grace through faith in Jesus. And what a blessing it was for him to translate the Bible into the German language and to bless all of Christendom with his marvelous hymns.

Yes, I am very grateful to Martin Luther, and I will always admire his courage, despite the fact that he turned out to be the worst anti-Semite in Church history. The pamphlet he wrote near the end of his life in which he denounced and condemned the Jews served as a blueprint for the Holocaust.

And then there is the example of C. S. Lewis. He was a brilliant Oxford professor of Medieval literature when he came to a belief in God and then later placed his faith in Jesus as his Lord and Savior. His Christian writings soon established him as the greatest defender of the Christian faith in the 20th Century. Those writings, like *Mere Christianity* (1943) and *The Problem of Pain* (1940), greatly impacted my life by drawing me deeper into the Scriptures and closer to the Lord. I will be forever grateful to him for his marvelous spiritual insights. He is going to be one of the first persons I will want to meet personally when I get to Heaven.

Yet, the incredible thing that most people do not know about C. S. Lewis is that near the end of his life he revealed in letters that he believed in Purgatory! To me, it is mind-boggling that a man with so many deep spiritual insights could have been spiritually blind concerning this doctrinal issue. Because he was so off-base on this point, should I throw out everything else he had to offer? I think not.

Bringing my examples more up to date, let's consider two great modern-day ministries whose leaders have recently been called home to the Lord.

The first is the ministry of Dr. James Kennedy who served for 47 years as the pastor of Coral Ridge Presbyterian Church in Fort Lauderdale, Florida. He was a powerful spokesman in behalf of the Christian heritage of America, and he was a man who spoke out fearlessly against the secular drift of our nation. I admired him greatly. Yet, he was one of the foremost proponents of Replacement Theology, a theology I consider to be absolutely abominable.

In like manner I highly valued the ministry of Chuck Colson. His conversion story was inspirational, and the prison ministry he established was an outstanding one. I also appreciated his syndicated columns in which he expressed a biblical worldview regarding political, moral and social issues. I praise God for him and his ministry despite the fact that he was a terrible Catholic compromiser and he lacked respect for God's Prophetic Word. Should I have just written him off and refused to pay attention to anything he had to say? I don't think so.

Let's take a look at some contemporary ministries that are alive and well today:

- I highly respect the preaching and teaching of Charles Stanley, and I have learned much from him, despite the fact that I abhor his hyper-Calvinism.

- I love the preaching of John MacArthur and his teaching of Bible prophecy. It would be hard to find a better expositor of God's Word. But when he starts talking about the Holy Spirit, I have to tune him out. To me, he just seems to have a spiritual blind spot in that area.

- I have always had great respect for the Pentecostal Movement — for its zeal, enthusiasm and passion. The praise music it has produced has blessed my soul, and I have been thankful for the Movement's appreciation and understanding of God's Prophetic Word. I am also thankful for the way God worked through the Movement to resurrect the gifts of the Spirit from the dead. But I have never been able to accept their core teaching that the baptism of the Holy Spirit must be manifested in the gift of tongues.

- I have always respected the wonderful ministry of David Barton and the insights he has provided regarding the Christian heritage of our nation. I hold him in high esteem despite the fact that he is a Postmillennialist who denies that Jesus could return anytime soon.

- I greatly admire the fantastic Creation ministry of Ken Ham, and I praise God for it, despite the fact that he thinks that a person's end time viewpoint is irrelevant.

I suspect that after having read the list above, some of you are ready to say that I am also spiritually blind in some ways — and that could well be. If you feel that way, I hope you will pray for me to be enlightened and not just write me off as hopeless.

The Point

The point is that I have learned much from each of the men and ministries mentioned above despite the fact that there are areas where I disagree with them and, in some cases, disagree with them strongly.

And I am convinced that I would have lost many great spiritual insights if I would have written off their teachings because I disagreed with some part of what they had to say.

The Ministry of Oral Roberts

The same is true of the ministry of Oral Roberts. I greatly admired his faith. And I appreciate the fact that he revived belief in God's healing power, returning that belief to mainline Christianity. I also respected the fact that he always insisted that those seeking healing had to first hear the Gospel preached. He cared about the welfare of people's souls as well as the health of their physical bodies. Another thing I respected about the way he operated his ministry is that before he would start praying for healing, he would always emphasize that if any healing occurred, it would come from God and not from him.

Oral Roberts was a great man of faith. He was a fabulous Gospel preacher. And he was anointed by God for healing.

I never agreed with his prosperity teachings. And I always felt like his dogged determination to build the City of Faith medical facility was based more on presumption than faith. I think its tragic fate proved that he had run out from under God's anointing on that particular project.

But he dramatically showed us the meaning of faith; he revived belief in healing; he established a great Christian university; and he pioneered Christian television. All of that should make us grateful to God for his life and ministry.

The Crucial Doctrines

So, where should we draw the line with regard to respect and support of a ministry? It has to do with the fundamentals of the faith. Those fundamentals are:

1) The Virgin Birth of Jesus
2) The Divinity of Jesus
3) The Atoning Death of Jesus
4) The Resurrection of Jesus
5) The Promise of Jesus to Return

When a Christian leader denies one or more of these fundamentals, his ministry should not be respected or supported, and it can be legitimately considered as apostate. Disagreements over other points of doctrine are important, but they should never serve to disrupt our fellowship in the Lord.

Truth is important, but not all truth is equally important. So, for example, whatever the truth may be about the Millennium, it is nothing compared to THE TRUTH that Jesus is Lord.

Disagreeing Amicably

When we as Christians disagree with doctrine being taught by some Christian leader, we need to do so in a Christ-like manner. We should avoid pejorative labels like "apostate." And we should avoid judging motives. We should simply deal with the issue of whether or not the questionable doctrine is biblical.

With regard to motives, one of my pet peeves is the way people seem compelled to sum up a doctrinal disagreement with me by saying, "I know the only reason you take that position is because it sells books." I hear that accusation over and over again. I want to emphasize that is a sinful accusation.

First, it is sinful because it is based on an evaluation of my motives, and that simply is not possible. We can judge words and actions, but we can never judge motives because we cannot know with certainty what each other's motives may be.

Second, the accusation is sinful because it attributes evil by asserting that I am guided only by monetary concerns. (I can assure you that money is not a motivator to me.)

I've never been able to understand why Christians must attribute evil motives to those they disagree with on a doctrinal point. It's as if they cannot conceive that people can honestly disagree about a biblical interpretation.

Increasing Shrillness

I have also become distressed in recent years by the increasingly strident tone of many Christian apologists. I'm sure this is due to the rapidly increasing apostasy in the Church and their sense of frustration in dealing with it. But this is no excuse for the attack dog mentality that seems to prevail.

A good example is the recent response to the best-selling book, *The Harbinger*, written by a Messianic Jew named Jonathan Cahn. I personally did not care for the book. I thought his method of scriptural interpretation was highly subjective in nature, and I thought his examples of prophetic fulfillment which he drew from the 9/11 attacks were highly strained. But I thought his overall conclusion that our nation is in rebellion against God and is therefore begging for God's destruction was right on target. So, I was thankful for the book.

But the apologetic attack dogs had a field day picking the book apart and slinging names at the author. One even called him a "false prophet"! They just couldn't seem to say anything good, despite the fact that the book's overall message was a sound one and a needed one.

Another fault of the modern day apologetic attack dogs is their tendency to attribute guilt by association. It's a good thing they were not around when the Apostle Paul delivered his sermon at Athens. They surely would have overlooked his words, while frying him for having the audacity to associate with heathens.

Outstanding Christian spokesmen like Joel Rosenberg have been viciously attacked and defamed simply because they participated in a prayer rally that was called by Governor Rick Perry of Texas. Why? Because there were people present at the rally who were considered unacceptable.

Others have been soundly condemned because they had the audacity to quote from the Bible paraphrase known as *The Message*. I don't endorse that paraphrase, but I don't believe for a moment that quoting from it renders a person apostate. I recently quoted favorably some words of an ancient Muslim poet. The words were beautiful and biblical, but because they were from a Muslim, I was severely condemned!

I knew that the moment I said anything positive about Oral Roberts and his ministry that the attack dogs would come growling and even, in some cases, howling. But I refuse to be intimidated by them and their rabid negativism.

Constant Condemnations

- I have had my Christianity questioned because I refused to condemn the Promise Keeper's Movement.

- I have had my Christianity questioned because I do not despise Bible paraphrases like the *Living Bible* and the *New Testament in Modern English* by J. B. Phillips.

- I have had my Christianity questioned because I do not dislike contemporary Christian music.

- I have had my Christianity questioned because I refuse to denounce modern Bible translations like the *New King James Version* and *The New American Standard Version.*

- I have had my Christianity questioned because I do not despise Billy Graham.

- I have had my Christianity questioned because I do not hold Charismatics in disdain.

Tragically, I could extend this list indefinitely!

There are many very fine apologetic ministries existing today who are earnestly contending for the faith. We have interviewed many of their leaders on our television program. But the self-proclaimed "watchmen on the walls" who constantly spew forth hateful condemnations are really nothing more than spiritual pit bulls who are trying to build themselves up by tearing other people down.

I know the attacks will continue, but I want to make it clear that I am not going to allow my Christianity to be defined by what I hate rather than what I believe. And what I believe is that Jesus is Lord!

Conclusion

My conclusion? Let's look for what is biblical, let's embrace it, and let's thank God for it. Criticize what you consider to be unbiblical, but do it in love, with a desire to correct and not defame. Pray for the person you disagree with, and remember, if God can show you grace with all your warts and hang-ups, surely you can show some grace toward those you disagree with.

Continuing to Laugh 38

If you have read the rest of this book up to this point, then you know that I have a great sense of humor.

Over the years, I have tried to always incorporate some humor into my presentations, particularly at the beginning of each sermon. In the years before PowerPoint, I usually did that by telling funny church related stories. But when PowerPoint came along, I felt a need to incorporate visual expressions of humor. I have done that in several ways, but the primary way has been by sharing my collection of church signs.

A Fascinating Collection

I began collecting church signs during the very first year of the ministry — in 1980. It all came about as a result of focusing my initial radio broadcasts on an overview of the Signs of the Times that point to the Lord's soon return.

One day I received a letter from one of our listeners in which she said, "I've been listening to you for three months talking about the Signs of the Times. I thought that a person so interested in signs might find the enclosed photo interesting."

The photo showed a church sign. The name of the church was "Little Hope Baptist Church."

I got a good laugh out of that picture, and I decided to mention it on my radio program.

Strange Church Names

That mention prompted a deluge of photos of church signs with very strange names. Here is a sampling:

Halfway Baptist Church
Bat Cave Baptist Church
French Broad Baptist Church
Hot House Missionary Baptist Church
Black Jack Baptist Church
The Exciting Singing Hills Baptist Church

The Baptists are not the only ones who come up with weird names. Here are some from other denominations:

Grenade Holiness Church
Lily White Church of the Living God
Church of Uncertain
Beaver Lick Christian Church
Whynot Wesleyan Church
Boring United Methodist Church
St. James Bond United Church
Lower Peach Tree United Methodist Church
Run for Your Life Chapel
The Driven Church
The Cool Assembly of God
The Desperation Church
The Non-Denominational Battle Axe Church

The Strangest Name of All

Perhaps the strangest church name I have in my collection is one for an Assembly of God in Corsicana, Texas. The name: "That Church." Can you imagine what Bud Abbott and Lou Costello could have done with that name?

"What church do you attend?"
"That Church."
"Which church?"
"That Church!"

"But what's its name?"

"That Church!"

"Are you playing games with me?"

Unusual Messages

To date I have 542 church signs in my collection. I have them divided into 32 categories. Most of the signs do not feature strange church names. Rather, they display unusual or funny messages. Here are some examples:

> There are some questions that cannot be answered by Google.
>
> Walmart is not the only saving place.
>
> God so loved the world that He did not send a committee.
>
> Don't be so open minded that your brains fall out.
>
> God does not believe in Atheists, therefore Atheists do not exist.
>
> Church parking trespassers will be baptized.
>
> Do not wait for 6 strong men to take you to church.
>
> Our church is like fudge — sweet with a few nuts.
>
> Why didn't Noah swat the two mosquitos?
>
> Tweet others as you would have them tweet you.
>
> Pobody is Nerfect — See U Inside.
>
> Whoever stole our AC units — keep one. It is hot where you're going!
>
> Honk if you love Jesus. Text while driving if you want to meet Him.

Odd Sermon Topics

Included in my collection are signs with unusual sermon titles. The weirdest one I have ever run across is one that announced the following topic: "No man has ever been shot while doing the dishes." Here are some others:

> Fruit Trees With Feet.
> Church: Why Bother?
> Christians Should Go To Hell!
> I'm Saved, You're Saved Maybe.
> Sacred Cows Make The Best Hamburgers.
> What To Do If Your Husband Is An Idiot!

Bible Prophecy Signs

Very few churches put any emphasis on Bible prophecy, and accordingly, there are very few prophecy signs in my collection. Here are my favorites:

> On Judgment Day you will meet God — not Mother Earth.
> Tomorrow's forecast — God reigns and Jesus shines!
> Jesus is coming. Look busy!
> Christ's return — don't miss it for the world!
> Satan: The fat lady is about to sing!
> Prophecy conference canceled due to unforeseen circumstances.

My all time favorite church sign is one about prophecy that one of our ministry's trustees photographed at a church near Denton, Texas: "The Rapture: Separation of Church and State!"

Signs About Pastors

I have a special place in my heart for pastors. I think being a pastor is God's highest calling, but it also has to be the most difficult. Pastors have to have supernatural patience and love to put up with all the abuse they and their families receive from their parishioners.

Three of my signs vividly illustrate this point. One announces the sermon topic: "Do you know what Hell is like?" Underneath this topic are the words: "Come hear our preacher." And then there is a sign that was actually shown on CNN news: "Come hear our pastor. He's not very good, but he's short." I also have a sign that reads: "Now is a good time to visit. Our pastor is on vacation."

The Impact of Humor

Some people object to humor in sermons. They argue that too much is at stake to joke around about anything. I understand their point, and I respect it. But I have found that humor has a way of opening the heart for the serious Scripture message to come.

Evaluating Success 39

Several years ago I gave a lot of thought to what have been the keys to the success of Lamb & Lion Ministries. In the process I came up with a list of 17 items:

1) Depending on the Lord by beginning each day with a staff devotional and prayer time.

2) Being faithful to the ministry's call by focusing on the proclamation of the Lord's soon return.

3) Avoiding speculation and sensationalism.

4) Being accountable by submitting to the control and oversight of a board of trustees.

5) Being transparent by sharing our financial records with anyone.

6) Operating debt free.

7) Providing staff members with good salaries and benefits.

8) Proceeding at the Lord's pace by neither running ahead nor lagging behind Him.

9) Investing in people and equipment.

10) Being willing to serve as a channel of blessings to other ministries.

11) Developing a dedicated supporter base through a partner program.

12) Communicating frequently, openly and in detail with supporters.

13) Being blessed with enthusiastic and encouraging supporters.

14) Being blessed with staff members who are dedicated to the Lord.

15) Being blessed with godly, generous and loving trustees.

16) Praying earnestly for the Lord to keep the ministry in the center of His will.

17) Attempting to be faithful to the ministry's founding scriptural passage (Psalm 127.1).

> "Unless the Lord builds the house,
> They labor in vain who build it . . ."

Let me comment briefly on a few of these items, and I will start with the most important, which is daily prayer.

Prayer

We begin each day at Lamb & Lion with a devotional service for all the full time staff members. A scripture passage is read, and then a devotional based on that passage is read. That is followed by an extended period of prayer for our personal needs and the needs of the ministry.

We normally pray also for such things as our nation, the Church and the nation of Israel. We include special prayer requests we have received from our supporters and the general public. We pray also for our Prophecy Partners on a rotating basis, covering ten each day.

All this takes about 45 minutes to an hour. We thus end up working a 7 hour day. Most people would consider committing so much time to prayer to be excessive, but I don't. I am fully aware of where our blessings come from, and I want to acknowledge and thank our God. I also want to ask Him each day to bless all our work to His Name's honor and glory.

Focus

As I have emphasized throughout this book, the Lord called me to establish Lamb & Lion Ministries for a very specific purpose: *to proclaim to as many people as possible, as quickly as possible, that Jesus is returning soon.*

Throughout the years, there have been many attempts to distract me from that call, and I have always tried to resist them.

However, looking back today with 20/20 hindsight, I believe that the reason our radio program was never as blessed as our TV program has been is because I failed to focus it on the Signs of the Times, the Rapture and the Second Coming. Instead, I got sidetracked by providing biblical commentary on national and international events — something I enjoyed doing and something I was qualified to do, but not what God called me to do.

By returning to a focus on the Lord's soon return when we shifted from radio to TV, the Lord's blessing on our media outreach has increased abundantly.

Avoiding Speculation and Sensationalism

The whole field of Bible prophecy has been discredited by irresponsible speculation and sensationalism — to the point that I am often embarrassed to admit that I specialize in the topic.

From the very beginning of Lamb & Lion, I have spoken out strongly and consistently against those who have converted the whole field of Bible prophecy into a playground for fanatics. And I have done everything possible to keep our ministry free of such nonsense.

One of the prophecy sensationalists wrote to me onetime and said, "The problem with your ministry is that it is boring. You keep teaching the same thing over and over."

I plead guilty to "teaching the same thing over and over," but it is anything but boring to learn about the glorious things that are going to happen when Jesus returns — things that most professing Christians are simply not aware of.

Accountability

Being accountable to a board of trustees is vitally important to keeping a ministry on an even keel.

Most ministries have a board of trustees in name only. That's because it has no power. At most, it is just an advisory board.

A good example that comes to mind is Jimmy Swaggart's ministry. Back when his ministry was at its peak, I had a lot of respect for him. He was a very talented musician and a great preacher and teacher, and his teachings were always grounded in the Word.

When *Time* magazine did a feature story on him, they asked if he had a board of trustees. He said he had. They then asked him who served on his board. He said himself, his wife, his son and his wife, and a lawyer who was his best friend. He was asked if his board had ever said no to him. He said he could not remember them ever doing so. They then asked what he would do if they ever rejected one of his proposals. He responded, "I would fire them!"

It was clear that his board existed in name only. And it was not long after this interview that Swaggart's ministry disintegrated.

He did not have a true board of trustees that could hold him accountable. Again, I have found this method of operation to be widespread. Usually, if an evangelist is challenged about not having a true board, he will respond that he "reports only to God." That is a cop-out. God works through people, and every evangelist needs a controlling board of trustees that has true power and is not made up of relatives.

That has always been the case with Lamb & Lion Ministries. The ministry belongs to the board, and not to me. And the board is the one that determines all the operating principles and policies. I am accountable to them, and they have the power to replace me at any time.

Debt Free

One of the policies that was established early on by the Lamb & Lion board is that we would operate debt free.

This has proved to be a great blessing. The Lord has always blessed our special fund-raising appeals for the construction of buildings and the purchase of equipment.

And by staying out of debt, we have been able to focus our funds on outreach instead of spending them on loan payments with interest.

Transparency

One of the most important keys to financial accountability, in addition to having an oversight by a board of trustees, is transparency with all financial records. This has also been a Lamb & Lion policy from the beginning.

We have always been willing to provide anyone with a copy of our monthly operating statement or with a copy of our yearly audit. I believe strongly that any organization that relies on donations should be willing to share all its financial records to the public. We even post our records on our website.

If you ever request a financial statement from a ministry and you are refused, you should never make a donation to that ministry. Period!

Staff

My dad was an outstanding businessman, and one of the principles he taught me was the importance of restraining one's self from personally using surplus funds by paying yourself a big salary. Instead, he stressed the importance of investing surplus funds in people and equipment so that the business would grow.

This is a principle I have followed in ministry. During the first seven years of Lamb & Lion Ministries, I asked the board of trustees to limit my salary to $1,000 per month so that we could invest any surplus funds in acquiring staff and equipment. My family lived basically on my wife's income as a first grade teacher. The bottom line is that most ministries never grow because the evangelist wants to keep all the surplus funds for himself.

There is another important principle we started following once the decision was made that we had reached the point in the ministry's growth where I could be paid a more reasonable salary. The decision was that the board would determine my salary and the board would pay my salary out of their own donations to the ministry. This meant that no funds donated by outsiders would ever come to me. They would be used exclusively to pay for the ministry's staff, equipment and outreach.

There was something else we did financially that resulted in big benefits for the ministry. We focused on providing generous salaries and benefits to our staff members. This resulted in very little staff turnover, giving the ministry stability.

I had always been annoyed by churches that paid their senior pastor a huge salary while all the other staff members barely scraped together a living. So, in addition to salaries being based on responsibility, we also included need — providing $125 a month extra for each dependent. This has nearly always resulted in some staff members making more money than me because they had several children, and I had none who were living at home.

Partners

Our Prophecy Partner Program that was established by our board of trustees in 1980 has proved to be one of the ministry's greatest blessings. Not only do our Prophecy Partners provide us with our financial foundation, they also pray for us regularly and provide us with a constant source of counsel and encouragement.

Such a program is essential if a ministry is to have any financial stability. Otherwise, the evangelist will be solely dependent on speaking engagements, which means constant travel and all the stress that goes with it. And should the evangelist become ill and have to cancel speaking engagements, the ministry is thrown immediately into financial crisis.

Communication

Effective communication is absolutely essential. It must be continual, regular and meaningful. And it must involve all segments of the ministry.

At Lamb & Lion, our staff members are involved in general communication with each other at our daily devotional meeting. This is supplemented with a weekly meeting of department heads and with weekly or bi-weekly department meetings.

I send several reports each month to our trustees to keep them aware of every aspect of the ministry. They also receive a financial statement at the end of each month. I keep in touch with our Prophecy Partners by writing them a special letter each month to inform them of our operations, goals and accomplishments. In that report I also include a list of our prayer needs.

"Out of sight, out of mind" is a truism. Every ministry needs to stay in contact with its people. But common sense needs to prevail, and that means not too much contact. I am on the contact lists of many ministries, and I become quickly annoyed at the ones that bombard me with spam over the Internet — usually begging constantly for money.

The ECFA and Charity Navigator

Many, but not all, of our operating principles are based on the guidelines that an organization must commit to follow in order to be a member of the Evangelical Council for Financial Accountability, an organization established in 1979 by the Billy Graham Evangelistic Association.

Some of those guidelines include:

1) Control of the ministry by a board of trustees that meets at least two times a year and consists of at least five members, a majority of whom are not family members of the chief operating officer.

2) Issuance of regular and accurate financial reports that are available to the general public.

3) Conduct of an annual audit that is available to the public.

4) Determination of the chief operating officer's compensation by the board in a manner that demonstrates integrity and propriety.

5) Truthfulness in requesting donations, using donations as directed by donors, keeping accurate records of donations and providing gift receipts.

An organization called Charity Navigator, which was established in 2001, is considered to be the most important evaluator of non-profit organizations in America today — both religious and secular. Its defined mission is "helping donors make informed giving decisions and enabling well-run charities to demonstrate their commitment to proper stewardship of donor dollars."

Charity Navigator currently evaluates more than 5,400 charities in the United States in addition to hundreds of organizations with international operations.

As we begin our 35th year of operation, we have received the organization's highest rating for ten years in a row. Only one percent of all the organizations they are currently evaluating have ever received their highest rating for ten years in a row.

This accomplishment on our part is a great testimony to the integrity of our board and staff and to their determination to operate Lamb & Lion Ministries according to the highest principles.

Conclusion

I will end this chapter where I began, by stressing the importance of prayer. There is no substitute for it. There is no way to overemphasize it.

When doing the Lord's work, you need Him much more than He needs you. Don't ever forget it.

Looking to the Future 40

At age 76, I doubt that I have much future on this earth to look forward to. Furthermore, the Signs of the Times clearly indicate that all of us who are believers do not have much time left before the Rapture. I'm expecting the Lord any day.

So, should I die or should I be forced to retire due to bad health before the Lord returns, I am doing all that I can to prepare the ministry for my successor. I want this ministry to continue proclaiming the Lord's soon return right up to the very day of the Rapture.

This has never been my ministry. It has always belonged to the Lord, and beneath His oversight, it has belonged to the ministry's trustees. That is one of the reasons that it is not named The Dave Reagan Ministry.

Legally, the ministry belongs to its trustees. I serve at their pleasure. I am willing to step aside whenever they think it is appropriate.

Our Transition Plan

Meanwhile, we have made careful plans for the day I will no longer be around to head up the ministry, should it come before the Rapture. We have prepared a detailed transition document called, "The Peter Marshall Plan."

Let me explain where we got the name. Several years ago I invited Peter Marshall, the son of the famous evangelist by the same name, to fly down to Dallas from Massachusetts to do two television interviews. I devoted the first interview to the marvelous books he had written about America's Christian heritage. The second interview concerned his famous parents, Peter and Catherine Marshall.

It was a wonderful time that I will never forget. Peter was 69 years old at the time, and he appeared to be in excellent health. His father had died of a massive heart attack at age 46, so Peter was very sensitive about keeping in good shape.

The next year we received the startling news that he had dropped dead at age 70 while playing basketball. We learned later that no plans had been made for the continuance of his ministry.

Thus, our "Peter Marshall Plan." It outlines in detail what is to be done, step-by-step, should I suddenly die or be rendered incapacitated by a stroke. An appendix to the plan lists possible successors, with my evaluation of each one.

Should my health hold up, and I am able to continue ministering into my 80s, as Hal Lindsey and Tim LaHaye are currently doing, I have asked the trustees to let me know when I should step aside, unless I feel led to retire first.

Our Plan for the Rapture

When our Web Minister, Nathan Jones, joined our staff in 2009, he started asking me why we had not made plans for the Rapture. He pointed out that if the Rapture were to occur without our having any plans for it, all our buildings, property, equipment and bank accounts could be confiscated by the government.

So, we brought this problem to the attention of our trustees. It was not an easy decision. After the Rapture, there would be many Christian leaders left behind who would be heading up churches and ministries. But they would be Christians in name only, and we did not want them to inherit our assets. Nor did we want our assets to go to any government, whether state or federal.

After much discussion and prayer, the decision was made to arrange for all our assets to be given to B'nai B'rith International, one of the largest Jewish philanthropies in the world, and one that specializes in defending Jewish people from persecution. We knew for sure that the leaders of this organization would be left behind at the Rapture, and we also knew that the Jewish people would be subjected to horrible persecution during the last half of the Tribulation. We want our assets to be used for their defense.

A Faith Challenge

One of the greatest challenges I have ever encountered in my Christian walk is the current severe illness of my beloved wife, Ann. She taught first grade for 30 years before she was forced to retire in 2002 due to a very acute Fibromyalgia attack. She currently suffers from Fibro, acute fatigue and other afflictions that require her to have an around-the-clock caretaker.

I have had to cut back my speaking schedule and stop taking groups to Israel. She is currently my number one ministry.

The irony is that she was never ill before 2002. She lived her life in as perfect health as it is possible to imagine. She has never had an operation of any kind, and when she was stricken with Fibro, she had accumulated 180 days of sick leave.

A further irony is that she ministers to me every day. She never complains. And when I express desperation over her afflictions, she always says, "Honey, remember, there are people suffering much greater afflictions than me."

I view her condition as an all-out attack of Satan on both of us. For her, it is a physical attack. For me, it is spiritual and theological. I say that because the greatest challenge to my faith has always been the suffering of the righteous amidst the prosperity of the wicked.

The Mystery of Suffering

I vividly remember an incident that occurred several years ago in Shelbyville, Kentucky. A physician, who was a member of a church there where I had ministered several times, decided to give up his medical practice and become a missionary to the Jewish people in Israel. He and his wife made several trips to Israel to scout out where they would live and to get a better idea of what type of ministry they would be doing.

They were ready to make the move, when they went to their home church in Shelbyville to talk with their pastor. While talking with him, the wife suddenly passed out and died from a stroke.

The news hit me like a hammer. I began to wrestle with the questions that were whirling around in my mind:

> God, are You really in control?

> Why, God, did you take the life of a person who was surrendering everything to serve you in a hostile environment?

> What purpose could there possibly be in this death?

It was hard enough to deal with this issue when I witnessed it in the lives of others, but now it has come home to me, and all my previous theological theories and doctrinal answers seem lame.

Continuing to Learn to Walk by Faith

I have to admit that my brain is drained looking for answers. I have come to realize, as never before, that I must have faith that God knows best and He has His reasons known only to Him. We currently "see in a mirror dimly" (1 Corinthians 13:12), but one day we will stand face-to-face, and we will understand.

Why do the righteous suffer? In many cases it is due to the fact that we live in a fallen world. In some cases it is due to personal sin. Often, it is because God uses suffering to refine us in righteousness. The most difficult situation for me is when suffering occurs to fulfill the perfect purposes of God which are known only to Him. It is at this point that living by faith is really put to the test.

In the meantime, I must remind myself daily to "trust in the LORD forever, for in God the LORD we have an ever-lasting Rock" (Isaiah 26:4).

A Concluding Thought

This is the last revision of this book I will ever write. I want to end it with a reflection on my life's experience with God.

Many times I have seen celebrities interviewed on TV, and invariably, the interviewer will ask, "Looking back over your life, do you have any regrets?" I am always amazed when they almost always answer, "None at all."

No regrets? Really? It makes me wonder if their consciences have been seared to the point that they no longer have any sense of sin

As I look back over my life, I have a host of regrets. And the greatest is the day I rejected the Lord's call on my life to serve Him full time in the ministry. Fortunately, it ultimately turned out to be a postponement and not a permanent rejection.

Based on my experience, I want to leave you with one word of advice: Never, never say "No!" to the Lord. If He places a call on your life to do anything, lift your hands to the heavens and shout "HERE AM I LORD, SEND ME!"

Meanwhile, the current shout of my heart is:
"MARANATHA, MARANATHA!
COME QUICKLY, LORD JESUS!"